An Important Message to Our Readers

This product provides information and general advice about the law. But laws and procedures change frequently, and they can be interpreted differently by different people. For specific advice geared to your specific situation, consult an expert. No book, software or other published material is a substitute for personalized advice from a knowledgeable lawyer licensed to practice law in your state.

2nd edition

Patent Searching Made Easy

How to Do Patent Searches on the Internet and in the Library

by David Hitchcock

edited by Patricia Gima and Stephen Elias

Keeping Up to Date

To keep its books up to date, Nolo issues new printings and new editions periodically. New printings reflect minor legal changes and technical corrections. New editions contain major legal changes, major text additions or major reorganizations. To find out if a later printing or edition of any Nolo book is available, call Nolo at 510-549-1976 or check our website at http://www.nolo.com.

To stay current, follow the "Update" service at our website at http://www.nolo.com/update. In another effort to help you use Nolo's latest materials, we offer a 35% discount off the purchase of the new edition of your Nolo book when you turn in the cover of an earlier edition. (See the "Special Upgrade Offer" in the back of the book.)

This book was last revised in: March 2001.

Second Edition	
Second Printing	**MARCH 2001**
Cover Design	TONI IHARA
Book Design	TERRI HEARSH
Production	SARAH TOLL
Illustrations	LINDA ALLISON
Index	PATRICIA DEMINNA
Proofreading	ROBERT WELLS
Printing	CONSOLIDATED PRINTERS, INC.

Hitchcock, David, 1956-
    Patent searching made easy / by David Hitchcock.--2nd ed.
        p.   cm.
    Includes index.
    ISBN 0-87337-554-8
    1. Patent searching. 2. Patent literature I. Title.
T210 .H58   1999b
608.7--dc21

                                99-045116
                                CIP

For information on bulk purchases or corporate premium sales, please contact the Special Sales Department. For academic sales or textbook adoptions, ask for Academic Sales. Call 800-955-4775 or write to Nolo, 950 Parker Street, Berkeley, CA 94710.

Acknowledgments

I wish to thank Steve Elias and Patti Gima for all their editorial input during the writing of this book. I also wish to thank the rest of the staff at Nolo, including Terri Hearsh and Sarah Toll, for the fabulous book design, Toni Ihara for the beautiful cover and Sheryl Rose and Robert Wells for crossing the t's and dotting the i's,

I would also like to thank the staff at the Inventors Connection of Greater Cleveland for their support during the writing of this book. Especially, Murray Henderson, Cheryl Sperie, Don Bergquist, Ruth Vinson, Cal Wight and Bill Bazik.

Finally, I wish to thank my wife Sylvia for her untiring support and encouragement.

Table of Contents

Part 2: Getting Started

3 Patent Searching at the PTO Internet Site

4 Patent Searching at the IBM Website

5 Patent Searching at the PTDL

Part 3: Maximum Performance

6 Advanced Internet Patent Searching

7 Advanced Patent Searching at the PTDL

8 Additional Patent Search Resources on the Internet

9 Additional Sources of Prior Art

10 Where Do I Go From Here?

Appendices

Glossary

Index

Preface

Many inventions have their beginnings as the recognition of a problem. Once the problem is clearly identified, an ideal solution often presents itself. Although this initial solution might not be practical, it is often possible to work backwards toward a more realistic approach. In my case, the problem was wildfires. Every year, millions of dollars worth of residential real estate are destroyed by wildfires. The methods used to protect houses from these infernos have changed very little in recent years.

So I asked myself, what would be the ideal way to protect a house from an approaching wildfire? I imagined an invisible giant standing over the house with a fireproof blanket in his hands. Just as the fire was about to engulf the structure, the giant would drop the blanket over the house.

So how do you work backwards from this scenario? Well, what are the desirable attributes of the solution?

- The fireproof blanket and deployment system remain hidden from view until needed.
- The blanket deploys within a few seconds and completely covers the house.
- The blanket reduces the flow of oxygen to the structure, separates it from the fire and provides a barrier to heat flow.

Using my background in physics and engineering, I began to design various configurations of folded blankets and deployment systems. Soon it became apparent that prior to investing a lot of time, effort and money, I needed to find out about previous related inventions. It was then that I became interested in patent searching.

I reviewed various books, pamphlets and information sources on the subject. These included written patent search guides, Internet patent search resources and specialized patent depository libraries. However, there was no single place where all the available patent search resources were combined and summarized in a logical, progressive manner.

So, I wrote *Patent Searching Made Easy*. With this guide, the novice patent searcher can learn about the various patent searching techniques and resources, and come to an initial judgment as to the originality of a particular invention.

In my case, the concept I developed (the Home Fire Shield™—www.HomeFireShield.com) was not present in the prior literature or inventions I uncovered. After performing my own patent search, I used *Patent It Yourself*, by David Pressmen (Nolo), to draft my patent application. The result was a very strong patent, with broad legal claims.

It is my sincerest hope that you find this guide informative, easy to use and helpful in your invention development efforts.

David Hitchcock
December 1999

Introduction

f you are an inventor or owner of a business engaged in research and development, this book shows you how to:

- quickly "check out" any new idea, to see if anyone else has already patented it
- verify the patent status of ideas submitted to you for development (if you are a potential developer)
- save lots of money in legal fees, and
- avoid reinventing the wheel.

A. Check Out New Ideas

You come up with what seems like a new way to solve a problem or accomplish a task. But you wonder if someone has already trod this ground before you, and either succeeded in obtaining a patent or proved that your idea is not feasible.

You have been told that to answer these questions you will need to have a lawyer or professional patent searcher perform a patent search for you at a cost of $500 or more—possibly much more. You know you can't afford to spend that much money on an idea that someone else may well have thought of already. Maybe you should just forget about it.

Well, think again. The fact is you can do your own patent search in your spare time, and with only a reasonable amount of effort. Even better, you can do this without spending more than a few dollars. If it turns out that your idea has never

before been addressed in a patent, it may be that its time for a patent has come. And depending on what you do with that patent, you may gain a new amount of independence and ability to fulfill your life goals.

As we explain in Chapter 1, an invention must be judged both novel and unobvious (surprising in light of prior developments) to receive a patent. The novelty of your idea will be judged not only against all previously issued patents, but also against all previous developments in the same field, whether or not they were ever patented. For instance, the grooves in an automobile steering wheel were deemed non-patentable because of the traditional use of grooves in sword handles. This rule means that to be absolutely sure that your idea is patentable you will have to go beyond the patent database and examine all written references to similar developments and all real-life items that may embody your idea. But that type of comprehensive search can wait until later. For now, a search of the U.S. patent database is a good place to start. If someone has thought of your idea before, and deemed it valuable, chances are the idea will show up in one or more patents. Keep in mind, however, that pending patent applications (patent applications that have already been submitted, but for which no patent has yet been issued) are kept confidential and cannot be searched. (See Chapter 10 for further discussion on pending patent applications.)

What Is the U.S. Patent Database?

The U.S. patent database contains all of the patents issued by the United States Patent and Trademark Office (PTO) from the beginning of the country. Individual patents are stored in patent file folders at the PTO in Virginia. Additionally, the PTO has created a computer database of patents issued since 1971.

The traditional method of searching the patent database is to hire a search professional to travel to the U.S. Patent and Trademark Office in Virginia and conduct the search there. While very effective, this process is also very expensive. However, you can save yourself some money by performing a preliminary search yourself. If your search reveals that your idea has already been described in one or more previous patents, you will have saved yourself the expense of hiring a search professional.

You don't have to go to Virginia to perform your preliminary search. For access to recent patents, you can use the World Wide Web. The PTO and the IBM corporation provide online databases where you simply type in words that describe your invention—called keywords—to search for patents as far back as 1971 that contain those same words. So if your idea involves technology that has arisen since 1971, you can perform a relatively thorough search over the Internet. However, if your idea involves something that is timeless (yet another way to core an apple), you'll need to search patents issued before 1971—which by and large can't be done over the Internet.

Where can you search these earlier patents? A great resource for complete patent searching is a network of special libraries called Patent and Trademark Depository Libraries (PTDLs). Every state has at least one and a complete list of all the PTDLs is provided in the Appendix. At a PTDL you can perform computer searches

of the PTO's electronic database. Additionally, patents can be searched via microfiche readers.

As you learn how to search for patents, you also will learn how to think about your ideas in the same way that the patent office would were you to apply for a patent on them. This knowledge will enable you to search for ideas that are not only the same as yours, but similar to yours. This process will allow you to determine not only if your invention is the first, but also whether it is the best. And if it is not, the search may inspire you to refine your idea in ways that will qualify it for a patent.

Key to assessing the patentability of your new idea is understanding what previous developments—known in the trade as prior art—the patent office will consider when deciding whether to issue a patent on your idea. This book will help you to:

- understand how the patent office classifies different types of inventions
- assign your idea to the right class
- compare your idea to other similar ideas in the same class, and
- tentatively conclude whether your idea is new enough to qualify for a patent.

By doing your own preliminary patent search, you will become educated about the true nature of your idea. Strangely enough, many people who come up with new ideas—including full-time inventors—often do not fully understand what they have invented. They may dwell on one particular aspect of their invention, and miss a much more valuable general concept that is revealed to them in the course of their patent search.

For example, suppose you want to invent a system to deploy a banner from a hot air balloon. For airplanes, banners simply need to be dragged behind the airplane. The speed of the aircraft, combined with the wake of the plane, will then cause the banner to be unfurled.

However, balloons travel much more slowly than airplanes. If you want to deploy a banner in the horizontal direction, you will need to insert a retractable rod into one side of the banner. You design an air cylinder and rod system, using compressed gas to deploy the rod. Since weight and cost are considerations, you use nitrogen as your compressed gas.

As an afterthought, you check the U.S. patent database for similar designs. You find out that no one has patented a retractable banner system for balloons using compressed nitrogen and a rod. Your search reveals that compressed nitrogen has been used to inflate air bags, but not banners. But wait, inflating air bags with compressed nitrogen makes you realize that the rod itself could be eliminated from your design. Compressed nitrogen alone could be used to inflate an inner chamber in the banner. This will greatly simplify the design. Hold on, why limit yourself to nitrogen when you could use any compressed fluid? You now have a much more general deployment system that can be used in several applications.

Performing patent searches is a great way to get familiar with patent terminology. This will come in handy during all aspects of the patent search as well as the patent application process itself. In particular, when dealing directly with the patent examiner who is reviewing your application, it helps if you are both speaking the same language.

B. Check Product Submissions

So far we have addressed you as if you are an inventor, whether formal or informal. But this book can also be of great benefit if you are a business owner who, because of the nature of your business, tends to be approached by people who want you to manufacture or distribute their new invention. The outside inventor wants you to invest thousands of dollars in special tooling and related manufacturing or marketing costs. The idea seems good. It looks as if it will enhance your existing product line. But how do you know that another company is not making the same or a similar product? If another company is manufacturing a similar product, you need to know about this before investing time, money and effort on the submitted idea. This does not necessarily preclude the submission, but gives you a warning flag to seek an expert opinion before proceeding.

Business owners often spend thousands of dollars on professional patent searchers to verify the uniqueness of new product submissions. This cost can add up quickly. As a business owner, you can save yourself considerable amounts of money by performing some of this searching yourself. Additionally, with the cost savings you realize, you will be able to evaluate more new products. This can be an especially valuable benefit if your business has a tight operating budget.

This book can help you "check out" new product ideas. You can also monitor new patents issued for devices in your line of business. By doing so, you can help your company advance with the leading edge of technology. You will also see what patents are owned by your competitors. This will help reduce the chances of having a nasty surprise product turn up on the shelves—a product which does everything that yours does, but at half the cost.

C. Save Time and Money

Performing your own preliminary patent search can save you a lot of money and time. If you want the patent office to grant you a patent on a particular invention, you will have to file what is known as a patent application. It is essential to perform a patent search before filing. Why? Because filing a patent application, with its associated specifications, drawings and fees, is an expensive, time-consuming process—often costing up to $5,000 if you have it done by a patent attorney. You can, however, do it yourself for far less money with the help of *Patent It Yourself* by David Pressman (Nolo). Either way, before setting out to file a patent application, you will want to be reasonably sure, at the very least, that your idea has not been trumped by a previous patent.

As mentioned, the average cost of a single preliminary patent search performed by a patent search professional is around $500. By using the techniques in this book, you will be able to do most, if not all, of this work yourself. If you have lots of ideas and you are trying to select the best one to patent, you can save some really serious money. This is because a professional patent searcher will charge you separately for each invention. For example, if you want four ideas searched, the cost easily could be $2,000. Even if you ultimately decide to use a professional patent searcher, you can perform some of the preliminary searching yourself. This may save you a portion of the search fees and make you a more knowledgeable client.

D. Avoid Reinventing the Wheel

By checking the U.S. patent database first, you can avoid spending a lot of time tweaking your invention, only to find out later that you have reinvented the wheel. For example, suppose your favorite hobby is amateur astronomy. You love to spend endless hours under the night sky with your telescope. One problem you have is reading the sky charts and comparing them with what you see through the eyepiece of the telescope. You purchased a red light nightlight because the red light does not interfere with your night vision. But you keep losing the nightlight or you have to hold the nightlight and fumble with the chart while switching your vision back and forth between the eyepiece and the chart.

Then it hits you. You will invent a special attachment for the nightlight, an attachment that will allow you to clip it to whatever is handy. Over the next several days you spend hours coming up with several designs. Nightlights with clips, nightlights with screws and nightlights with rubber bands. Finally, you have it. The best solution is a nightlight with a flexible housing that can be wrapped around any convenient nearby structure. You've invented the flexible astronomy nightlight! Wrong, you've reinvented the snake light.

E. How to Use "Patent Searching Made Easy"

Learning how to perform a preliminary patent search is analogous to learning how to drive a car. First, you have to study the rules of the road and the controls of the vehicle. Then, you perform a few simple stops, turns and accelerations. You take local trips to the store, the bank and around town. Finally, you learn to drive with confidence on the highways and byways of America.

Similarly, this book is arranged in three parts:
- Part One: The Basics
- Part Two: Getting Started
- Part Three: Maximum Performance

⚠️ **Patent Searching Is Not a One-Stop Process.** *You will soon learn that different websites offer different patent searching services. One important feature of this book is that it educates you on which sites to use for which purposes, and how to use all of the sites to accomplish the best possible patent search.*

Part One—The Basics (Chapters 1–2): Part One provides a basic orientation to the tools and techniques used in patent searching. Here, we help you come up with words to describe your invention. These are known as keywords or search words. Once you come up with these words, you can use your computer to search the U.S. patent database for patents that contain these words. In addition to searching for isolated occurrences of your individual search terms, you can also search for combinations of search terms. Often, the use of words in combination will produce much more targeted or specific search results. For your information, the rules of logic that control how we combine keywords are known as "Boolean logic." In Chapter 1, we will review Boolean logic in detail and show how you use it to get the best possible search results.

Part One also covers:

- The required hardware, software and Windows skills necessary for doing patent searches on the Internet, and
- An introduction to the tools and resources available at the various Patent and Trademark Depository Libraries (PTDLs). This includes the Automated Patent Search (APS) system—a type of computer search system used for searching the PTO's computer patent database, CASSIS (Classification And Search Support Information System)—a type of search system used for searching patent and trademark information on CD-ROM, and the use of microfilm readers.

Part Two—Getting Started (Chapters 3–5): You will take your first trips in the patent search car (to continue the metaphor) in Part Two. You will perform simple patent searches using the Internet and the PTDL. You will use different keywords and vary their combinations with Boolean logic. We will also introduce you to the PTO's classification system. These are the categories that the PTO uses to classify or sort the various types of inventions. Here we will help you discover what category the PTO will most likely use for your invention. Once we identify these categories, we will show you how to search for other patents within the same category. This will tell you what patents have been issued for inventions similar to yours.

Part Two also covers:

- Which Internet resources to use and how to use them to provide the best preliminary patent search results,
- Detailed instructions on how to use the CASSIS and APS computer search systems, and
- Searching techniques for older patents stored on microfilm.

Part Three—Maximum Performance (Chapters 6–10): We will slip into high gear in Part Three, and cruise the highway of discovery. Here we will cover advanced patent search methods and the advantages of more advanced patent searching. We will review often-overlooked resources, certain specialized databases and provide some information about international patent offices.

Part Three also covers:

- Powerful Internet search commands and techniques that let you fine-tune your search results,
- Advanced methods and strategies for getting the most out of your visit to the Patent and Trademark Depository Library (PTDL), and
- Often-overlooked resources for patent searchers.

The best way to use this book is to:

- Read all the material in Part I (The Basics), Chapters 1 and 2, for basic skill building.
- Proceed to Part Two (Getting Started) and read Chapters 3 and 4. These two chapters give you your first exposure to Internet patent searching.
- After reading Chapters 3 and 4, try some simple patent searches using the techniques covered.
- Return to Part Two and read the material in Chapter 5. This will give you an introduction to what's available at a typical Patent and Trademark Depository Library (PTDL).
- Consult Appendix A and locate the PTDL nearest you. Take a trip to the PTDL and try

the methods and tools covered in Chapter 5. For reasonably thorough and accurate preliminary patent searches, it's important to use both the Internet and the PTDL.

- When you are comfortable with all the materials in Part Two (Getting Started), move on to the advanced methods of Part Three (Maximum Performance). Chapter 6 introduces you to advanced Internet patent search commands and techniques. The best way to learn them is to read over the chapter, and then try them yourself over the Internet. Similarly, Chapter 7 provides additional training in the use of PTDL search tools. Plan another visit to the PTDL to take advantage of these techniques as well. The rest of the material in Part Three will provide further insight into often-overlooked patent search resources and methods.

- Finally, Chapter 10 will help you assess the results of your search in terms of their effect on the patentability of your invention.

Alternatively, you may simply follow the "Jump To" icons located throughout Parts One and Two to locate the related advanced techniques discussed in Part Three. By doing so, you can immediately follow up your study of a basic technique with its more advanced features.

So, if you are ready, let's start our engine, and slip on our driving gloves. It's time to start our journey which will lead us to the answer you seek. Is your new idea in the running for a patent?

An Alternative Way to Use This Book

Some readers may feel a bit impatient at our phased approach to learning how to search for patents and other prior art references. If so, here is an alternative method for using this book:

- After reviewing Chapters 1 and 2, read Chapters 3, 4 and 6. This will arm you with both the beginning and advanced techniques for searching the PTO and IBM Internet patent sites. These are the main Internet patent search resources covered in the book. Then proceed with your Internet-based patent searches.

- Read Chapters 5 and 7. This will give you the beginning and advanced techniques for searching in the Patent and Trademark Depository Library.

- Locate and visit the PTDL nearest to you using Appendix A and use the techniques that you have learned.

- Review Chapter 8 for additional Internet and online patent searching options and Chapter 9 for how to search for non-patented prior art on the Internet. Use the information in these chapters to augment your previous search results. Return to the book as necessary to refresh your understanding of a particular technique or resource.

- Finally, when you have accumulated some patents or prior art references that are relevant to your invention, read Chapter 10 for some tips on how to evaluate the results of your search.

Part 1

The Basics

I n this part of the book, we introduce you to the tools and techniques used to perform a basic preliminary patent search. In Chapter 1, we discuss what a patent is and how word-based patent searches work. In Chapter 2, the computer hardware, software, and Windows skills that you will need are reviewed. Chapter 2 also introduces us to the resources available at the Patent and Trademark Depository Library (PTDL).

1

Introduction to Patents and Patent Searching

A. What Is a Patent, and What Does It Do for Me?

A patent is a right, granted by the government, to a person or legal entity (partnership or corporation). A patent gives its holder the right to exclude others from making, using or selling the invention "claimed" in the patent deed for 20 years from the date of filing. (For patents issued before June 8, 1995, 17 years from the date the patent was issued by the U.S. Patent and Trademark Office.) Once the patent expires, the invention covered by the patent enters the public domain and can be used by anyone. The scope of a U.S. patent is limited to the borders of the United States and its territories.

The right of exclusion given to a patent owner can best be thought of as an offensive legal right. This right of exclusion allows the patent owner to file a lawsuit in federal court against an infringer (anyone who violates the right of exclusion). Because the right of exclusion is not a defensive legal right, the patent owner can't rely on law enforcement agencies to automatically prosecute someone who infringes (copies) his or her patented invention.

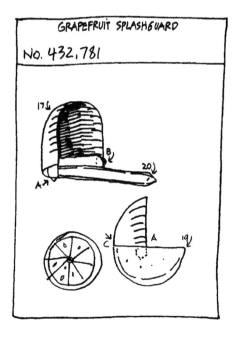

The Patent Application Process

When you submit your completed patent application and filing fee to the PTO, you will be assigned a filing date. After a six- to 18-month waiting period, a patent examiner will review the application. While it is possible that your application will be allowed as is, this is usually not the case. More often than not, the patent examiner will object to one or more of your claims, or require changes to your patent drawings or specifications. This results in what is known as an "Office Action." The office action is an official communication (letter) from the patent office, outlining the objections to your original patent application. You then have the choice of either modifying the application or convincing the examiner that he/she was in error.

After you successfully respond to the office action the patent examiner will allow your application and you will have to pay an issue fee. After a few more months' delay, your patent will finally issue. The entire process, from initial patent application submission to issued patent, usually takes from 1.5 to three years.

For more information about how to complete and file a patent application, see Patent It Yourself, *by David Pressman (Nolo).*

In the sense that a patent gives the patent holder the right to sue anyone who tries to develop, use or manufacture the invention covered by the patent, the patent can be a valuable commodity. It can be sold outright or licensed in exchange for a royalty. Additionally, the patent owner may choose to manufacture and distribute the invention, thereby keeping all the proceeds for him or herself.

For more information about licensing inventions, see License Your Invention, *by Richard Stim (Nolo).*

Patents As a Type of Intellectual Property

A patent falls under the larger category of Intellectual Property. Other forms of intellectual property are Trademarks, Trade Secrets and Copyrights. Depending on the type of invention, one of these other forms of intellectual property may give you greater offensive legal rights. For example, a trademark would be appropriate if your innovation is a new type of symbol, or word associated with a particular product, or a family of products. Examples of popular trademarks are Diet Coke and Mr. Coffee. A trade secret would generally be described as any information that, by being kept a secret, gives its owner a competitive business advantage. The formula for Kentucky Fried Chicken is one of the best-known examples. Copyright law is used to protect the expressive works of authors, computer programmers, movie producers and other artistic creators.

For more information about trademarks, trade secrets and copyrights, consult the following resources: Trademark: Legal Care for Your Business & Product Name, *by Kate McGrath and Stephen Elias (Nolo),* Patent, Copyright & Trademark, *by Stephen Elias (Nolo) and* The Copyright Handbook, *by Stephen Fishman (Nolo).*

1. Categories of Patents

There are three main types of patents: utility patents, design patents and plant patents. In this book, we will focus on utility patents because they are more common. Not surprisingly, a utility patent covers the functional aspects of an invention. As an example, assume that the hammer hasn't been invented yet. Ivan Inventor conceives of the hammer as an invention after he accidentally smashes his thumb with a rock he was using to pound a square peg into a round hole. If Ivan applies for a patent and his patent application describes his hammer invention in general enough terms, the patent would cover all variations of the hammer as a utilitarian device. It would cover common household hammers, sledgehammers, rubber hammers and the like. Perhaps even hydraulic hammers would be covered.

A design patent only covers the appearance of an invention. In our example, Ivan might apply for a design patent for a hammer with a horsehead etched into the shaft of the hammer. Removal of the horsehead would not affect the utility or functioning of the hammer. Design patents are easy to work around. A competitor could design a hammer with a slightly different horsehead (longer mane or bigger eyes), and the new hammer design most likely would not infringe on the original design patent.

Plant patents are for new types of plants. Because plant patents are uncommon we don't cover them in this book.

2. Patent Eligibility Requirements

In order to get a utility patent (as opposed to a design patent), your patent application has to satisfy four legal criteria. (Novelty, unobviousness and other patent requirements are discussed in greater detail in Chapter 10.)

1. Your invention has to fit into an established Statutory Class.
2. Your invention must have some Utility. In other words, it has to be useful.
3. Your invention must have some Novelty. It must have some physical difference from any similar inventions in the past.

4. Your invention must be Unobvious to someone who is skilled in the appropriate field.

In order to fit within an established Statutory Class (the first legal criterion), your invention must be either a Process, a Machine, an Article of Manufacture, a Composition of Matter or a New Use invention.

- A Process is just the performance of a series of operations on something.
- A Machine is a device consisting of a series of fixed or moving parts that direct mechanical energy towards a specific task.
- An Article of Manufacture can be made by hand or machine. As opposed to machines, Articles of Manufacture are inventions that are relatively simple, with few or no moving parts.
- A Composition of Matter is a unique arrangement of items. Chemical compositions such as glue and plastics are good examples of compositions of matter.
- A New Use process is simply a new way of using an invention that fits in one of the first four statutory classes.

The second criterion your patent application has to satisfy is that it must be useful. Fortunately, any new use will satisfy this requirement. In general if your invention is operable (if it functions), it will satisfy this requirement.

The next requirement is Novelty. To get a patent, your invention must be somehow different from all previous inventions documented in the prior art. Generally, there are three types of difference categories.

1. Physical differences between your invention and previous inventions.
2. New combinations made by using previous aspects of two or more different inventions.
3. A new use of a previous invention.

As mentioned, your patent will also have to be deemed unobvious. This is the toughest of the patent requirements. Essentially, what it means is that your new concept must be a significant step forward in the field of the invention. In other words, if a skilled worker who is thoroughly familiar with developments in the area of your invention would consider the idea obvious, you would fail this test.

3. The Patent Document

In one sense a patent is an abstract notion. The PTO issues a patent. The patent gives you certain affirmative rights. The patent expires in 20 years. You can sell or license your patent. In all these uses, the term patent is an abstraction. In reality, the terms of a patent are spelled out in a document called a patent deed that is produced by the PTO. More commonly, the patent document is simply referred to as a patent or patent reference. The patent database consists of hardcopy, microfiche or electronic copies of patent documents.

Every utility patent document, which we'll simply refer to as a patent from this point on, has several identifiable fields or sections. Understanding the different parts of the patent will be especially important when we cover computer searching. This is because we will conduct our search in certain subsections of the patent, and it helps to know what sort of information to expect to find there. Below is a table showing the typical sections that appear in a patent, along with a brief description of what is in each one.

Our table introduces us to several terms commonly used in the patent world. "Class" and "subclass" refer to the complex system used by the PTO to categorize each and every patent that it issues. Conceptually, the system is similar to an alphabetical library index file. For example, to search a library for a book about baseball, one would first go to the subject card index. In the file drawer for subjects beginning with the letter S, you would most likely find a Sports section. Under the sports section, you would go to the subsection for Baseball. There you would find the titles of several books related to baseball. The PTO currently has over 100,000 classes and subclasses.

Table of Patent Sections

Patent Section	Description
Title	Patent title.
Inventor information	Inventor's name and address.
Patent number	The number assigned to the issued patent.
Patent filing date	The date the patent application was filed with the PTO.
Patent issue date	The date the patent was issued by the PTO.
Classification	Class and subclass information. These are the categories that the PTO uses to classify or sort the various types of inventions.
Referenced patents	The patent numbers of previous patents referred to in the patent application, along with their classes and subclasses.
Abstract	Usually one concise paragraph that summarizes the invention in plain English. Appears on the front page of the issued patent. This is the most frequently referenced section of the patent.
Drawings	Drawings of the invention from different perspectives.
Background of the invention	Discussion of any previous inventions that were related to this invention. This is known as "prior art."
Summary of the invention	A discussion of the invention that captures its essential functions and features.
Brief description of drawings	A one-sentence description of each patent drawing figure.
Detailed description of the preferred version of the invention	An in-depth discussion of the various aspects of the invention. Painstaking references to the patent drawings are made.
Claims	This section defines the legal scope of the patent (as a deed describes the boundaries of real estate).

An "abstract" is simply a summary of the most important features of the invention covered by the patent. The abstract appears on the front page of the issued patent. Patent searchers consult the abstract to get a quick overview of the invention. This in turn helps them decide whether it is worthwhile to review the entire patent. The abstract is the searcher's way to separate the wheat from the chaff. Figure 1 below shows a typical abstract. This is from patent # 5,712,618, an automatic turn signaling device for vehicles.

ABSTRACT:
An automatic signaling device for a vehicle which automatically initiates a method and apparatus for an automatic signaling device warning signal to pedestrians and to other vehicles in connection with lane changes and upon turns. The present invention is activated and deactivated automatically providing significant safety advantages for all of those using the roads and highways.
15 Claims, 2 Drawing Figures

Figure 1

The "background of the invention" is a discussion of previous inventions that are related in some way to the current invention. These inventions are known as the prior art of the current invention. These previous inventions may embody some of the same or similar elements as the current invention. For example, sprinkler systems and fireproof blankets are two vastly different products. However, they are both related by the fact that they are fire suppressant devices. So, if you invented a modern-day fire suppression device (for instance one using nanotechnology—tiny microscopic machines—to deprive the fire of oxygen), both sprinkler systems and fireproof blankets would be considered prior art related to your invention.

BACKGROUND OF THE INVENTION

The invention disclosed herein relates to preferred methods and apparatuses for an automatic signaling device which automatically activates a warning signal. The following patents form a background for the instant invention. None of the cited publications is believed to detract from the patentability of the claimed invention.

U.S. Pat. No. 3,771,096 issued to Walter on Nov. 6, 1973, discloses a lane changing signaling device for vehicles employing a rotary electrical connector joined to the steering wheel. The principal disadvantage of the device is that it fails to measure the angle of rotation of the steering wheel.

Figure 2

Figure 2, above, shows the first two paragraphs from the background section of patent number 5,712,618. The first paragraph is a general summary of the background of the invention. The next paragraph begins the discussion of the advantages of the current invention over previously patented inventions.

Prior art is not limited to inventions patented in the U.S. Patents issued in other countries are considered valid prior art, and, if you apply for a patent, will be compared against your invention. Also, any other published information, from any corner of the globe, can prevent a patent from being granted. Even unpublished works, such as a Master's thesis, can be considered valid prior art. In Chapter 10 we explain how to evaluate your invention in light of the relevant prior art.

The "detailed description of the preferred version of the invention" (*embodiment* in patent terms) is a detailed description of an actual, "nuts and bolts" version of the current invention. It is essentially the inventor's best-guess (preferred embodiment) description of the product, at the time the patent application is written. By reading the detailed description, a person who is familiar with similar products should be able to build and operate the current invention. It is important to note that the legal scope of the patent is not defined (the language of patents calls it "limited") by the details of the description of the preferred embodiment. Rather, the scope of the patent is determined by the "claims" (see below).

Figure 3, below, shows the first paragraph of the detailed description of the preferred embodiment for patent number 5,462,805, a fire safety glass panel. Reading through the description we see that specific numbered elements of figure number 1 (from patent 5,462,805) are referenced. This figure is shown as Figure 4 below. Here we have a glass plate (element 10), another glass plate (element 11), an intermediate resin layer (element 12), and first and second adhesive layers (elements 13 and 14). By following along with the detailed description, and matching the numbered elements of the description with the labeled elements of the drawing, a person familiar with fire safety glass would be able to construct this invention.

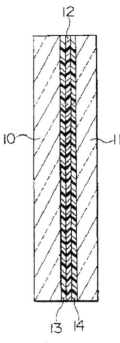

Figure 4

DESCRIPTION OF THE PREFERRED EMBODIMENT

Referring to FIG. 1, a fire-protection and safety glass panel according to a preferred embodiment of this invention comprises a first glass plate **10**, a second glass plate **11** opposite to the first glass plate, and an intermediate resin layer between the first and the second glass plates **10** and **11**. At least one of the first and the second glass plates **10** and **11** is a heat-resistant glass plate. The intermediate resin layer comprises a polyethylene terephthalate film (namely, a PET film) **12** and first and second adhesive agent layers **13** and **14** and has a thickness which is not greater than 200 μm. The first adhesive agent layer **13** adheres the PET film **12** to the first glass plate **10**. The second adhesive agent layer **14** adheres the PET film **12** to the second glass plate **11**.

Figure 3

The "claims" of the patent are a series of tersely worded statements that precisely describe and define the underlying invention. As we suggest in the chart, patent claims operate in much the same way as do real estate deeds—they precisely delimit the scope of the patent in the same way as the real estate deed describes the precise location of the property.

From the patent applicant's viewpoint, the claims should be as broad as possible, thus covering many possible versions of the same basic invention. Broad claims make it difficult for someone to defeat the patent by making a minor change to the invention. On the flip side, if patent claims are too broad, there is always the possibility of someone finding a previous invention (prior art reference) that falls within the patent's scope. This could make the patent susceptible to being ruled invalid if the patent holder ever finds it necessary to bring an infringement case.

Figure 5, below, shows the first claim from the fire safety glass patent (5,462,805). While calling out the same elements of the invention as described in the preferred embodiment, the specific element references have been omitted. This is because the claim is meant to be general enough to include different designs based upon the same invention concept.

Also note that here the glass plates are referred to as "low-expansion crystallized glass." This is broad enough to include many types of glass that do not readily expand when exposed to heat. If a specific type of low-expansion glass were claimed, then the patent could be "worked around" by simply claiming a different type of low-expansion glass.

What is claimed is:

1. A fire-protection and safety glass panel comprising a first glass plate, a second glass plate opposite to said first glass plate, and an intermediate resin layer between said first and said second glass plates, at least one of said first and said second glass plates being a low-expansion crystallized glass plate of a low-expansion crystallized glass, wherein said intermediate resin layer comprises a polyethylene terephthalate film, a first adhesive agent layer for adhering said polyethylene terephthalate film to said first glass plate, and a second adhesive agent layer for adhering said polyethylene terephthalate film to said second glass plate, said intermediate resin layer having a thickness which is not greater than 200 um.

Figure 5

B. Understanding How Databases Are Created

The PTO has created an electronic database consisting of patents issued since August, 1971. This database can be searched by computer and patent text data can be extracted and examined. However, the data records are incomplete between the years 1971 and 1975. Not all of the patent text data was captured electronically during that time.

In order to get the most benefit from a word-based computer search, it is useful to first understand how searchable databases are put together.

Creating a computer database is basically a two-step process. First, the information has to be entered into the computer. Then, the information has to be processed by a special kind of computer program so that the information can be easily retrieved in a meaningful form.

There are generally two ways to get information into a computer (not including voice recognition hardware and software, which is still not commonly used). Someone can physically type the data in at the keyboard, or a person can make use of a device called a scanner. A scanner is similar to the everyday copy machine. A page is placed on a surface and a machine records an image of what's on the page. However, when a scanner is connected to a computer, it is possible to capture an image of a document and store that image on the hard disk of the computer.

When a document is scanned into a computer, it may take one of two forms:

- an image, or
- text that has been extracted from the scanned document by software known as OCR (Optical Character Recognition).

For the purpose of searching by computer, there is a big difference between an image of a document that hasn't been subjected to OCR software and the text that an OCR scan produces. If, for example, a patent is scanned into a computerized database without OCR treatment, the contents of the image can't be searched; after all, it's just a picture. The computer has no way of knowing what the picture contains. You can pull up the patent on your computer screen the same as any other graphical image, but you can't search for the patent according to the words contained in it. However, if the text in the patent document is read by an OCR program before it makes its way into the database, the database will be able to index the text and pull up the patent document according to the words contained in a keyword search.

The database that gets created as a result of OCR processing (or of text that is manually entered or already in computer-readable form) is essentially a huge lookup table. The program that builds this table searches through all the entered text and extracts all the meaningful words. Then, these words, along with a link to the original document they were found in, are placed in the lookup table.

When you use a computer program to perform a word-based search, the program matches the search words you type in with words stored in its lookup table. The search words that you enter are called "keywords" and the search process is called a keyword search. If the computer finds a match, the program will report back to you the document in which the word was found and, in some cases, the location of the word within the document.

The lookup table ("database" in computer talk) is similar to indexes found in the back of many books. In book indexes, words are listed alphabetically, along with a comma-separated list of each page in the book where the word was used.

C. Understanding Keyword Searching

When you use a computer program to search for patents, you often must search for them by entering words into a "query" box and asking the search program to match your words with words stored in its database.

As you might expect, performing keyword searches is a skill with a learning curve. Sure, anyone can put one or two words into a box and pull up all the patents with those words. No skill there. But the overall number of patents you pull up is likely to be huge and the number of the patents that are relevant to your search are likely to be low. To pull up a manageable number of patents and to assure that most of them will have some relevance to your own invention, you will need to know at least some of the basic techniques for choosing your search terms and combining them into meaningful search queries.

1. The Role of Wildcards in Keyword Searching

One powerful tool that is often used during keyword searching is called the wildcard. A wildcard is a special character inserted into your keyword. This character tells the computer search program to do something special with the keyword within which it's used. The two most often used wildcard symbols are the asterisk (*), and the question mark (?).

The asterisk wildcard is used at the end of a word root to take the place of any number of additional letters that may come after that root. For example, assume you have invented a new type of dance shoe. The shoe can be used for ballroom, ballet and tap dancing. In addition to the keywords "ballroom," "ballet" and "tap," you will certainly want to search for the word "dance." But there are several variations of the word "dance," "dancing," "dancer," "danced," and even "danceable." By using "danc*" as your keyword, the asterisk replaces any other possible characters that would follow the four letters, "danc."

Figure 6, below, contains the search results from searching the titles of U.S. patents issued in the years 1997–1998 for the word "dance." The patent titles that have the word "dance" in them are listed and numbered. As you can see, there are four patents that have the word "dance" in the title. The first title relates to a dance practice slipper, the second title concerns the sole of a dance shoe, the third title relates to a type of dance and the fourth title relates to a portable dance floor.

Searching 97-98...

[Search Summary]
Results of Search in 97-98 db for:
TTL/dance: 4 patents.
Hits 1 through 4 out of 4

| Refine Search | TTL/dance |

Pat. No. Title
1. **D388,592** *Dance* practice slipper
2. **5,682,685** *Dance* shoe sole
3. **PP9,938** Peach tree "Snow *Dance*"
4. **5,634,309** Portable *dance* floor

Figure 6

Searching 97-98...

[Search Summary]
Results of Search in 97-98 db for:
TTL/danc*: 8 patents.
Hits 1 through 8 out of 8

| Refine Search | TTL/danc* |

Pat. No. Title
1. **D388,592** *Dance* practice slipper
2. **5,682,685** *Dance* shoe sole
3. **5,669,117** Buckle for line *danc*ing
4. **D382,902** Unit for teaching *danc*ing
5. **5,659,229** Controlling web tension by actively controlling velocity of *danc*er roll
6. **PP9,938** Peach tree "Snow *Dance*"
7. **5,634,309** Portable *dance* floor
8. **5,602,747** Controlling web tension by actively controlling velocity of *danc*er roll

Figure 7

Figure 7, below, contains the search results from searching the titles of U.S. patents issued in the years 1997–1998 for the word "danc*." As you can see, we now have eight patents listed. The first two titles are the same ones that we obtained before. However, title numbers 3 and 4 contain the word "dancing" as opposed to "dance." The first four letters (danc) are the same as in the word "dance," but the wildcard (*) was used for the letters "ing." Similarly, title numbers 5 and 8 contain the word "dancer," as opposed to "dance." Here, the wildcard (*) was used for the letters "er."

The question mark (?) wildcard can be used to replace any single character in a word. Continuing with our dancing example, the words "foot" or "feet" could be searched by using "f??t" as our keyword. Obviously, you would not want to use the keyword "f*," as this would return every word that started with the letter "f." By using "f??t," every four-letter word that starts with "f" and ends with "t" would be searched for by the computer. For example, along with the words "feet" and "foot," the words "flat" and "fast" would also be reported to you in the search results.

In Figure 8 below, we show a portion of the search results obtained from the IBM electronic patent database when searching for the word "f??t" in patent titles for the years 1995–1998. The first patent (Patent Number 5,697,106) contains the

5697106 Liquid impervious <u>foot</u> receiving article

5696529 <u>Flat</u> panel monitor combining direct view with overhead projection capability

5696435 <u>Fast</u> battery charger for a device having a varying electrical load during recharging

5695530 Method for making high charging efficiency and <u>fast</u> oxygen recombination rechargeable hydride batteries

5695527 Coil prosthetic <u>foot</u>

5695526 One-piece mechanically differentiated prosthetic <u>foot</u> and associated ankle joint with syme modification

Figure 8

word "foot" in the title, whereas the next patent (Patent Number 5,696,529) contains the word "Flat" in the title. The third and fourth patents listed have the word "Fast" in their titles. Finally, the fifth and sixth patents listed (Patent Numbers 5,695,527 and 5,695,526) contain the word "foot" in the title.

There are other wildcards used on the various computer search systems available to the public. However, the asterisk (*) wildcard is, by far, the most popular.

2. The Role of Boolean Logic in Keyword Patent Searching

A search technique known as Boolean logic can be used to combine individual keywords into powerful searches. Boolean logic uses a total of four words (called "logical operators") to define the search: AND, OR, XOR and ANDNOT. The AND operator is by far the most useful. A graphical representation known as a Venn diagram will help you to understand how these operators work.

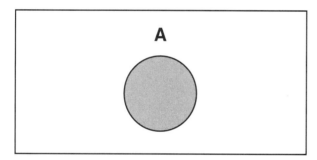

Figure 9

In Figure 9 above, we have a circle that has been shaded. The area inside the circle represents all of the patents that contain the keyword represented by the letter A. The area outside the circle represents all the other patents that do not contain the keyword represented by A. In other words, if we were to search a database of patents for all the occurrences of the keyword A, our search results would be contained in the shaded circle above.

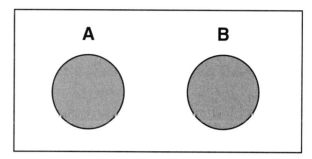

Figure 10

In Figure 10, we have two keywords represented by the circles A and B. Searching for individual occurrences of the keywords A or B would result in a lot of search results. It would take a long time to review these results and most of them would be irrelevant.

For example, let's suppose we have an invention idea for a new type of telephone cable. A search for the keyword telephone would return numerous references to different types of telephones. Similarly, a keyword search for the word cable would return patents related to cable television, bridge support cables, cable cars and so on. What we need is a way to search for both the keywords telephone and cable within the same patent. This is where Boolean operators come into the picture.

3. The AND Boolean Operator

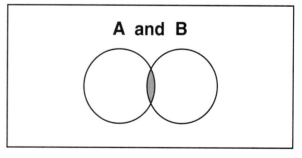

Figure 11

In Figure 11 above, we have used the Boolean operator AND to combine the keywords A and B. The shaded area where the circles overlap represents the search results that contain both keywords A and B. As you can see, the AND operator is a great way to narrow the scope of the search.

When a match is found between a keyword (or a combination of keywords) and a patent, the result is called a "hit." When patent searches are conducted, the number of hits, or occurrences, of a keyword match is usually reported to the user. By using the AND operator, the user reduces the quantity of hits that need to be reviewed.

For example, let's suppose that you have invented a new type of steam engine. A steam engine is a machine for converting the heat energy in steam into mechanical energy by means of a piston moving in a cylinder.

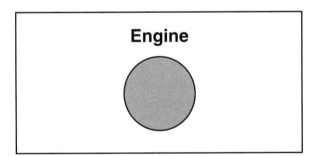

Figure 12

The search results using the keyword Engine are shown in Figure 12 above. The shaded circle represents all of the patents that contain the word Engine. This could be quite an extensive list. For example, all the various types of internal combustion engines would be included in this list. A steam-powered vehicle is an external combustion device; the steam is usually obtained from an external boiler. However, if we only searched for the word Engine, we would have to review search results that contained references to gasoline-powered engines for cars, trucks, trains and all other engine-powered devices.

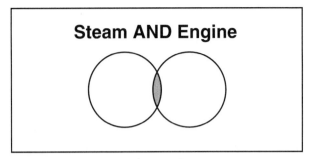

Figure 13

Figure 13 above shows the search result obtained when using the Boolean AND operator to combine the keywords Steam and Engine. The resulting number of hits is represented by the small shaded area in the diagram, where the two circles overlap. We can see at once why AND is the most often used Boolean operator. It allows the searcher to narrow the scope of the search and obtain more meaningful results.

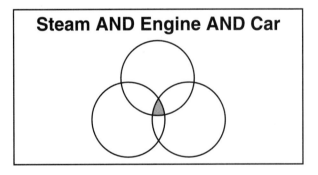

Figure 14

In Figure 14 above, we see the results of a search using the keywords Steam, Engine and Car. In this case the overlapping area is even more precisely defined. It would be necessary for a patent to contain all three keywords before being reported as a match.

Throughout this book, we will identify critical concepts used for effective patent searching. We call these concepts *Searcher's Secrets*. The use of the AND operator brings us to Searcher's Secret #1.

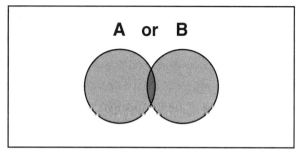

Figure 16

4. The OR Boolean Operator

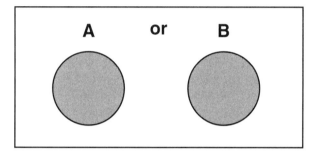

Figure 15

In Figure 15 above, we have used the Boolean operator OR to combine the keywords represented by the letters A and B. The shaded area within the circle labeled A represents all of the patents that contain the keyword represented by the letter A. Similarly, the shaded area within the circle labeled B represents all of the patents that contain the keyword represented by the letter B. When you use the Boolean OR operator, you can't tell from your search results whether a particular reference contains just one of your key words or both. Using our Venn diagrams to represent one possible set of search results, we see that in Figure 15, above, there were no hits that contained both of the keywords represented by the letters A and B. If the search results did have some patents that contained both keywords, the resulting Venn diagram would look like Figure 16 below.

In Figure 16 above, we have the two circles, A and B, with a small overlapping area. The lightly shaded areas of A and B that do not overlap represent patents that contain only one of our keywords. The heavily shaded, overlapping area represents patents that contain both keywords.

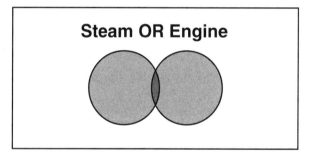

Figure 17

Returning to our steam engine example, Figure 17 represents the number of hits returned when we use "Steam OR Engine" to search the patent database. What this means is that any patent that contained the word Steam or the word Engine would be returned as a match. The lightly shaded areas of the circles represent patents that contain the keyword Steam or the keyword Engine, but not both. The heavily shaded area, where the two circles overlap, represent patents that contain both keywords. Remember, however, that you couldn't tell this from your research results; the Venn diagrams are only being used to explain what happens in fact. Use of the OR operator brings us to our next Searcher's Secret.

5. The XOR Boolean Operator

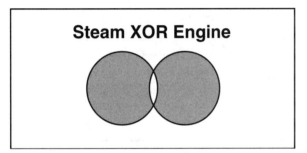

Figure 18

The exclusive OR operator is symbolized by the
XOR letters. This operator is very similar to the OR
operator, but with one important difference. The
overlapping area is not included in the search
results. So, if we used "Steam XOR Engine" to
search our database, we would obtain a list of
patents that contained the word Steam, or the
word Engine, but not both. This brings us to our
third Searcher's Secret.

6. The ANDNOT Boolean Operator

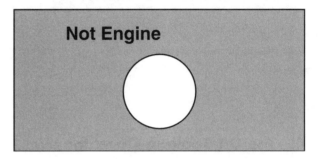

Figure 19

The final Boolean operator we will be reviewing is
the ANDNOT operator. The ANDNOT operator is
actually a combination of the AND and NOT
operators. The NOT operator, by itself, simply
finds all the patents that do not contain the
keyword used. The reason the NOT operator is
combined with the AND operator can be seen in
Figure 19. If you were to use the NOT operator, by
itself, with just the keyword Engine, your search
results would include all the patents that do not
contain the word Engine—a very large search
result indeed.

An example of the correct use of the ANDNOT
operator is shown below. If you wanted to search
for steam engines used in all devices except trains,
you could compose a query like:

(Steam AND Engine) ANDNOT Train

This would return patents concerning steam
engines in cars, boats, etc. However, any patent
containing the word Train would be excluded.
This is true even if the words Steam and Engine
were contained within the train-related patent.
Figure 20 below shows the search result obtained
when using the above query. The resulting number

of hits is again represented by the small shaded area in the diagram where the circles representing the keywords Steam and Engine overlap. However, a small section of that overlapping area has been excluded. This excluded area represents the patents that contain the keyword Train.

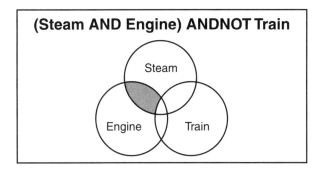

Figure 20

Use of the ANDNOT operator brings us to our next Searcher's Secret.

Searcher's Secret Number 4

The ANDNOT operator is used to exclude specific keywords from the search results.

7. Use of Parentheses

Also, notice that we have made use of left and right parentheses— ( )—around the words Steam and Engine. This means that the words within the parentheses are evaluated first, then the ANDNOT condition is applied.

We will cover the use of parentheses for advanced keyword searches later in this book (Chapter 6).

You can also combine wildcards with Boolean operators. To return to our dance shoe example, we can combine the keyword "danc*" with the keyword "Shoe," and exclude the keyword "Tap" with the following query.

(Danc* AND Shoe) ANDNOT Tap

The resulting patents would have the words "shoe" and one or more words like "dancing," "dancer" or "dance," but not the word "tap."

Summary

What Is a Patent, and What Does It Do for Me?
- A patent is a right of exclusion, granted by the government, for a term of years. It is a document as well as an abstract right.
- A utility patent covers the functional aspects of the invention. A design patent only covers the appearance of an invention.

How Keyword Searches Work
- A computer program matches the words you type in (keywords) with words stored in its database.

How Wildcards Work
- The asterisk (*) wildcard can take the place of any number of letters following its location in the word.
- The question mark (?) wildcard can be used to replace any single character in a word.

Boolean Logic
- Use Boolean logic to combine keywords into powerful searches.
- The more keywords used with the AND operator, the smaller the number of matches obtained and the more meaningful each match is to the searcher.
- The OR operator is used to widen the scope of the search results.

- One, and only one, of the keywords combined with the XOR operator will appear in each of the patents in the search results.
- The ANDNOT operator is used to exclude keywords from the search results.

- Left and right parentheses—( )—are used in complex Boolean logic to determine which terms are evaluated first.
- You can also combine wildcards with Boolean operators.

■

2

Tools and Resources

Here we introduce you to the tools you'll need to use this book and the resources that will help you carry out your preliminary patent search.

You can skip ahead to Section F of this chapter if you already have a computer and Internet browser and a basic understanding of how the Internet works.

A. What Is the Internet?

The Internet is commonly described as a network of computers linked by telephone lines. Not so. The Internet is actually a network of computer networks. The Internet is an international "web" of interconnected government, business, university and scientific computer networks. These networks are connected via dialup phone lines, fiber optics, satellites and microwave links. This network of computer networks is currently made up of over 90 million individual computers worldwide. Every day, approximately 375 million individual users tie into this "web" of networks. Most users connect to the Internet via a personal computer, modem, telephone line and some software. Using the Internet gives us access to thousands of databases all over the world. Almost every subject imaginable is covered to some extent.

B. How Does the Internet Work?

Without getting too technical, information on the Internet is broken down into chunks of data called packets. A computer image (such as a patent drawing), or a document (such as a patent abstract), will be divided into several data packets. These packets of information are sent from the source computer, over the various interconnected networks, to the destination computer. In addition to the image, or document data, each data packet contains some header information. This header information contains the address of the sending and receiving computer, and the order (or sequence) in which the packets must be assembled to produce the finished document.

An analogy would be moving a building from New Mexico to Florida. You could take the building apart, label all the pieces, and ship everything out. You may use more than one common carrier. For the medium weight sections, you could use trucks. For the heavier sections, you may choose railroad. Some of the building parts would arrive at their destination out of order. The roof may arrive before the walls, the second floor may arrive before the first, and so on. But none of this makes any difference. With careful labeling of all the components, you will know which section goes first, which section goes second, and so on. In a similar fashion, the receiving computer on the Internet knows how to read the header information of each arriving data packet. These packets are then assembled into a finished document for your viewing pleasure.

C. Computer Hardware Requirements for Using the Internet

In order to access the Internet, your computer system will have to meet certain minimum performance requirements. The typical home computer system is composed of a few key components. Each of these components has to perform at a certain level. These key components are the CPU (central processing unit), the computer display, computer RAM (random access memory), hard disk storage capacity, CD-ROM drive, floppy disk drive, keyboard, mouse and modem.

If you are using a personal computer (PC), you will need Windows 95 or better, with 16 MB or more of RAM and a modem that runs at 28,800 baud or faster. If you are using a Macintosh (MAC), you should have at least 12 MB of RAM and MAC operating system (Mac OS) version 7.5 or later. The key to keeping your sanity while using the Internet is enough computer RAM and a fast modem. The faster the modem, the less time you have to spend waiting to transmit Internet search requests and receive search results.

Older computer systems may not perform at the required level. For example, older 386 computers were usually shipped with a Video Graphics Array (VGA) monitor. These monitors typically display only 16 colors with high resolution. Newer computer systems use Super Video Graphics Array (SVGA) monitors, with 256 (or more) colors and high resolution. Since most Internet sites use 256 colors or more, you really need an SVGA monitor.

Other common computer system components are the keyboard, mouse, CD-ROM drive and speakers. The CD-ROM is not really required for Internet-based patent searches, but comes in handy for accessing CD-ROM patent products published by the PTO. In Chapter 5, Section B, we will show you how to order a valuable, free CD-ROM resource.

Once you have your computer system squared away, you will need to find an Internet service provider (ISP). An Internet service provider is a company that provides you with telephone number access to the Internet. There are several well-known ISPs, like America Online (AOL) and Netcom. There are also many smaller, local companies that can provide Internet access. Check your local Yellow Pages, newspapers, magazines and television ads for listings of these companies. The current average cost for unlimited Internet access is around $20 per month. For this fee, you should be able to use the Internet for as long as you want, at any time of the day, seven days a week.

In addition to the monthly service charge, the other important thing that you will need is a local dialup number. This is the local telephone number that your modem will dial to access the Internet. When you have a local dialup number, every time you access the Internet, you are simply making a local phone call. It makes no difference if you are accessing information from an Internet site in Australia, England or Bora Bora. It's still a local telephone call. If your ISP does not have a local dialup number, you will have to pay an extra charge every time you access the Internet.

Other methods of accessing the Internet (besides a modem and standard telephone lines) include the use of ISDN (Integrated Services Digital Network) telephone lines and direct cable connections. ISDN is a numerical telephone network. This network can transport not only voice data (like the standard telephone network), but caller identifications, images, facsimiles and Internet data as well. Using ISDN lines is faster than standard telephone line access. However, there are additional charges for this service and some additional computer equipment is required. Your telephone company undoubtedly has literature about ISDN that it will be happy to send you.

Another Internet access method uses existing cable television networks which have been upgraded with fiber optics. Internet data is then transmitted over cable, directly into your computer. Again, additional computer equipment (special cable-ready modems and network cards) is required. However, the increase in speed can be up to 100 times greater than with a residential telephone line. Road Runner is an example of one company providing such service. Call your local cable company for further information.

D. Computer Software Requirements

In addition to your computer system setup and your local ISP connection, you will need some computer software to perform Internet patent searches. In this book, we will assume that you are using the Microsoft Windows operating system. Typically, when you purchase a new computer, Windows is already installed on the system.

There are two versions of Windows that are currently in wide-scale use: Windows 95 and Windows 98. In order to follow the examples in this book, you will need one of these versions of Windows installed on your computer. Since Windows 98 is currently the most recent version, we will use it in most of the examples in this book. However, where the Windows 98 presentation differs significantly from Windows 95, both versions will be discussed. Macintosh users will need Mac OS 7.5 or higher. Again, where the MAC presentation differs significantly from Windows 98, both versions will be discussed.

In order to view information on the Internet, you will also need computer software that provides an easy way of looking at information on the World Wide Web (WWW). This software is called a "browser." What is the WWW and how does it differ from the Internet? Well, the WWW is just one part of the Internet. The WWW consists of a worldwide series of computers and computer networks that adhere to the same strict software protocols. These computers allow public access to information stored on their respective hard disks. By following the same software protocols, different computers from all over the world can transmit and receive data from each other. The World Wide Web uses the HyperText Transfer Protocol (http), which allows you to click your way from one site or document to another.

A browser handles all of these details for you, so you don't have to think about them. A browser allows you to visit what is known as a website. A website is a specific location on the WWW. The browser program reads the information at the website, and displays it for you on your computer monitor. Each website on the WWW has a specific address, which defines its location of the WWW. We will discuss addressing in detail, when we visit some of the various websites that provide patent search resources.

There are other computers on the Internet that do not use the protocols necessary for the WWW. However, due to the lack of a browser type of program, access to these machines is not as easy. As a result, the vast majority of Internet users limit their activities to the WWW. All of the Internet resources that we will be using in this book are available on the WWW.

The browser also drives the system performance requirements discussed in the previous section. As more sophisticated browsers become available on the market, the computer platform that supports them must perform at a higher level. For example, most Internet sites contain multiple images of high-resolution graphics. In order to retrieve and display these images, large amounts of computer RAM are required. In addition to performance problems, older systems may also have compatibility issues with modern browser programs. A browser program may not even load or run if sufficient computer RAM is not available.

Currently, the most popular browser programs are Netscape Navigator and Microsoft's Internet Explorer. In order to follow the examples in this book, you will need one of these programs installed on your computer. Since Netscape Navigator is currently the most widely used browser program (but perhaps not for long) we will use it in the examples given in this book. The presentation with Internet Explorer does not differ significantly from that for Netscape Navigator.

For Macintosh users the latest version of the Macintosh operating system (Mac OS 8.1) includes Netscape Navigator and has an integrated version of Internet Explorer. So you can use the Web browser of your choice.

When you purchase Netscape Navigator or Microsoft's Internet Explorer, installation instructions are included. Usually installation just involves inserting an installation CD into the CD-ROM drive, or a few floppies into the floppy disk drive. For Windows 98, the operating system will usually start the installation process automatically. Occasionally, a run command may need to be executed. In either case, detailed installation instructions are either printed directly on the software CD (or floppies), or included on a printed insert. Infrequently, compatibility issues occur between previously installed software and WWW browser programs. (Conflicts can also occur between the most recent versions of browsers and older versions of system software.) These issues can be resolved by referencing your computer user's manual and the documentation that accompanies your software.

Although not essential for patent searches, you should have a professional word processing program installed on your system. Later in this book, we will be using a word processor to assemble a summary of our patent search results. Although small word processing programs, such as Notepad and Wordpad, usually ship with Windows 95 and Windows 98, these programs lack the tools that a full-blown word processing application has. We recommend installing Word for Windows or WordPerfect. Both of these programs have spell check capability and a thesaurus. A thesaurus comes in handy when you try to think of words that describe your invention.

E. Windows Skills

There are only a couple of basic Windows skills that are essential for Internet-based patent searches. At a minimum, you need to be able to enter search words with the keyboard and you need to be able to use the mouse. For those of you that have never used a mouse before, don't worry. There are only a couple of essential mouse skills that you need, namely, the "click" and the "double click." A click means simply pressing the left mouse button down once, and then releasing it. A double click means pressing the left mouse button down and releasing it twice, in rapid succession.

F. What's Available at the PTDL?

As an alternative to using the Internet, if you happen to live near Arlington, Virginia, you can perform patent searches at the U.S. Patent and Trademark Office (PTO) itself. The patent search room is located at: 2021 South Clark Place, Crystal Plaza 3, Room 1A01, Arlington Virginia, 22202. The hours of business are: weekdays (except holidays) from 8:00 a.m. to 8:00 p.m. For information, call 703-308-0595.

For the rest of us, there is the Patent and Trademark Depository Library (PTDL) system. A network of 84 PTDLs are located in 50 states, the District of Columbia and Puerto Rico. (See Appendix A for a list of PTDLs, showing locations and telephone numbers.) A PTDL library can provide access to patent materials not available on the Internet. For example, most PTDLs maintain a complete patent image microfilm collection. This collection contains the facsimile images of every page of virtually every patent issued since patent #1. The size of this collection is approximately 30 million patent image pages, or around six million patents. These files are updated on a weekly basis (new patents are issued every Tuesday). Each update contains approximately 2,000 patents.

To search for your idea in the vast sea of information available at the PTDL (or on the Internet), it is necessary to know how the PTO will classify your invention. The PTO uses a complex system of classes and subclasses to categorize each and every patent that it issues. In order to determine where your idea would fall in this scheme, a searcher consults three different reference publications, which are available at every PTDL:

- *Index to the U.S. Patent Classification*
- *The Manual of Classification*
- *The Classification Definitions.*

Every PTDL also has a CD-ROM version of these manuals. This computer search system is known as CASSIS (Classification And Search Support Information System). The results of searches performed on CASSIS can be saved to a floppy disk.

Additionally, 28 PTDLs (noted in Appendix A) offer access to the APS (Automated Patent System) text search program. Patent text data can be searched via computer for patents that have been issued since August, 1971. A PTDL that allows access to the Automated Patent System will have one or more computer terminals available for public use. These terminals are connected via modem to the Patent Office in Virginia. By typing in search commands, you can automatically search through the entire APS database.

An enhanced version of the APS, which allows the viewing of patent images and text, is called the CSIR (Classified Search and Image Retrieval) system. This system is available at three specially designated Partnership PTDLs. These are located in Sunnyvale, California; Houston, Texas; and Detroit, Michigan.

 We show you how to use the PTDL and its many useful resources in Chapter 5.

Summary

What Is the Internet?
- The Internet is a worldwide web of interconnected government, business, university and scientific computer networks.
- Approximately 500 million individual users tie into this "web" of networks every day. Most users connect to the Internet via a personal computer, modem, telephone line and some software.

- Using the Internet gives us access to thousands of databases all over the world. Almost every subject is covered to some extent.

Computer Hardware Requirements for Using the Internet
- If you are using a Personal Computer (PC), you should have 16 MB or more of RAM, and a modem that runs at 28,800 baud or faster.
- If you are using a Macintosh (MAC), you should have 12 MB of RAM and a 28,800 modem.

Computer Software Requirements
- The Windows 95 or better operating system.
- For the Macintosh, version 7.5 or higher of the Mac operating system (Mac OS).
- Netscape Navigator or the Microsoft Internet Explorer browser program.
- Preferably Word for Windows or the WordPerfect word processor program.

Windows Skills
- Keyboard entry and mouse skills are the essential skills needed for performing patent searches using the computer. The most important mouse skills are the "click" and the "double click." Understanding the various parts of a window (maximize/minimize button, title bar, etc.) would be a plus.

What's Available at the PTDL?
- Microfilm images of issued patents
- Classification reference publications
- The CASSIS computer search system
- The APS text search program.

Part 2

Getting Started

In this part of the book, we will use the patent searching tools and techniques discussed in Part 1. This part consists of three chapters, each of which provides a sample search to prepare you for your own. The first two chapters—Chapters 3 and 4—should be read together. They introduce you to two patent search Websites—the PTO site and the IBM site. Chapter 3 explains what you can accomplish by starting with the PTO site. Chapter 4 goes on to explain how the IBM site works and why you should follow up your PTO search with a visit to the IBM site.

In Chapter 5 we leave behind the Internet and the World Wide Web (WWW), and enter the world of the Patent and Trademark Depository Library (PTDL). While it might be tempting for inventors with Internet experience to limit their searches to Internet-based resources, and therefore skip the PTDL, *don't do it!* Most Internet patent databases only go back to the early 1970s. Unless your field of research is based completely on recent technology, you will almost certainly miss some important patents by limiting yourself to post-1971 data. Examples of new technology inventions (i.e., post-1971 technology) would be: CD-ROMs, lasers and nanotechnology.

For those inventors with limited or no computer experience, it is tempting to skip learning computer skills and concentrate on using just the PTDL. After all, successful patent searches were performed manually long before the computer age. Also, why learn a new skill when old techniques will suffice? Well, many hundreds of thousands (perhaps millions) of hours have been spent making modern computer programs efficient and easy to use. By taking advantage of the information these programs offer, the patent searcher can save a lot of time and effort.

There are three classification manuals that the PTO uses to categorize patents: *Index to the U.S. Patent Classification, Manual of Classification* and *Classification Definitions.* As we shall soon see, finding out which classes and subclasses apply to your invention is crucial to a successful patent search. While the Internet provides access to selected sections of these manuals, their entire text is available at the PTDL. Every PTDL also has a CASSIS (Classification And Search Support Information System) computer system. The CASSIS computer system is used to search the electronic versions of the classification manuals and to extract a list of patents issued within a given class/subclass.

In Chapter 5, we will also explore the functionality of the Automated Patent System (APS) text search program, which allows you to search the entire text of patents issued since 1971. Also in Chapter 5, we will perform manual searches of pre-1971 patents using microfilm readers.

These three chapters are a necessary first step towards developing strong patent search skills. Once you have mastered the material in these three chapters, you should move on to the advanced searching methods in Part 3. However, if after learning a basic skill covered in Parts 1 and 2, you decide you'd like to learn the more advanced portion of that skill right away, use the Jump To icons to help you locate the corresponding advanced section in Part 3. ■

Patent Searching at the PTO Internet Site

This chapter introduces you to the U.S. Patent and Trademark Office's website. You are best served by starting your Internet patent search at this location. However, as we point out in Chapter 4, you can and should extend your search by running the results of your search here past the IBM patent database described in Chapter 4.

A. Simple Keyword Searches at the PTO's Website

Now that you have a pretty good idea what a patent consists of and you understand the mechanics of a keyword search, it's time to try some actual patent searches at the U.S. Patent and Trademark Office's patent search website (a different website from the general website maintained by the PTO at http://www.uspto.gov). This site allows you to search the full text and drawings of all U.S. patents issued since 1976.

1. Up and Running

In order to access the PTO over the Internet, you must be running Windows 98 or better, along with your favorite Web browser software. If you are a Mac user, you should be running Mac OS version 7.5 or higher and your browser of choice.

In the examples given below, we will be using Netscape Navigator as our browser of choice. You should follow along with the examples and try out the various commands. To start the Netscape Navigator running, just double click on its icon. Depending on your configuration, a separate dialup process may have to be started first. The Netscape Navigator icon for a typical Windows installation is shown in Figure 1 below.

Figure 1

After the Navigator program starts running, it will connect with the Internet location you selected during installation. This will most often be your Internet service provider's homepage or the homepage for Netscape Communications, Inc. The Netscape homepage is shown in Figure 2 below. Across the top of the figure, you will see the words File, Edit, View, etc. This is the main command menu for the Netscape Navigator program. We will be exploring some of these functions later in this chapter and throughout this book.

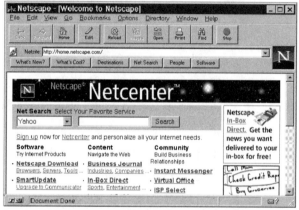

Figure 2

There is a series of buttons immediately below the menu line. They are called buttons because their purpose is to make something happen when you click on them, much like buttons in real life. From the left, these buttons are labeled Back, Forward, Home, etc. We will be using some of these buttons, as well as the menu commands, in this chapter.

The Internet address entry area is located directly below the row of buttons. This is where we type in the address of the Internet location that we want to visit.

2. Connecting to the PTO's Website

In order to get to the PTO's patent searching website, you need to type the following address in the address window:

http://www.uspto.gov/patft

Another way to get to the PTO's patent search site is through the PTO's homepage at http://www.uspto.gov. After typing in the address, just press ENTER on the keyboard. After a few seconds' delay (occasionally longer, depending on Internet traffic), you should see the homepage for the PTO'S patent searching site, as shown in Figure 3 below.

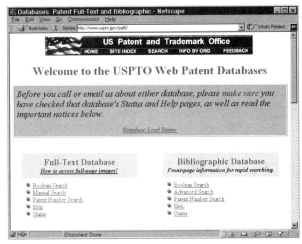

Figure 3

Web Jargon

Electronic documents that are published on the WWW are called *Web pages.* As mentioned in Chapter 1, the address (physical location on the WWW) of a Web page is referred to as its *website.* For multi-level documents that reside at the same website, the topmost document is usually called its *homepage.* If you look closely at the PTO's Web page for patent searching (Figure 4), you will notice that some text items are highlighted and/or underlined. On the WWW, these items are known as *hypertext links,* or just *links.* If you click on a link, the browser will take you to the document indicated by the link.

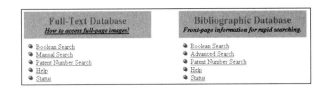

Figure 4

3. Understanding the PTO's Boolean Search Page

There are two databases available for patent searching at the PTO's website. These are the Full-Text Database and the Bibliographic Database. The Bibliographic Database lets you search only the front page of issued patents. The Full-Text Database allows you to search every word contained in the issued patent. Why two databases? Why not always search through the maximum amount of patent text available? As we shall soon see, it is more efficient to search the Bibliographic Database first, then proceed to the Full-Text Database for more detailed searching.

Figure 4 is a close-up screen shot of several hypertext links from the PTO's patent search homepage. Under the title, Bibliographic Database, there are five links:

- Boolean Search (explained in Chapter 1)
- Advanced Search
- Patent Number Search
- Help, and
- Status.

To perform a Boolean search, you need to position your mouse on the Boolean Search link. When correctly positioned, the shape of your mouse will change from an arrow to a hand. Then simply click once to jump to the Boolean Search Web page, shown in Figure 5.

Advanced Search Page. *We feature the Boolean search Web page in this chapter because it is the easiest way to get started. However, if you wish to search for a precise phrase, or you want to include more than one Boolean operator in your query (such as using both "and" and "or"), you* *can do this by using the Advanced Search page. We explain that page in detail in Chapter 6, Section A, if you wish to jump ahead.*

As you can see from Figure 6, there are several fields that can be filled in. We will discuss them one at a time. The buttons at the top of the screen, Help, Home, etc., are called "navigation aids." They are used to quickly move you from one location in the PTO's online hierarchy to another. For now, we will ignore these and move down the page.

the empty circle to the left of the Specify label, and click once. To choose which years to search, position your mouse cursor over the down arrow on the right-hand side of the rectangular box, next to the Specify radio button. Click the left mouse button and you will see a pull-down menu of searchable year ranges as shown in Figure 6.

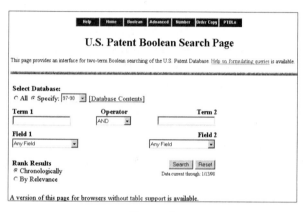

Figure 5

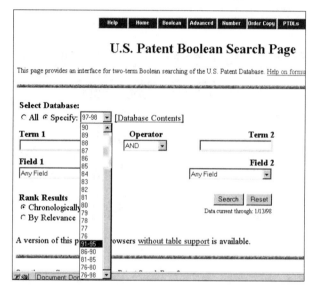

Figure 6

a. Select database

Below the horizontal bar separating the top and bottom of the page, we are presented with several text entry boxes and menu selection items. The first area that we want to address is the *radio buttons* below the Select Database title. Radio buttons are circles that can be selected with a mouse click. When selected, the circle has a dot in the center. Radio buttons are arranged in groups. Each group allows you to select one, and only one, button.

The Select Database radio buttons allow you to choose the range of years that you wish to search. By selecting the Specify button, you can limit your search to patents issued within the specified years. To choose Specify, just position your mouse over

To select the specific year or range of years that you wish to search, simply highlight that year (or years) by positioning the mouse over that selection. Then click once with the left mouse button. If you wish to search the entire patent database from 1976 to the present (that is, the front pages of all the patents in the database), select the All radio button with the mouse. This action will cause the PTO's search engine to ignore any year ranges selected in the pull-down box.

For this first example, let's select the Specify radio button. Then select the year range of 91-95, as shown in Figure 6. This means that the program will only search through the patents issued in the years 1991 through 1995.

b. Search terms and field selection

Next, below the Select Database entry and selection fields, is the field labeled Term 1. Here is where you enter your search words (keywords). Directly below the Term 1 entry box is the Field 1 entry box. This is another pull-down selection menu. By positioning your mouse cursor over the down arrow and clicking once, you can see all of the searchable fields that are available. This action is shown in Figure 7 below.

Here you can limit the scope of your search to a particular section of the issued patent's front page. For example, if you only wish to search the abstract of the patent, you can scroll down (move the mouse over) to that entry point. The item will be highlighted, click with the mouse to select it. Limiting your search to certain sections of the front page has many advantages. Chief among them is to precisely define your search in order to find just the patents you are looking for, and nothing extra. Later in this chapter we will illustrate this feature with a search of a single field from the front page.

For this example, we wish to search the entire front page of all the issued patents in the year range of 1991 through 1995. To accomplish that, select the entry "Any Field" (as shown in Figure 8) at the top of the list.

To the right of the Term 1 and Field 1 entries, we have the Operator selection boxes shown in Figure 8 below. By selecting the down arrow, you will be able to choose among the four Boolean operators (AND, OR, ANDNOT and XOR) that we discussed in Chapter 1. For the purposes of this first search, let's select the AND operator, which is the default.

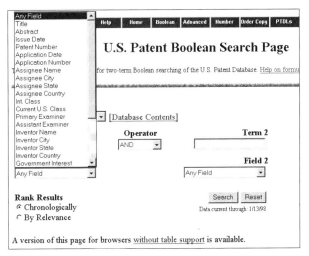

Figure 7

Figure 8

Further to the right of the page, past the operator selection box, are the Term 2 and Field 2 entry boxes. These work identically to the Term 1 and Field 1 entry boxes.

For example, let's suppose that your invention is related to a device that is involved in fire protection. You could type in "fire" for the first search term, select the logical operator AND, then enter "protection" for the second search term. This is shown in Figure 9 below.

c.   Rank the search results

Finally, you will see the Rank Results radio button selection area towards the bottom of the page. Here you can select the order in which the results will be displayed. By selecting Chronologically, patents found to have words that match your keywords will be displayed in chronological order with the most recent patents listed first. Selecting Relevance will place the search matches (or hits) in the order of most relevant first.

Figure 9

Relevance is often a difficult concept to define. The PTO uses a complex information science algorithm to determine which documents most closely match your submitted query. Some of the criteria used are the frequency of occurrences of hit terms and the proximity of terms to each other. Other factors include which field on the front page of the patent is searched and the location of the keyword within that field.

Ranking the results chronologically is the most frequently used option of the Rank Results button. Often, the search engine's idea of relevance will not match your own. For this example, we will choose to rank the results chronologically.

4.   Doing the Search

Now we are ready to begin our search. The search program will search for the terms "fire" and "protection" in all the fields of the first page of all the patents issued between the years 1991–1995. To start the search, click the button labeled Search located at the lower right side of the screen (as shown in Figure 9). Adjacent to the Search button is the Reset button. Clicking on this button will clear all of the entries and selections that you have made. This comes in handy when starting a new search.

The time it takes the PTO's search engine to complete its task will depend on several factors: the number of persons using the system at a given time, the Internet traffic returning the information to your site, and in particular, the magnitude of the range of years you selected for your search. In any case, the time delay should seldom be longer than 30 seconds.

5.   Understanding the Search Results

The results of our sample search are shown in Figure 10 below. Under the heading Search Summary, the system has reported 132 "hits" or patents in which our two search terms were found. Remember that with the use of the AND Boolean operator, both search terms "fire" and "protection" must be present for the system to report a match.

Achieving a Sharper Focus in the Search.
With only two words, we managed to produce a list of only 132 patents. But reviewing 132 patents can still be a lot of work. In Chapter 6, Section A, we explain how to further narrow your search by using the Advanced Search box and adding additional terms and conditions to your query.

Reading the search summary, we see that hits 1 through 50 are listed from the 132 total patents found. Looking below the "Pat. No." and "Title" headings in the middle of Figure 10, we see the matching patents. Notice that the patent numbers start with the most recently issued (highest number) patent first, and then proceed backward in time. This is our chronological order listing in operation.

Each of these listed patent numbers is accompanied by a patent title. Only the first eight patents fit within the initial display. You can use the *scroll bar* at the far right of the display to scan the search results. The scroll bar is a feature that is available on both Windows and Macintosh systems. It lets you use the mouse to see objects that are outside the normal viewing area.

Using the Scroll Bar

There are several ways to use a scroll bar. By clicking once on the arrow at the bottom of the scroll bar, you move the display window down one line. Similarly, by clicking once on the arrow at the top of the scroll bar, you move the display window up one line. If you press and hold the left mouse button down while positioning the mouse over the darkly shaded area on the scroll bar (shown at the top of the scroll bar in Figure 10), you can move the entire display area up and down with up and down movements of the mouse. Finally, by clicking inside the scroll bar, but outside the darkly shaded area, you can move the display up and down a page at a time.

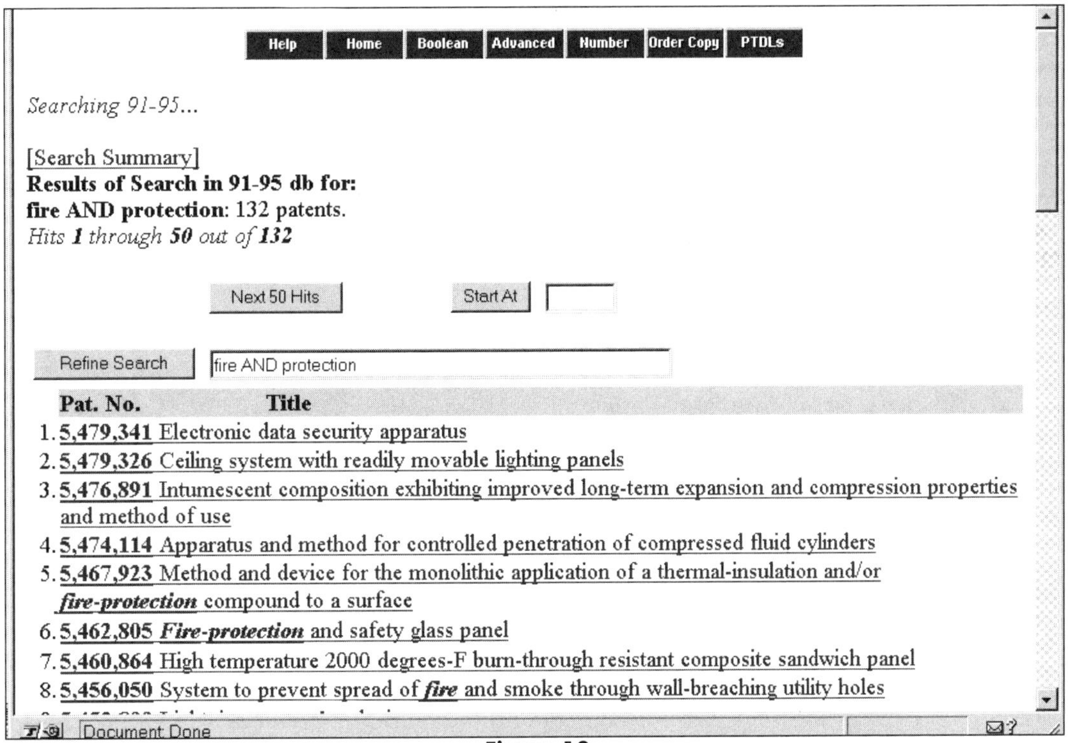

Figure 10

44. **5,350,019** *Fire protection* system
45. **5,347,767** *Fire* retardant sleeve
46. **5,344,108** Pipe surge restrainer for use with pipe hanger
47. **5,343,124** Shock-hazard-free lighting means
48. **5,340,612** Sprayable portland cement-based fireproofing compositions
49. **5,339,876** Apparatus and methods for removing hazardous contents from
50. **5,337,793** Cylinder rupture vessel

Next 50 Hits   Start At

Refine Search   fire AND protection

Search Summary

fire: 4847 occurrences in 2196 patents.
protection: 8828 occurrences in 5767 patents.
(fire AND protection): 132 patents.

Search Time: 0.59 seconds.

Figure 11

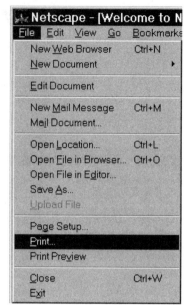

Figure 12

If you don't find what you are looking for in the first 50 hits, you can select the Next 50 Hits button (shown below the 50th patent listed in Figure 11) to see the next 50 matches.

You can get a feel for the power of a succinctly constructed Boolean search by looking at the bottom of Figure 11. Here we see that there were 4,847 occurrences of the word "fire" in 2,196 different patents. There were also 8,828 occurrences of the word "protection" in 5,767 different patents. However, the words "fire AND protection" together occurred in only 132 patents.

6. Saving and Printing the Search Results

You can get a printout of the displayed patent numbers and titles by using your browser's print feature. Simply move your mouse to the File menu item at the upper left corner of the Netscape screen display and click once. Then scroll down to the Print function. This action is demonstrated in Figure 12 below.

When you select the Print function, a printer control window similar to Figure 13 will open up. On our computer, the default printer is an HP Laserjet II (yours may be different). The down arrow next to the printer name will allow you to select from among any installed printers that you have. To obtain your printout, just click the OK button at the bottom of the window.

Figure 13

When you find a patent whose title seems appropriate to your search, you can view the entire front page of that patent by simply clicking on that title. This is because the search results listing is actually a list of hypertext links. Let's suppose that patent number 5,462,805 is one that we are interested in. This is item number 6, as shown in Figure 14 below. To view the front page of this patent, just select the link with the mouse and click once.

The front page of the patent will then be displayed, as shown in Figure 15. Here, you can review the inventor's name, patent issue date and patent abstract. By scrolling down the image, you can see the current classification of this patent. This is shown in Figure 16. Scrolling down further, we see a list of referenced patents (Figure 17). These are the patents that were determined to be the prior art for patent number 5,462,805. The front page of recently issued, referenced patents can be

5. **5,467,923** Method and device for the monolithic application of a thermal-insulation and/or *fire-protection*
6. **5,462,805** *Fire-protection* and safety glass panel
7. **5,460,864** High temperature 2000 degrees-F burn-through resistant composite sandwich panel
8. **5,456,050** System to prevent spread of *fire* and smoke through wall-breaching utility holes

Figure 14

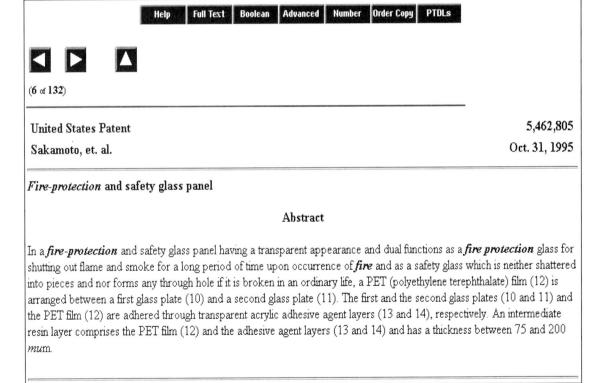

Figure 15

viewed by clicking on the patent number. Older referenced patents can be searched at your local PTDL (see Chapter 5).

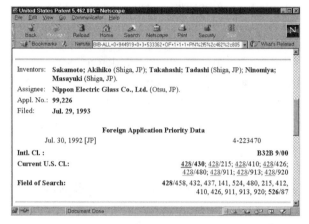

Figure 16

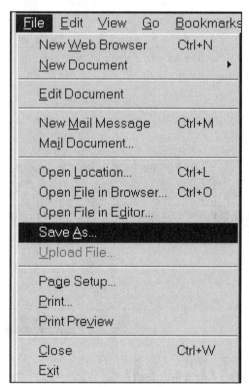

Figure 18

References Cited | [Referenced By]

		U.S. Patent Documents	
3,900,673	Aug., 1975	Mattimoe et al.	428/339
4,358,329	Nov., 1982	Masuda	156/106
4,382,996	May, 1983	Mori et al.	428/442
4,910,074	Mar., 1990	Fukawa et al.	428/215
4,911,984	Mar., 1990	Parker	428/428
4,952,460	Aug., 1990	Beckmann et al.	428/429
5,002,820	Mar., 1991	Bolton et al.	428/215
5,091,258	Feb., 1992	Moran	428/437
5,091,487	Feb., 1992	Hori et al.	526/87
5,145,746	Sept., 1992	Tomoyuki	428/458
5,219,630	Jun., 1993	Hickman	428/38
5,230,954	Jul., 1993	Sakamoto et al.	428/332
		Foreign Patent Documents	
684017	Jul., 1966	BE	
1905619	Aug., 1970	DE	
480276	Dec., 1969	CH	

Figure 17

The first thing to do to determine if this patent represents relevant prior art is to read the abstract of the patent. If it is germane to your invention, then you will want to save this information. (Chapter 10 helps you evaluate the relevance of the patents you uncover during your preliminary search.) Again, you can obtain a hardcopy printout, as discussed above. However, you can also save an electronic copy. To do this, we again

move our mouse to the File menu item at the upper left corner of our Netscape screen and click once. Then we scroll down to the Save As... selection, as shown in Figure 18 below.

When you click Save As... you will have a choice of whether to save the file as an *HTML* document or a *TXT* document. An HTML document has special codes in it that allow the browser programs (Netscape Navigator, Microsoft Internet Explorer and others) to display and link the document with other documents on the Internet. Saving the document in HTML format will preserve the hypertext links. However, you probably won't need these links since you will be assembling your patent search results in a word processor. Therefore, you should save the file in a TXT format. A TXT format is a common format that any word processor can read.

In addition to the patent abstract, you can determine the class and subclass of the patent from the front page. The PTO uses classifications to group patents according to their subject matter. In short order, we will see how to use this classification system to jump-start your patent search.

The front page also lists the class and subclasses of the referenced patents. For example, in Figure 17, the listing of cited references for the Sakamoto patent are arranged in columns. From left to right, the columns represent patent number, issue date, inventor and major Class/Sub-class. For referenced patent number 5,230,954, also by Sakamoto, Class 428 and subclass 332 are listed. Class 428 is also shown in Figure 16 as the current classification for this patent. Class 428 is actually a hypertext link. To view a description of this class, just click on it with the mouse.

Figure 19 shows the very top of a lengthy document which describes the types of inventions that are classified under Class 428. If you were to print out this class description, it would consume over 200 pages of printout. That's a lot of pages to print and read! In the next section, we will show you how to use the Find feature of Netscape Navigator to greatly simplify this task.

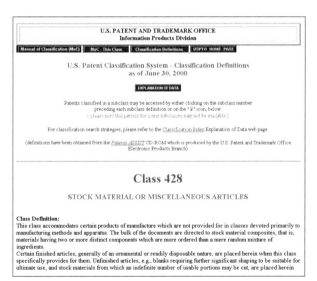

Figure 19

B. Searching the Manual of Classification

In the previous section, you searched the front pages of issued patents. You may have gathered information about patented inventions that were similar to your invention idea. This information includes the one-paragraph abstract (or description) of the patent and the class/subclass that the patent was filed under. But how do you know that you found all of the relevant classes and patents? The search results that you obtained so far depended entirely on the keywords that you used. Suppose other inventors used different words to describe similar, patented inventions. In that case, you may have missed entire classes of related patents. One way to help prevent this from happening is to search for patents according to how they've been grouped by the PTO (that is, by class and subclass).

In the previous section, we used several hypertext links to get a description of Class 428. To summarize, we performed a Boolean search of the front page of several years' worth of issued patents. Then, we looked at a list of results and selected one patent from that list. Next, we jumped to a description of that patent. From there, we jumped to a description of Class 428, which was referenced in the patent.

1. Using Navigation Aids

Now would be a good time to discuss the various ways of navigating through the PTO's hierarchy of patent search Web pages. Our description of Class 428 is actually four hypertext links away from the main PTO homepage. To keep you from getting lost as you search for patents, most of the Web pages used by the PTO have a row of navigation button across the top. The easiest way to navigate from place to place is to click on these buttons. The most common navigation buttons are shown at the top of Figure 15. Starting from the left, these buttons are labeled: Help, Full Text, Boolean, and so on. To move to the Boolean search page, just click on the Boolean button.

Another way to navigate from website to website (and Web page to Web page within the same site) is through the use of the Netscape forward and backward arrow buttons. The program maintains a running tally of which sites you visited during an Internet session. By using these two buttons, you move forward and backward along this list of locations. These buttons (along with several others) are shown in Figure 20 below. To quickly return to a previous website, just click once on the button labeled Back. To return to a website that you viewed several hypertext jumps ago, just keep clicking the Back button until you get there. If you go too far, you can click the Forward button to move forward. For example, return to the main PTO patent search homepage, from the description of Class 428 in Section A, you must click the Back arrow four times.

Figure 20

A third way to navigate is by clicking on the Go menu. This is shown in Figure 21 below. The Netscape program will list the most recently visited sites by title. To go to a particular site, just click on its title.

Figure 21

2. Using the "Browse U.S. Patent Classes" Feature

The navigation buttons across the top of the class description for class 428 (Figure 19) are different from the most common navigation buttons shown in Figure 15. These buttons are used to browse the PTO's online classification manuals. For example, to browse through the various major patent classifications click on the furthest left button, labeled "Manual of Classification (MoC)", at the top of Figure 19. You will then be presented with the Web page illustrated in Figure 22 below.

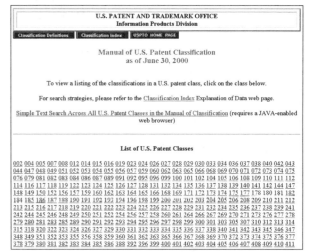

Figure 22

Each class number within this list is a hypertext link to a description of the class. By scrolling down this Web page, you can read the titles of the various classes as shown in Figure 23. Proceeding further down this Web page, you could continue to browse until you encountered one or more relevant classes. But, as we explain below, there are more efficient methods.

Before continuing, let's stop and ask: What good will this classification information do us? Suppose you came up with a new idea for a nightlight. Since many nightlights are used in bathrooms, you reason that shining a light off the reflective surfaces of porcelain fixtures (sinks and toilet bowls) would help light up the bathroom. You design your bathroom nightlight to mount to a wall fixture. In order to have the nightlight shine at the appropriate angle, you position the bulb at the end of a flexible support.

It seems simple enough to search for a classification called "lights" or "light." You would think that the PTO should have a huge listing of subclasses under the class "light." To check this assumption, we will use the Find feature of Netscape Navigator.

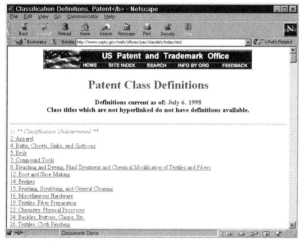

Figure 23

To activate the Find feature, just click on the Find button at the top of the Netscape display. This is the far right button with the binoculars on it, as shown in the row of buttons in Figure 20. After selecting the Find button, the little window shown in Figure 24 below will pop up. This utility will allow you to search for any word occurring in the list of class titles.

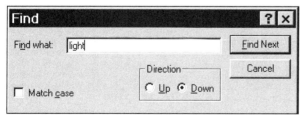

Figure 24

To search for the word "light" in the title of any of the classes, enter the word "light" in the Find box, as shown in Figure 24. Make sure the direction radio button is set to "down," then click "Find Next." Each time the Find function encounters the word "light" in a class title, the word will be highlighted. After viewing each occurrence of the word "light" in a classification title, you can proceed to the next occurrence by clicking Find Next.

You may be surprised to learn that there is no major classification using the word "light." How can this be? Isn't the lightbulb the universal symbol for a new idea or invention? The case of the word "light" should serve as a warning that the PTO may use a term you don't expect to see for a class title. First-time patent searchers often make the mistake of searching for obvious keywords only. This has a serious impact on the reliability of their patent search results. In this case, common sense tells us that all of the patents related to lights must be classified somewhere else. This is where a thesaurus comes in handy. Use the thesaurus to find alternatives for the keywords you used the first time.

Searcher's Secret Number 6

The PTO may use a term you don't expect for a class/subclass title. Use a thesaurus as necessary to find alternative descriptive words for your class titles.

One alternative form of the word "light" is "illumination." Trying our search again with the word "illumination" inserted into the search box, as shown in Figure 25, we eventually get to Class 362. This is shown in Figure 26, below. (When conducting a new search, reposition yourself at the top of the document again using the scroll bar. Be sure to select the proper search direction with the direction radio buttons.)

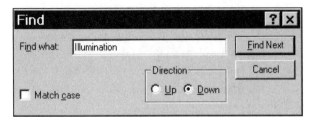

Figure 25

Figure 27

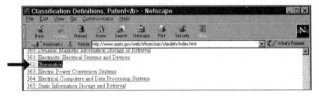

Figure 26

The listing of class titles shown in Figure 26 are actually links to descriptions of each class. Therefore, to view a description of Class 362: Illumination, just click on it. The result is shown in Figure 27 below. This Web page shows an indented list of all the sub-classes that can be found under class 362. Reading this entire Web page to see if there is a subclass title that might pertain to your invention could be very time consuming. Instead, we will again make use of Netscape's Find feature.

Recall that besides having a light, another feature of our invention was the use of a flexible support. Might there be a subclass, under the class "illumination," that refers to lights with flexible supports? To find out, we'll use our Netscape search window as in Figures 24 and 25, but this time we will use the word "flex". This will find all the derivatives of the word ("flexible," "flexing," and others). Here, we don't have to use an asterisk (*), as we do with Boolean searching.

Eventually, our Find function will bring us to subclass number 198, as shown in Figure 28 below. To read a description of this sub-class, click on the link at the left of Figure 28, labeled "198". This will load the Web page description for the entire class 362 and position you at the exact location of the subclass 198 description. This is shown in Figure 29 below.

At this point we seem to have identified one of the primary classes and subclasses of our invention, namely, Class 362, subclass 198. Wouldn't it be nice to be able to get a comprehensive list of all the patents issued in this class/subclass combination? Well, we can by using the Boolean search page.

195	. . Battery terminal sole support of lamp
196	. Mating-halves type flashlight casing
197	. Lamp bulb or lamp support axis adjustable or angularly fixed relative to axis of flashlight casing
198	. . Flexibly or extensibly mounted lamp bulb or lamp support
199	. . Separate lamp housing or lamp support pivoed to flashlight casing
200	. Flat flashlight casing
201	. . Lamp terminal directly contacts a battery terminal

Figure 28

Subclass: 198
This subclass is indented under subclass 197. Subject matter wherein the light source or light source support is connected to the casing by a means which is movable to permit the light source or light source support to be moved to various locations consistent with the length of the means or by an electric cord of such length to permit the light source or light source support to be moved to various locations consistent with the length of the cord. (1) Note. The means of this subclass type may be, for example, telescopic, flexible, and sectional pivoted members.

Figure 29

3. Using the Boolean Search Page to Find All Patents Under a Particular Class and Subclass

To return to the Boolean search page, use the Netscape back arrow. You will have to arrow back several times to return to the main PTO homepage. Then select Boolean Search.

The Boolean search page is shown in Figure 30 below. To search for all the patents in a particular class and subclass, we select the down arrow for Field 1 and change the setting from "Any Field" to "Current US Class." In the Term 1 entry box, we need to type "362/198." That is, the class 362, followed by a slash, and then the subclass 198. Next we need to specify a range of years to search. In this case, let's select 91-95. These selections and entries are shown in Figure 30.

After selecting the search button, the list of patents shown in Figures 31 and 32 will be returned. As shown in the figures, there were 17 patents issued between the years 1991 and 1995 in Class 362, subclass 198. These are patents issued for inventions that involve a light with a flexible support. Recall that our invention involves a nightlight for the bathroom that casts reflections off the porcelain fixtures. In scanning the list of patents, we see that item number 16 (in Figure 32), patent number 5,136,476, toilet bowl illuminator, sounds similar to our idea.

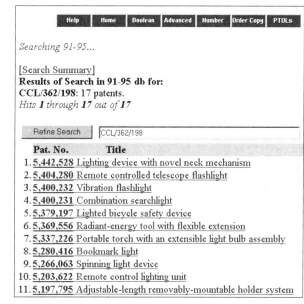

Figure 31

| | Help | Home | Boolean | Advanced | Number | Order Copy | PTDLs |

Searching 91-95...

[Search Summary]
Results of Search in 91-95 db for:
CCL/362/198: 17 patents.
Hits 1 through 17 out of 17

Refine Search   CCL/362/198

Pat. No.	Title
1. 5,442,528	Lighting device with novel neck mechanism
2. 5,404,280	Remote controlled telescope flashlight
3. 5,400,232	Vibration flashlight
4. 5,400,231	Combination searchlight
5. 5,379,197	Lighted bicycle safety device
6. 5,369,556	Radiant-energy tool with flexible extension
7. 5,337,226	Portable torch with an extensible light bulb assembly
8. 5,280,416	Bookmark light
9. 5,266,063	Spinning light device
10. 5,203,622	Remote control lighting unit
11. 5,197,795	Adjustable-length removably-mountable holder system

Figure 31

U.S. Patent Boolean Search Page

This page provides an interface for two-term Boolean searching of the U.S. Patent Database. Help on formulating queries is available.

Select Database:
○ All ⦿ Specify: 91-95 ▾ [Database Contents]

| **Term 1** | **Operator** | **Term 2** |
| 362/198 | AND ▾ | |

| **Field 1** | | **Field 2** |
| Current U.S. Class ▾ | | Any Field ▾ |

Rank Results
⦿ Chronologically   Search   Reset
○ By Relevance   Data current through: 1/13/98

Figure 30

12. 5,176,438	Integral clipboard and reading light
13. 5,158,356	Ornamental lamp with internal switch
14. 5,154,483	Flashlight with flexible extension
15. 5,136,477	Miniature battery-powered lighting device
16. 5,136,476	Toilet bowl illuminator
17. 5,012,394	Hand portable light with extendable lamp housing

Refine Search   CCL/362/198

Search Summary
CCL/362/198: 17 occurrences in 17 patents.

Figure 32

To get a listing of the front page of this patent, just click on the patent number or title. We are then presented with the front page of patent number 5,136,476, issued to D. Horn on Aug. 4, 1992 (Figure 33). By reading the patent abstract, as shown in Figure 34, we see that some aspects of our idea have been anticipated by the Horn patent. Clearly, patent number 5,136,476 requires further study. For that, we will use the Full-Text Search techniques illustrated later in this chapter.

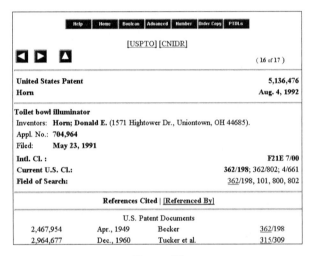

Figure 33

Figure 34

4. Using the "Search Across All U.S. Patent Classes in the U.S. Manual of Classification" Feature

Another method of finding relevant classes for our invention is to directly search the class descriptions. You can accomplish this by using the link labeled "Simple Search across All U.S. Patent Classes", shown in Figure 35 below. This link can be seen towards the bottom of Figure 27 for the Manual of Classification entry for Class 362.

> Simple Text Search Across All U.S. Patent Classes in the Manual of Classification (requires a JAVA-enabled web browser)

Figure 35

Whereas, the first link allowed us to list class titles, which we subsequently searched via the Netscape Find button, this link, allows us to search for keywords across all the class descriptions. As such, it is a very powerful search tool. After clicking on this link, you will see the query box shown in Figure 36 below. To search for the word "light" across all the patent classes, enter the word "light" as shown in the Figure, and click on "Find".

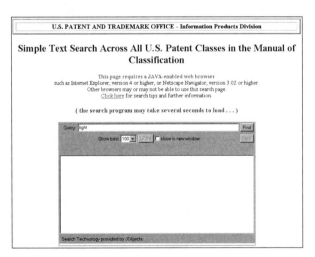

Figure 36

The results of the search will be similar to those shown in Figure 37 below. What you will get is a listing of classes that contained your keyword. The classes will be listed in order of most frequent usage. To jump to a class description from these results, just double click on any class listing.

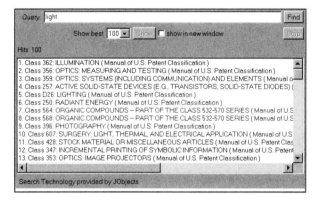

Figure 37

After you have collected the most relevant classes, you can return to the Boolean search page and search for all the patents within those classes.

C. Search by Patent Number

Let's suppose that you have a patent number and wish to quickly look up a description of that patent. This can come in handy for sudden inspirations or for detailed product research. For example, suppose you are doing some interior decorating and you are working with a stud finder. Stud finders are used to find the wooden studs hidden behind plasterboard on interior walls. It's important to drive support nails into wooden studs when hanging heavy wall decorations.

After missing a stud and driving a nail through the wall, you decide that there has to be a better design for a stud finder. A quick look at the back of the device you are using reveals a patent number in raised plastic. Wouldn't it be great if you could review a patent document just by typing in a patent number?

The PTO provides just such a feature. Here's how it works. After returning to the PTO main patent search Web page, by using one of the methods described in Section B1, you will see the links shown in Figure 38 below. To search by patent number, select the "Patent Number Search" link, under the Bibliographic Database heading.

Figure 38

You will then be presented with the Web page shown in Figure 39, below. To review the front page of a particular patent, just enter the patent number into the query box, as shown in the figure, and click on Search. Here we have entered patent number 5,148,108. The results are shown in Figure 40 below.

Figure 39

Here we see the patent number and title for our stud finder. To review the front page of this patent, just click on the patent title.

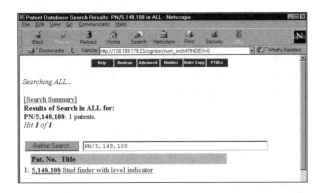

Figure 40

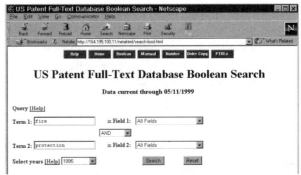

Figure 41

D. Full-Text Search

Using the keyword search methods explained in Section A above, and the patent class search techniques described in Section B, you probably found one or more patents that are related to your area of invention. After reviewing the abstracts and class definitions of these patents, you will probably be left with several patents that should be studied in further detail. You can now review the complete patent document by using the Full-Text Search feature of the PTO.

1. Selecting Full-Text Searching

To perform full-text searching of U.S. patents, select the Boolean Search link under the Full-Text Database, as shown on the left side of Figure 38. Be sure to click on the correct Boolean search link. Up to this point in the book, we have been using the links under the Bibliographic column (right-hand side of Figure 38). Now we are using the links under the Full-Text column (left-hand side of Figure 38). The resulting Web page is shown in Figure 41, below.

2. Doing the Full-Text Search

The various keyword entry fields and selection boxes work exactly the same as the Boolean Search page under the Bibliographic Database. In Figure 41, we have used the same search terms as in Section A. Namely, searching for the words "Fire" and "Protection." Also, as in Section A, we have set the range of the patent text to be searched to "All Fields." However the range of years has been reduced from 1991-1995, to just the year 1995. After clicking on the Search button, the results are shown in Figure 42, below.

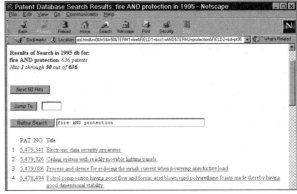

Figure 42

3. Understanding the Full-Text Search Results

Here we see that there are 636 patents that contain our two search terms. This is a lot more than the 132 hits obtained with our search of the Bibliographic Database. Why the difference? Instead of just reviewing the front page of issued patents for our keywords, we are now reviewing the entire text of the patent. Also, note that the 636 hits were obtained by only searching through the year 1995. If we had set our search range to 1991-1995, as was the case for the Bibliographic Database, we would have received many more hundreds of hits.

However, we can quickly reproduce the reasonable results of the Bibliographic Database by limiting the range of our patent search to the abstract of the patent. This action is shown in Figure 43, below. The results of this new search are shown in Figure 44. Here we see that 22 hits were obtained.

As in the case of the Bibliographic Search results, to review a patent document, just click on the appropriate link. From Figure 44, we see that patent number 5,462,805 (item number 3) is again listed among the results. This is because patent 5,462,805 was issued in 1995. To review the entire text of this patent, just click on the patent title. The various sections of patent text can then be reviewed by using the scroll bar. The claims section of patent 5,462,805 is shown in Figure 45. The background of the invention and the detailed description are shown in Figures 46 and 47, respectively.

Figure 45

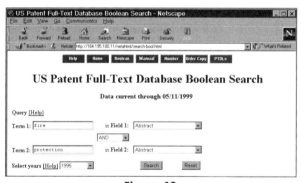

Figure 43

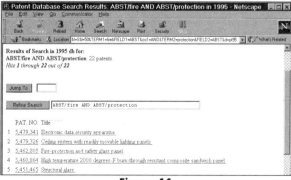

Figure 44

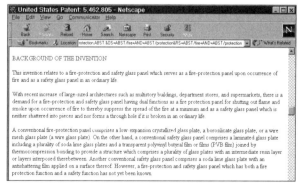

Figure 46

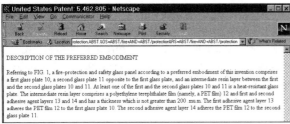

Figure 47

To review the full text of patents located via the patent keyword searches of Section A, and the class/sub-classes searches of Section B, return to the PTO main patent search Web page. Then click on the patent number search link, under the Full-Text Database as shown in Figure 48, below. Then enter the number of the patent you wish to review. This link works exactly like the patent number search link shown in Section C. The major difference here is that the entire text of the resulting patents can now be reviewed.

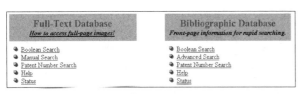

Figure 48

E. Patent Images

In addition to searching through the full text of all patents issued since January 1, 1976, you can look at images of each page. What's the advantage of looking at scanned images of a patent page? After all, recalling the discussion of Optical Character Recognition in Chapter 1, Section B, an image can't be searched. The big advantage is that viewing scanned images of issued patents allows you to review the patent drawings. The detailed descriptions of patents contain painstaking references to the patent drawings. By reading the detailed

description and referring to each of the numbered elements of the patent drawings, a reviewer can gain a detailed understanding of the patent.

1. Loading the Image Viewer

The first step to viewing patent images on the PTO's website is to load a separate patent image viewer program into your computer. The good news is that the program is free and can be downloaded over the Internet. At the upper left of Figure 48, just below the Full-Text Database title, is a link to an online patent image viewer program. This link is labeled: "How to access full-page images!" By clicking on this link, you will be presented with the Web page shown in Figure 49, below.

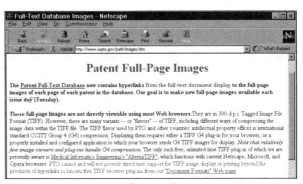

Figure 49

This Web page provides some background information about PTO compatible image viewer programs. Currently, the only freely available image viewer program that will work with the PTO's online database is the Medical Informatics Engineering "AlternaTIFF" program. To gain access to this program, click on the link labeled "Medical Informatics Engineering's AlternaTIFF" shown in the center of Figure 49. You will then be presented with the Web page shown in Figure 50.

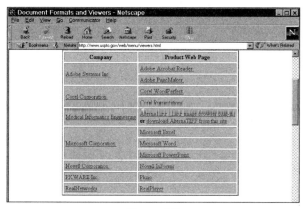

Figure 50

This Web page provides information about various document formats found on the PTO website. It also contains links to the manufacturers who offer free viewers for those formats. The link of interest here is in the center of the right hand column. It is the link labeled "AlternaTIFF." To access the manufacturer's website, select this link. You will then see the Web page shown in Figure 51, below.

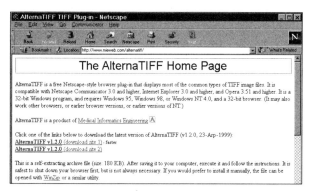

Figure 51

Here we can download the actual viewer program by clicking one of the download links shown in the middle of the Figure 51. As this book goes to print, the latest version of the program is version v1. 2.0, dated April 23, 1999. As a rule, you should always download the latest version.

After clicking on the download link, you should see a small window pop up on your screen. Its appearance will be similar to the image shown in Figure 52, below. This screen allows you to select a directory on your computer for storing the image viewer program. You can click on the small pulldown arrow shown at the top center of Figure 52 to change directories. In this case, the program will be saved in the Patent Searching directory.

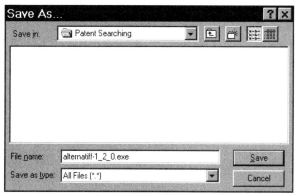

Figure 52

The name of the program is shown at the bottom of Figure 52. In this case, the program name is "alternatiff-1_2_0.exe." The program name you see may be slightly different as new versions are released. Before clicking the Save button, be sure to write down the name of the program and the directory where it is stored. If you forget, you can always use the Windows Find feature to hunt for the file later.

To start the download process, click the Save button at the lower right of Figure 52. As the program is being saved on your hard disk, you will see a display similar to that shown in Figure 53. Transfer times will vary, but this program is fairly small and should take around a minute or less to download.

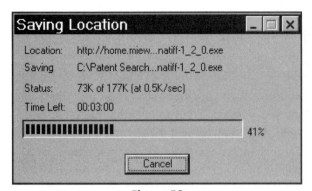

Figure 53

shown in Figure 55, below. To continue the extraction process, just click on the Setup button located at the upper right of the window.

Figure 55

2. Installing the Image Viewer

After downloading, the AlternaTIFF image viewer is stored on your hard disk in compressed mode. What this means is that the file has to be expanded prior to use. Files are transferred over the Internet in compressed format, because they take up less space that way, and therefore require less time to transfer.

The next step in the setup process is to select the location on your hard disk where the image viewer will be stored. Figure 56 shows the default location for Netscape Communicator. Notice that the check box next to the label "Install into Netscape Navigator" has been selected. To install the image viewer with the Microsoft Internet Explorer, simply click in the check box directly below.

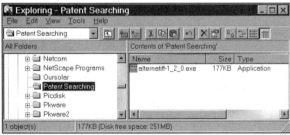

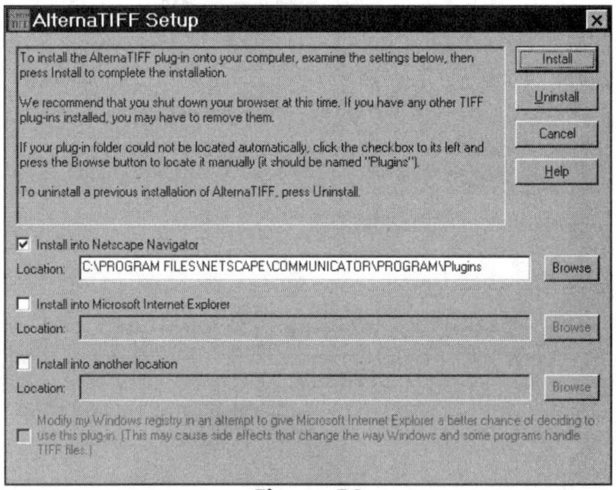

Figure 54

Fortunately, uncompressing the file to fully functional format is very simple. First, to avoid any installation problems, you should close any open applications, including any browser programs you have running. Next, locate the file using the Microsoft Windows Explorer program. This file management program ships with every version of Windows. Figure 54 shows the compressed AlternaTIFF file, located in the Patent Searching directory. To uncompress the file, simply double click on it. You will then see the small window

Figure 56

After selecting the appropriate browser for your system, click on the Install button as shown at the upper right on Figure 56. After the image viewer has been successfully installed, you will see the small popup window shown in Figure 57. Click on the OK button to continue.

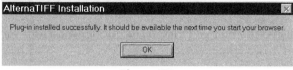

Figure 57

3. Using the Image Viewer

After successfully installing the AlternaTIFF image viewer, we can return to the PTO's patent search website and view the scanned images of each page of our relevant patents. At the PTO patent search home page, click on Patent Number Search under the Full-Text Database (see Figure 48). For example, let's look at the scanned images of patent number 5,462,805, the fire-protection and safety glass panel. After entering the patent number and clicking on Search (see Section C to refresh your memory on how to do this), you will see the Web page shown in Figure 58, below.

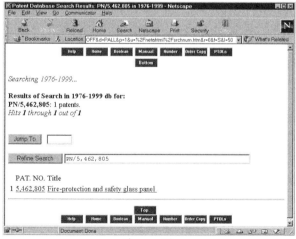

Figure 58

Figure 58 simply shows our patent number and title. To review the patent document, click on the

title. You will then be presented with the Web page shown in Figure 59, below. Figure 59 shows the patent name, issue date, and abstract as seen before in Section A. However, there is now one important difference. Across the top of Figure 59 are several navigation buttons. The center button labeled Images is an activation button for our patent image viewer program. To start the viewer, click on the Images button. You will then see the Web page shown in Figure 60, below.

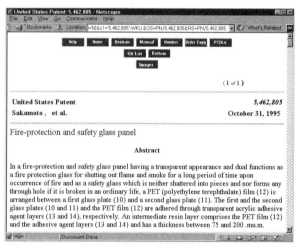

Figure 59

Figure 60 shows the image viewer program with the first page of patent 5,462,805 already loaded. The left side of Figure 60 shows several controls for the image viewer. We will discuss these one by one.

Towards the center left of Figure 60 there is an entry box labeled "Go to Page." You can make the image viewer display any selected page of patent 5,462,805 by typing in the page number and clicking on the button labeled Go immediately to the right.

Below the "Go to Page" box are a series of arrows. They work in a similar fashion to the indicators on a tape recorder. The left-most arrow will rewind the image viewer to the beginning, or first page of the patent. The next arrow reduces the page number of the current display, one page at a time. Similarly, the third arrow from the left advances the displayed patent page, one page at a time. Finally, the forth arrow advances the displayed page to the last page of the patent.

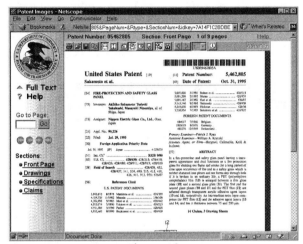

Figure 60

Below the arrows, hypertext links have been set up for the major sections of the displayed patent. As shown in the figure, these sections are the Front Page, Drawings, Specifications and Claims. Clicking on any of these links will cause the respective section of the patent to be immediately displayed in the viewer. This can come in handy if, for example, you want to jump directly to the patent specifications section. This way you don't have to search for it by advancing one page at a time through the entire patent.

One of the primary reasons for using the image viewer is to review the patent drawings. Figure 61 shows the image viewer display after the "Drawings" link has been selected. As you can see from the top of the display, this particular patent has three drawing pages. The image viewer has jumped to the first drawing page.

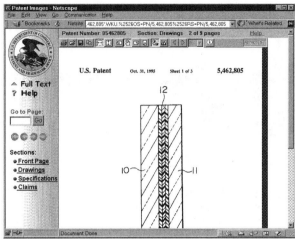

Figure 61

Enlarged images of the patent drawings can be displayed by moving the mouse cursor over the displayed area. The shape of the cursor will change from an arrow to a magnifying glass. An enlarged display of a section of a patent drawing can be obtained by positioning the cursor over the selected area and clicking once. An enlarged display of the top area of patent drawing number 1 is shown in Figure 62. This clearly shows where drawing element 12 is used in this patent. The image is returned to normal size by clicking once again with the mouse.

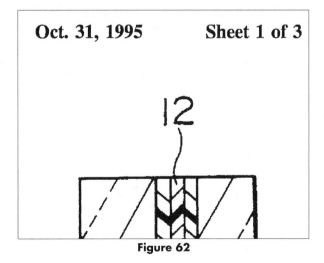

Figure 62

4. Printing and Saving Patent Images

Images of any displayed patent page can be printed or saved to hard disk for future reference. To print the currently displayed page, just click on the button with the small image of the printer. This is shown in the top left of Figure 61. A close-up view is shown below, in Figure 63.

To save the displayed patent page to the hard disk, click on the third button from the left. This is the button with the small image of a floppy disk shown in Figure 63.

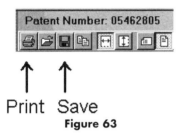

Print Save

Figure 63

F. An Effective Strategy for Basic Patent Searches

When searching the patent database, there are two goals that you must keep clearly in mind. The first goal is to find the most relevant classes and sub-classes for your invention. Relevancy is determined by reading the class descriptions and applying them to your invention. The second goal is to review all of the issued patents within those classes and determine if your idea has been anticipated by the prior art. Anticipation means that all the main aspects of your idea have been documented in previously issued patents or other sources of prior art. We explain anticipation in more detail in Chapter 10.

You can approach this problem in one of two ways. First, as shown in Section B, you start from a keyword search of the patent classes. By reviewing the class descriptions, you determine where your invention might fit in. Then you review all of the issued patents within those classes. Alternately, as shown in Section A, you can start from keyword searches of the patents themselves, and after reviewing the matching patents, extract the relevant patent numbers and classes.

Starting from a keyword search of the classes first is usually more efficient. However, we recommend using both methods. That way, you are less likely to miss an important prior art reference. Figure 64 shows a flowchart for searching the patent classes. Notice that you can start from keyword searches of the class titles or of the class descriptions. Figure 65 shows a flowchart for searching the front page of the patents themselves.

This is what we would call a one-level-deep search. In other words, you have made one pass of your keywords through the Internet PTO database and hopefully extracted some relevant prior art. You have probably found two or three classes and several patents that speak to different aspects of your invention.

After saving the front page of all relevant prior art patents, you can assemble these documents into a quick search results report. For example, using the "Insert..File" function of the Word for Windows word processor (see Figure 66), we can insert each of our saved patent front pages into a single document.

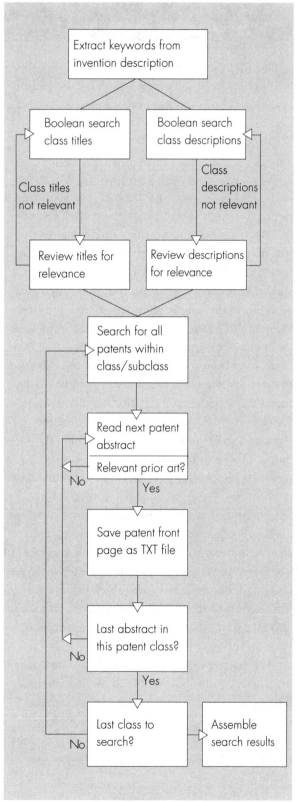

Figure 64

Figure 65

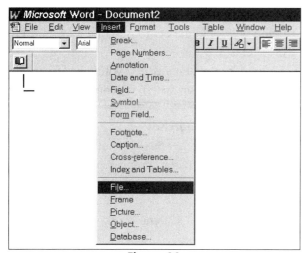

Figure 66

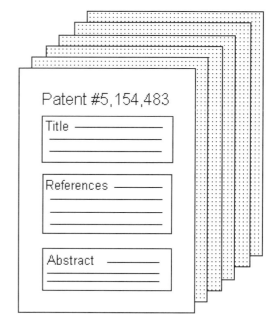

Figure 68

After inserting all of the front patent pages into your new document, just use the "File..Save As" command (see Figure 67), with a new file name. This is shown schematically in Figure 68.

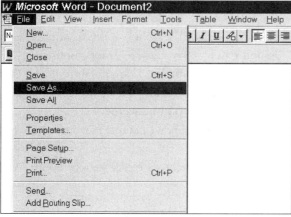

Figure 67

Now you can use your saved patent summary to assist you with the Full-Text patent database. Using the patent number search feature of the Full-Text Database, you should review the entire text of each of the patents you uncovered. Use the patent image viewer to print out and save images of each page of relevant patents.

In order to do a reasonably thorough patent search, you should make a second-level pass through your results. This means reviewing the referenced patents listed on the front of each of those prior art patents. This action is shown in Figure 69. This can lead to a lot of reading. For example, if you found ten patents related to yours, and each of these referenced ten older patents, then you have an additional one hundred patents to review. It's worth the effort, however, because this may lead you to an important class or patent that you might have otherwise overlooked.

For patents issued before 1971, you will have to make a trip to your local Patent and Trademark Depository Library (see Chapter 5). However, the good news is that by arming yourself with a list of prior art patent numbers, you'll have a reasonable head start and save yourself a lot of time.

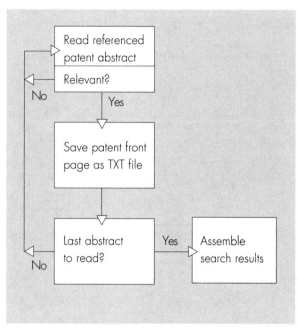

Figure 69

- Be aware that the PTO may use different words than you would expect to describe a given class of patents.
- Search for all patents issued within a class using the PTO's Boolean search function.

Patent Number Searches

Use the Patent Number Search feature to review the text of a given patent number.

Full-Text Search

- Perform keyword searches of the full text of issued patents
- Review the full text of suspected prior art patents located from patent front page searches.

Patent Images

- Load the image viewer onto your computer.
- Install the viewer.
- Use the image viewer to review, save and print each page of prior art patents.

Summary

Simple Keyword Searches

- Perform keyword searches of the PTO's Internet database using simple Boolean logic.
- Review abstracts of matching patents for relevance.
- Use the "File..Save" command to save your results.

Searching the Manual of Classification

- Perform keyword searches of classification titles using the Find function.
- Perform keyword searches of classification descriptions using the PTO's search function.

An Effective Strategy for Basic Patent Searches

- Perform keyword searches of classes first, then find all patents issued within those classes. Save the front pages of relevant patents.
- Perform keyword searches of the front pages of issued patents. Save any relevant results.
- Use the Patent Number search feature of the Full Text Database to review the entire text of each relevant patent you uncovered.
- Review the referenced patents of your results for further prior art.
- Assemble results into a quick search report. ■

Patent Searching at the IBM Website

n Chapter 3, we explained how to search the PTO patent database at the PTO's patent searching website. In this chapter, we first introduce you to the IBM patent database located on IBM's website and then explain how you can use this database to augment your PTO search results.

As a general proposition, you're better off starting with the PTO site because it lets you search by classification and offers a more precise type of search. However, the IBM database lets you extend your online patent searching back to January 1971. That's a full five years additional coverage. So the best strategy is to start with the PTO database, and then extend your patent searching using the IBM website. This strategy requires that you read Chapter 3 first, if you haven't already done so. Then return here.

Searcher's Secret Number 8

Always start your Internet patent searches at the PTO website. Then proceed to the IBM website to take advantage of the extended range of years covered.

A. Introduction to the IBM Patent Search Site

The IBM corporation has provided an important patent search resource on the Internet. To get to the IBM patent search website, you need to type the following address into the address window of your browser:

http://www.patents.ibm.com

New Location for IBM's Search Site

On May 24, 2000, Internet Capital Group and IBM announced the formation of a new company, "Delphion". The new company has acquired IBM's existing Patent Search Site. It is anticipated that the look of some of the Web pages presented here will change. However, the basic functionality should remain the same. Check the website http://www.delphion.com for details.

Figure 1

The PTO's website, covered in Chapter 3, provides you with two methods for searching its patent database. You can search the front page of issued patents via their Bibliographic search method, or you can search the full text of issued patents with their Full-Text search engine. The IBM website has a slightly different patent search interface. At the IBM website, you can search the front page and the claims section of all patents issued from January 1971 to the present. The IBM website also allows you to view, but not search, graphic images of the entire patent text and drawings. Limited searching of European patents is also available.

Figure 1, above, shows the homepage of the IBM patent search website. As you can see, it appears different from the PTO's patent search homepage discussed in Chapter 3. At the PTO website, you have to click on a link to get to a Boolean search Web page. While the IBM patent search homepage also has a link to a Boolean search Web page, you can perform "text only" searching right from the homepage.

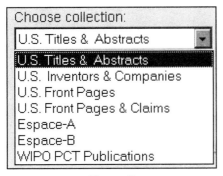

Figure 2

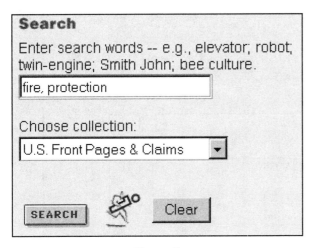

Figure 3

What's the difference between a text-only search and a Boolean search? The difference is that the Boolean operators (AND, OR, XOR and ANDNOT) are not available.

To perform a text-only search, you enter one or more keywords separated by commas. The other available selections are shown in Figure 2. For example, in Figure 3, we have entered the words "fire, protection." The second search collection we have selected is U.S. Front Pages and Claims. We then click on the search button to obtain our results.

The results are shown in Figure 4 below. As you can see, we obtained 131,340 hits from this simple search. What this means is that 131,340 patents, issued between the years 1971 to the present, contained the word "fire," the word "protection" or both, on the front page and/or in the claims section.

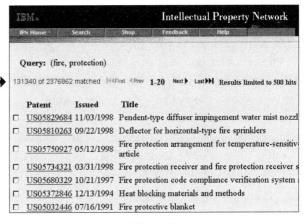

Figure 4

More selective searches can be performed by using the three hypertext links below the text search box. These links are called "Patent Number," "Boolean Text" and "Advanced Text." To get back to the IBM patent search homepage, just click once on the back arrow of your browser.

To get to the IBM Boolean search page, click Boolean Text. You will then be presented with the Web page shown in Figure 5 below.

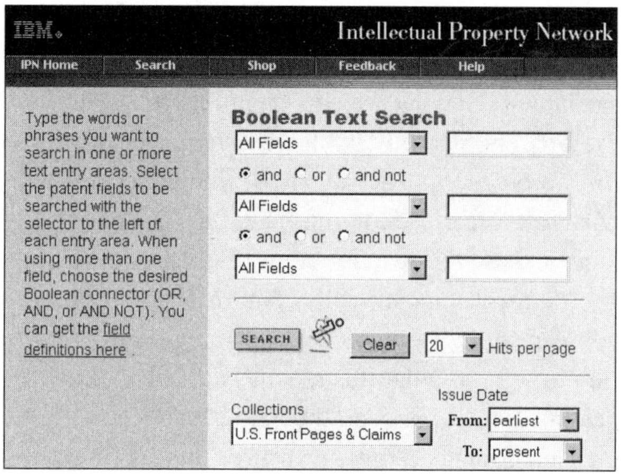

Figure 5

IBM's Boolean search page is similar to the PTO's Boolean search page in that there are text entry boxes separated by a Boolean operator box. The entry boxes at the IBM website are above one another, whereas the PTO has the boxes side-by-side.

To see the available search fields, just click the down arrow to the left of the first text entry box. Figure 6 shows the available fields that can be searched at the IBM site. Figure 7 shows the available Boolean search collections. Later in this chapter, we will have a side-by-side comparison of the capabilities of the two databases.

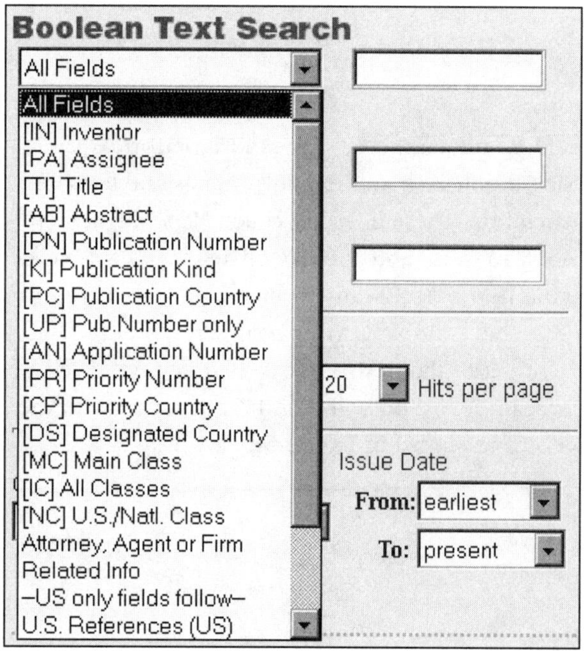

Figure 7

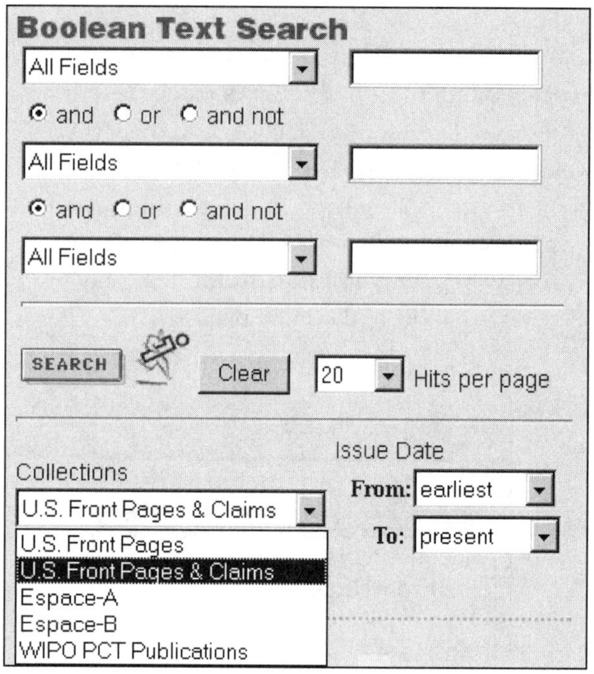

Figure 6

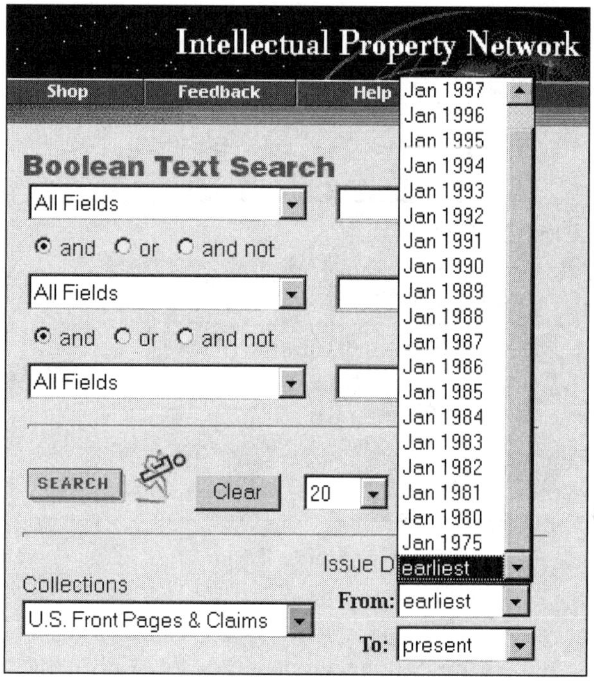

Figure 8

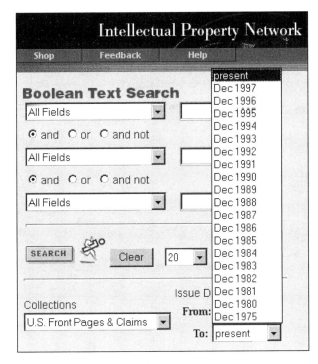

Figure 9

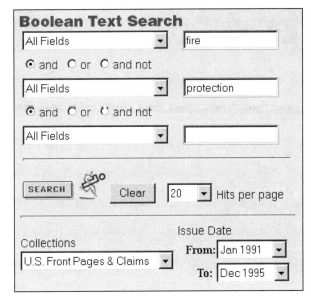

Figure 10

To select the specific year, or range of years, that you wish to search, use the "From:" and "To:" selection boxes shown in Figures 8 and 9, respectively.

Figures 8 and 9 also show the Boolean operators available from the IBM website. The desired operation is selected by clicking on the radio button adjacent to the operator name. In Figures 8 and 9, the AND operator has been selected.

To see the differences between the IBM and the PTO's patent databases, let's perform a Boolean search similar to the one performed in Chapter 3, Section A. Namely, we will search for the words "fire" and "protection" as shown in Figure 10 below. In the figure, we have selected the All Fields operator for both of our keywords, and selected the AND Boolean operator. The patent collection we have selected is: "U.S. Front Pages and Claims," and the range of years is set to 1991–1995.

Using IBM's Built-In Thesaurus Operator. *In Chapter 6, Section B, we explain how to use IBM's built-in thesaurus operator to automatically search for synonyms of your selected keywords.*

To start the search, just click the Search button shown at the bottom of Figure 10. The results are shown in Figure 11 below. As you can see there are 401 patents that contain the words "fire" and "protection." This is quite an improvement over the 131,340 patents obtained with a simple text search.

However, 401 is still a lot more than the 132 patents obtained in a similar search of the PTO's Bibliographic database. Why the difference? Well, recall that with the IBM database, you are searching through more of each patent than with the PTO's Bibliographic search. When you select Any Field with the PTO Bibliographic database, you are searching only the front page of the issued patent. When you select All Fields with the IBM database, you are searching through the front page and the claims of the issued patent.

Searching Patent Claims

The claims of the patent are a series of tersely worded statements that precisely describe and define the underlying invention. Searching the claims section is a good way of finding those patents dealing with subject matter similar to your invention. As described in Chapter 1, patent claims operate in much the same way as do real estate deeds—they precisely delimit the scope of the patent in the same way as the real estate deed describes the precise location of the property.

Figure 12

Using Advanced Text Search to Narrow Your Search. *In Chapter 6, Section B, we explain how to use the Advanced Text Search to greatly narrow the number of patents in your search results list. After you master the text search material in this chapter, study the material in Chapter 6.*

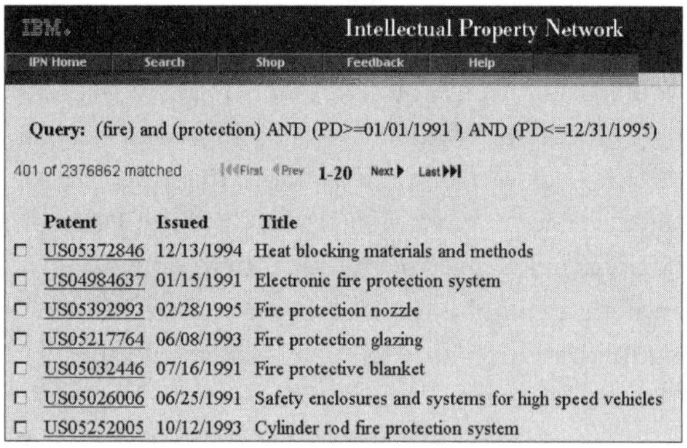

Let's refine our search results by limiting our search to the abstract of the issued patent. You do this by changing the All Fields selection for both keywords, to the Abstract selection. This action is shown in Figure 12 above. After clicking search, we get the results shown in Figure 13.

Here, we have reduced the number of patents matching our query to 159. As in the PTO database, each patent number listed is actually a hypertext link to the patent itself. Since the Sakamoto patent of Chapter 3 (Patent Number 5,462,805) was issued in 1995, it is included in our list of hits. To view the patent on the IBM system, just scroll down to Patent Number 5,462,805 (you will have to select the "Next 20 Hits" button three times since only 20 patent titles are displayed at one time), and click on it. The results are shown in Figure 14 below.

While similar to the PTO's patent front page presentation, there are several important differences to note. The most important difference can be seen

Figure 11

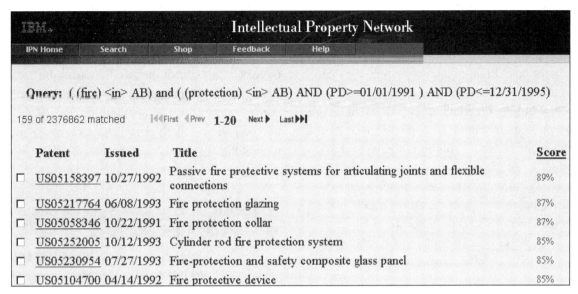

Figure 13

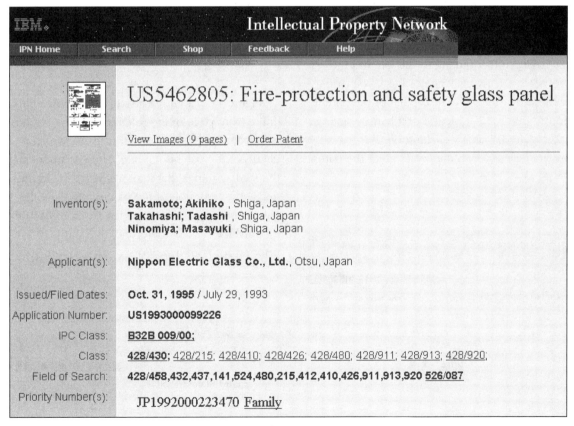

Figure 14

at the upper left corner of Figure 14. There you will find a "View Images (# pages)" hypertext link. By clicking on this link (or the small graphic image of a patent page immediately to the left), you can view each page of the patent.

After you select the link, a special patent image viewer program is started. As opposed to the PTO's image viewer program, you do not have to download and install this program on your system. This program will run in a separate browser window. The first page of the patent is automatically loaded into the viewer. This action is shown in Figure 15 below. The IBM system defaults to a display of the first page only. To load graphic images of all the patent pages, select the "Fetch Remaining Pages" link at the upper left of Figure 15. Figure 16 shows the IBM patent image viewer with all the images of the Sakamoto patent displayed. Across the top of the viewer are the controls, which are also shown in Figure 16. At the far left, there is a picture of a hand with the index finger pointing left to a vertical bar. When you click on this picture, the viewer displays the first page of the patent. The next two images have hands pointing to the left and the right respectively. By clicking on these, you display either the previous or the next page of the patent. The fourth control is a picture of a hand pointing right to a vertical bar. By clicking on this control, you move the viewer to the last page of the patent.

In Figures 16 and 17, the two leftmost controls are grayed out. This is because we are viewing the first page of the patent, so there is no previous page. To the right of the hand controls are "+" and "-" controls with magnifying glasses. By selecting the "+" control, you can enlarge the size of the displayed page. Similarly, by clicking on the "-" magnifying glass, you shrink the page.

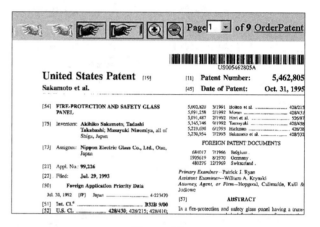

Figure 16

Figure 18 is a reduced size view, showing the entire front page of the Sakamoto patent. Figure 19 is a magnified view of the front page, which reveals details of the patent drawing. The great benefit of the IBM system is that it allows you to read the detailed description of the patent and view the patent drawings. This provides a relatively straightforward method for determining if this patent is prior art for your invention.

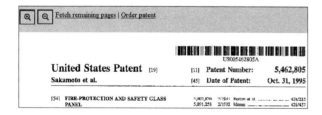

Figure 15

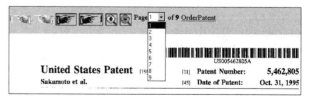

Figure 17

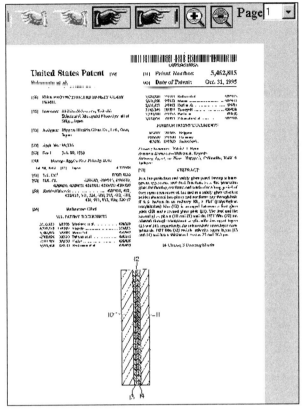

Figure 18

To the left of the "magnify" controls is a page number control. As shown in Figure 17 above, by clicking the down arrow you can quickly jump to any page of the patent.

To the left of the page number control is a link that allows you to order copies of patents. By selecting the link, you will be presented with the patent order form shown in Figure 20 below. At the bottom of the order form (Figure 21), the number of the patent that you are currently viewing has already been filled in for you.

To order nice clean copies of patents from IBM, you will need an Optipat account number. To get an Optipat account number, call Optipat at 800-445-9760 within the U.S., or call 703-916-1500 outside the U.S. The cost is $2.50 per patent, for up to 100-page patents. Patents over 100 pages in length will cost you $2.50, plus an additional $2.50 for each additional 100 pages or portion thereof. You can select from several delivery options, including U.S. mail, 2nd day delivery and Priority Mail. You can also have the patents faxed to you (one-hour service) for $9.00 per patent (up to 20 pages per patent), and 40 cents per page after 20 pages. In general, Optipat will process your order within 24 hours.

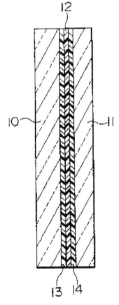

Figure 19

Customer Number:	
Docket Number:	
Firm:	
Attention to:	
E-mail address:	
Fax number :	
Voice number :	
Address :	
City:	
State:	
Zip Code:	
Country:	

Figure 20

Patent	Qty	Patent	Qty
5462805	1		

Please wait to receive your order confirmation number or further instructions after submitting the order. Orders are not complete until a confirmation number is shown.

☞ Submit Order   Clear

Figure 21

To return to the patent image viewer, click the back arrow on your browser. When you have finished viewing the images of the patent, you can close the graphics viewer. You do this by selecting File, and then Close, as shown in Figure 22. You will then be returned to the front page of the Sakamoto patent, as shown in Figure 16.

Netscape - [5462805.tif P

File Edit View Go Bookmark

New Web Browser   Ctrl+N
New Document   ▶

Edit Document

New Mail Message   Ctrl+M
Mail Document...

Open Location...   Ctrl+L
Open File in Browser... Ctrl+O
Open File in Editor...
Save As...
Upload File...

Page Setup...
Print...
Print Preview

Close   Ctrl+W
Exit

Figure 22

Figure 23

If you scroll down the front page display of the Sakamoto patent (Figure 16), you will see the three alternate search links shown in Figure 23. Instead of further Boolean searches, let's perform a Patent Number search. You do this by selecting the Patent Number link.

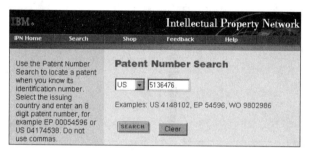

Figure 24

This Web page, shown in Figure 24, allows you to retrieve a particular patent by typing in the patent number. In Chapter 3, Section B, we determined that patent number 5,136,476 (toilet bowl illuminator) might be prior art for a bathroom nightlight. Let's look at the same patent using the IBM system. To see the front page of the patent, just enter the patent number, as shown in Figure 24, and click Search. We are then presented with the results shown in Figure 25 below.

From this point, you can proceed to view images of each page of the patent. As with the Sakamoto patent, just click on the view pages hypertext link at the upper left of Figure 25.

The IBM patent search system does not allow you to search the *Manual of Classification*. Nor can you directly search for all the patents issued within a particular class/subclass. However, once you have located a patent of interest, you can obtain a list of other patents issued within the same class as the patent.

Figure 25

Figure 25 illustrates this situation. Recall from Chapter 3, Section B, that Class 362 (Illumination), subclass 198 (flexibly or extensibly mounted lamp bulb or lamp support), was the major classification for this invention. The IBM search system has a hypertext link for this class/subclass, as shown in Figure 25. However, when we click on this link, instead of getting class descriptions, we get a listing of all of the patents issued with this class/subclass. These results are shown in Figure 26.

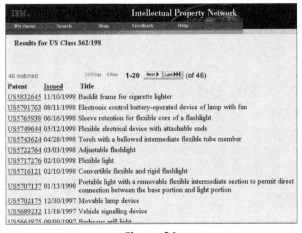

Figure 26

B. An Effective Strategy Using the PTO and IBM Websites

Earlier we suggested that the best strategy is to use both the PTO and IBM websites to do your patent search, starting with the PTO site. Let's take a closer look at why this is so.

Why should you start with the PTO site? The biggest reasons are:

- The PTO site allows you to search the full text of patents back to January 1976, whereas the IBM website allows you to search only the front page and claims of the same patents.
- The PTO site allows you to search the *Manual of Classification*. This is extremely important since the *Manual of Classification* tells you how your invention will be classified.

Why should you finish with the IBM site? The biggest reason is that the IBM site allows you to search the front page and claims sections of patents back to January 1971. The PTO site only provides searching back to January 1976.

Starting at the PTO website, follow the flowcharts shown in Chapter 3, Section C. After assembling a quick report with all of the patent front pages, use the PTO's Full-Text database to review each patent in detail. Then jump to the IBM site and repeat your Boolean searches. This takes advantage of the extended range of years available.

It's important to start from the PTO website because you could miss an entire category of patents if you don't search through the *Manual of Classification*. Also, by reading the class descriptions, you get a clearer definition of what types of patents are listed within that class. Once you have identified the appropriate class and subclass, it's easy to get a listing of every patent issued in that class.

It's also important to view each of the patents that you think are relevant to your invention. Sometimes it can be difficult to determine just what an invention does from a one-paragraph abstract. Viewing the drawings and reading the detailed description really help determine if the patent is germane to your idea.

C. Comparison of the PTO and IBM Websites

Functions	PTO	IBM
Search the Manual of Classifications?	Yes	No
Search Patent Front Page?	Yes	Yes
Search Patent Claims?	Yes	Yes
Search Full Patent Text	Yes	No
View Images of All Patent Pages?	Yes	Yes
Range of Years Covered	1976–Present	1971–Present
Number of Boolean Operators	4	3

Table 1

While using the IBM and PTO websites, it is helpful to keep in mind what functions are available at which site. In Table 1 above, we have summarized the major capabilities and differences of the IBM and PTO Internet patent search systems.

⚠ **Incomplete Searches.** *Except for inventions based completely on recent technology, any Internet-based patent search will almost certainly be incomplete. Examples of new technology inventions (post-1971 technology) would be: nanotechnology, CD-ROMs and Buckminsterfullerene applications (C_{60} molecules—a closed cage structure molecule with a carbon network).*

At this point, you should continue on to Chapter 5 and learn about Patent and Trademark Depository Libraries (PTDLs). The time it takes to make the trip to your nearest PTDL will be well worth the effort. Each PTDL contains a complete record of all patents issued in the United States.

Summary

Introduction to the IBM Patent Search Site
- The IBM website allows you to search the claims, as well as the front page of issued patents back to 1971.
- The IBM website allows you to view images of every page of the issued patent.

At the PTO's Website
- Use the PTO to perform keyword searches of classes first, then find all patents issued within those classes. Save the front pages of relevant patents.
- Perform keyword searches of the front pages of issued patents. Save any relevant results.
- Review the entire text of each of the patents you think are relevant prior art for your invention.
- Review the referenced patents of your results, for further prior art.
- Assemble results into a search report.

At IBM's Website
- Perform keyword searches of patents to take advantage of extended coverage of claims section and years back to 1971.
- Review the entire patent for relevance.
- Order copies of relevant patents.

■

5

Patent Searching at the PTDL

In this chapter, we leave behind the Internet and the World Wide Web and enter the world of the Patent and Trademark Depository Library (PTDL). Every PTDL has patent information available in three formats: printed manuals, microfilm and computerized databases. See Appendix A to locate the PTDL nearest you.

The printed manuals we will be using are the *Index to the U.S. Patent Classification, Manual of Classification* and *Classification Definitions*. In this chapter, you will learn how to use these manuals to determine which classes and subclasses apply to your invention. Once you have identified the appropriate class/subclass, you can then obtain a listing of every patent that has been issued within that class by using one of several methods. As you will see, this method of patent searching is far more efficient than randomly searching for matching keywords within issued patents.

In addition to printed manuals, every PTDL has a CASSIS computer system installed. The CASSIS computer system is based on a series of CD-ROMs. Each CD in the series is devoted to a certain topic. The CASSIS system can be used to:

- search the electronic versions of the classification manuals,
- extract a list of patents issued within a given class/subclass, and
- access bibliographical data for utility patents issued from the year 1969 to the present.

The current classification of all utility, design and plant patents issued from patent number 1 to the present can also be accessed. However, you can't search through the text of U.S. patents with the CASSIS system (for that you will need the APS system described below). In this chapter, we will cover CASSIS functions in detail and show you how you can get a free demo CASSIS CD-ROM for home use.

Though you may have a preference of using either the printed manuals or the CASSIS computer system, it's important to understand both resources. Having the flexibility to use either can save you the inconvenience of waiting. For example, most PTDLs have only one CASSIS

system available and it may be in use. Then too, there are only a limited number of copies of the classification manuals available.

Selected PTDLs (see Appendix A) have the Automated Patent System (APS) text search program installed. With this system you can search the entire text of patents issued since 1971. This is a more comprehensive type of search than can be performed with the Internet resources covered in Chapters 3 and 4. For instance, with the PTO search, you can only search the full text of patents issued since 1976. With the IBM search, you can search all the way back to 1971, but you are limited to the patent's front page (mainly the abstract) and the patent claims.

Call Ahead Regarding APS Use

It would be wise to call ahead before traveling to your local PTDL to use their APS system. Be sure to ask if there are any connection charges associated with using the APS. For example, you can use the APS for free at the Cleveland, Ohio, PTDL. At the PTDL in Toledo, Ohio, (2–3 hours' drive from Cleveland), the connection charge is $50 per hour.

Finally, you can perform manual searches of patents using microfilm readers. Some PTDLs have complete microfilm records of all patents issued in the United States. However, these microfilm collections vary from location to location. At a minimum, a PTDL is required to maintain at least a 20-year backfile. The good news is that this will change some time in the next three years. The PTO is starting a project to convert all patents from as far back as 1790 to DVD-ROM. The PTO will release this resource to the PTDLs as it is completed.

Searching these older records is especially important because, with the exception of recent technology-based patents, any computer based patent search will almost certainly be incomplete. Examples of new technology-based patents (post-1971 technology) would be CD-ROMs, lasers and nanotechnology.

There is some overlap with these PTDL resources. For instance, some of the data available in book form is also available on computer or in microfilm format. However, it is important to understand how to use all of the available patent search tools. Remember, you will have to share the available resources at the PTDL. The system that you would prefer to use may be occupied or otherwise unavailable.

A. Hitting the Books

Let's start with a hypothetical new idea you want to check out for possible patentability.

A common occurrence for people who drive is to see a vehicle with its turn signal stuck in the "on" position. This happens occasionally when automobiles negotiate gentle curves or during lane changes. This is a problem because other drivers can't tell if the signaling car is about to change direction or remain traveling straight ahead. While seeing this happen during your drive to work one day, you come up with an idea for a turn signal timer. This device would automatically cancel the turn signal after a given period of straight-ahead travel time.

After locating the nearest Patent and Trademark Depository Library, you decide to do a patent search for your idea. As discussed in Chapter 3, Section B, the most efficient way to start is to search for the class and subclass of your invention. Then proceed to search through the patents issued under each of the relevant classes.

Your first task is to come up with a list of words that describe your idea. Then use the *Index to the U.S. Patent Classification* to look for those words. The *Index to the U.S. Patent Classification* contains two very useful resources:

- An alphabetical listing of all of the classes used by the PTO.

- A cross-reference list of all known subject areas of invention, along with the appropriate class and subclass.

Let's suppose that you have selected the following words to describe your invention:

Car

Turn Signal

Timer

Electrical

These descriptive terms are arranged in order, from the general to the specific. In other words, the term "car" describes the general product that uses your invention. The term "turn signal" refers to the device upon which your invention will operate. Finally, the terms "timer" and "electrical" pertain to the type of turn signal and the timer function used to turn the signal off.

The classification system used by the PTO also flows from the general to the specific. By using this strategy we will attempt to capture all of the classes related to your invention.

The alphabetical listing of all of the classes used by the PTO is at the beginning of the *Index to the U.S. Patent Classification*. You will use the alphabetical listing of classes to find a class for each of the words on your list. Since there are only about 430 classes, it is quite possible that you will not find a match for each of your descriptive terms. For this reason, it is helpful to come up with a few synonyms for your descriptive terms. For example, in addition to the word "car," you can add the following two descriptive terms:

Automobile

Vehicle

Figure 1, below, shows a typical page from the alphabetical listing of classes in the *Index*. Here, we have boxed class 116, Signals and Indicators. You should write down the class name and number for any classes that match your descriptive words. The search results from the alphabetical list of classes is shown in Table 1 below.

The next section of the *Index to the U.S. Patent Classification* (right after the alphabetical listing of classes) is the cross-reference list of all known subject areas of invention. This cross-reference list makes up the bulk of the *Index*.

CLASSES ARRANGED IN ALPHABETICAL ORDER -- Continued

Class	Title of Class	Class	Title of Class
271	Sheet Feeding or Delivering	505	Superconductor Technology: Apparatus, Material, Process
413	Sheet Metal Container Making	248	Supports
270	Sheet–Material Associating	312	Supports: Cabinet Structure
114	Ships	211	Supports: Racks
116	Signals and Indicators	128	Surgery
117	Single–Crystal, Oriented–Crystal, and Epitaxy Growth Processes; Non–Coating Apparatus Therefor	600	Surgery
		604	Surgery
508	Solid Anti–Friction Devices, Materials Therefor, Lubricant or Separant Compositions for Moving Solid Surfaces, and Miscellaneous Mineral Oil Compositions	606	Surgery
		601	Surgery: Kinesitherapy
		602	Surgery: Splint, Brace, or Bandage
241	Solid Material Comminution or Disintegration	607	Surgery: Light, Thermal, and Electrical Application
206	Special Receptacle or Package	520	Synthetic Resins or Natural Rubbers –– Part of the Class 520 Series
75	Specialized Metallurgical Processes, Compositions for Use Therein, Consolidated Metal Powder Compositions, etc.	521	Synthetic Resins or Natural Rubbers –– Part of the Class 520 Series
		522	Synthetic Resins or Natural Rubbers –– Part of the Class 520 Series
267	Spring Devices	523	Synthetic Resins or Natural Rubbers –– Part of the Class 520 Series
365	Static Information Storage and Retrieval	524	Synthetic Resins or Natural Rubbers –– Part of the Class 520 Series
249	Static Molds	525	Synthetic Resins or Natural Rubbers –– Part of the Class 520 Series
52	Static Structures (e.g., Buildings)	526	Synthetic Resins or Natural Rubbers –– Part of the Class 520 Series
428	Stock Material or Miscellaneous Articles	527	Synthetic Resins or Natural Rubbers –– Part of the Class 520 Series
125	Stone Working	528	Synthetic Resins or Natural Rubbers –– Part of the Class 520 Series
126	Stoves and Furnaces		
127	Sugar, Starch, and Carbohydrates		

A–9

Figure 1

Search Results from Listing of Classes

General Terms Used for Cars

Term	Class Found
Car	None
Automobile	None
Vehicle	Motor Vehicles: Class 180, Land Vehicles: Class 280

More Specific Terms Pertaining to Turn Signals

Term	Class Found
Turn Signal	None
Turn	(Turning): Class 82
Signal	Signals and Indicators: Class 116

Terms Pertaining to the Type of Turn Signal

Term	Class Found
Timer	None
Electrical	Communications: Electrical: Class 340 Electricity: Electrical Systems and Devices: Class 361

Table 1

Here, you look up each of the classes found from Table 1 and write down the class and subclass of any matching references. For example, from Table 1 you found Class 340 while searching for the term "Electrical." A section from the *Index* cross-reference for Class 340 is shown in Figure 2. Here we see a small section of the listings under the topics Electric & Electricity. These results would indicate that Class 340, subclass 425.5+, was highly relevant to vehicle mounted electric signals. The plus sign (+) following the subclass 425.5 indicates there are subclasses that further differentiate vehicle mounted electric signals.

The search results for all our descriptive terms are summarized in Table 2. For the general terms "Car," "Automobile" and "Vehicle," the most relevant class/subclass would appear to be Class 340, subclass 425.5+ (as shown in Figure 2). The more specific terms, "Turn signal," "Turn" and "Signal," lead us to Class 116, subclass 28R+ for Signals and Indicators. Finally, the most specific terms, "Timer" and "Electrical," again lead us to Class 340, subclass 425.5+. Clearly, classes/subclasses 116/28R+ and 340/425.5+ warrant further examination.

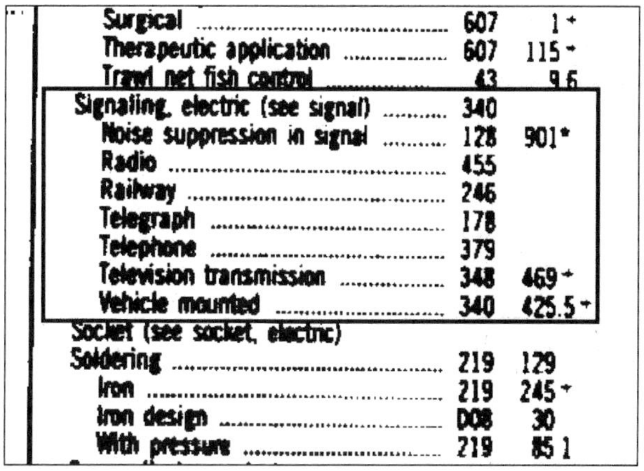

Surgical	607	1+
Therapeutic application	607	115+
Trawl net fish control	43	9.6
Signaling, electric (see signal)	340	
Noise suppression in signal	128	901*
Radio	455	
Railway	246	
Telegraph	178	
Telephone	379	
Television transmission	348	469+
Vehicle mounted	340	425.5+
Socket (see socket, electric)		
Soldering	219	129
Iron	219	245+
Iron design	D08	30
With pressure	219	85 1

Figure 2

Search Results from Cross-Reference List of Inventions

General Terms Used for Cars: Car, Automobile and Vehicle

Subject Area	Class	Subclass
Land Vehicle	280	
Vehicle Mounted	340	425.5+

More Specific Terms Pertaining to Turn Signals: Turn Signal, Turn and Signal

Subject Area	Class	Subclass
Signals & Indicators	116	28R+

Terms Pertaining to the Type of Turn Signal: Timer and Electrical

Subject Area	Class	Subclass
Electrical	340	425.5+

Table 2

We have now proceeded as far as we can in the *Index to the U.S. Patent Classification*. Next we turn to the *Manual of Classification*. This manual has an indented list of all the subclasses to be found under each main class. The classes are listed in numerical order. Each class is covered by its own page or group of pages. Here we can easily look up each of the class/subclass numbers found in the *Index to the U.S. Patent Classification*.

Why should we look up the class/subclass numbers in this manual? Don't we already have our class/subclass information from the *Index*? Well, yes and no. What we have so far are a few individual class/subclass combinations. By using the *Manual of Classification*, we can see all of the subclasses within each major class. Furthermore, this listing of subclasses is indented. This gives you a visual aid towards understanding how the various subclasses are related. By reviewing this indented list of subclasses, you may find more classifications of interest.

Figure 3 below is a page from the *Manual of Classification* for Class 340. The figure shows a partial listing of the indented list of subclasses under the subclass 425.5—Land Vehicle Alarms or Indicators. The dots or periods to the left of the subclass title indicate how specific that subclass is. The more dots there are, the more specific the subclass. For example, subclass 442 has two dots to the left of the title and refers to tire deflation or inflation. Subclass 443 has three dots to the left and refers to a specific measurement means of deflation or inflation, namely, tire height.

```
425.5   LAND VEHICLE ALARMS OR INDICATORS
426     .Of burglary or unauthorized use
427     ..Of motorcycles or bicycles
428     ..Responsive to changes in voltage or current in a vehicle
          electrical system
429     ..Responsive to inertia, vibration, or tilt
430     ..With entrance/exit time delay
431     .For trailer
432     .For bicycle
433     .For school bus
434     .For taxi
435     .Of relative distance from an obstacle
436     .Of collision or contact with external object
437     ..Curb
438     .Internal alarm or indicator responsive to a condition of the
          vehicle
439     ..Operation efficiency (e.g., engine performance, driver
          habits)
440     ..Tilt, imbalance, or overload

441     ..Speed of vehicle, engine, or power train
442     ..Tire deflation or inflation
443     ...By indirect detection means (e.g., height measurement)
444     ....Relative wheel speed
445     ...With particular telemetric coupling
```

Figure 3

From a close examination of the indented list of subclasses, it would appear that subclass 465—Turning or Steering would be the most relevant for our turn signal canceling invention. Figure 4 below shows the appropriate section from the indented list of subclasses. Here we see that subclass 463 refers to the general topic of External Alarms or Indicators of Movement, and subclass 465 limits those movements to turning or steering.

```
463     .External alarm or indicator of movement
464     ..Plural indications (e.g., go, slow, stop)
465     ..Turning or steering
466     ..Speed
467     ..Acceleration or deceleration
```

Figure 4

The process of finding the appropriate subclass moves from the general to the specific. Figure 5 summarizes this process for Class 340, subclass 465. First, we start with the general topic, "Communications: Electrical." Then we proceed to electrical communications that are used for land vehicle alarms or indicators. Then we further limit the topic to external alarms or indicators of movement. Finally, the patents issued under subclass 465 are limited to electrical signals that are used on land vehicles for the purpose of external indicators of turning or steering.

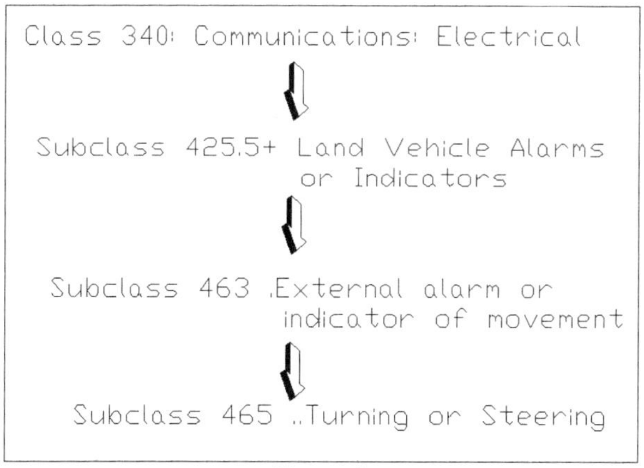

Class 340: Communications: Electrical

Subclass 425.5+ Land Vehicle Alarms or Indicators

Subclass 463 .External alarm or indicator of movement

Subclass 465 ..Turning or Steering

Figure 5

Now we proceed to our third manual, *Classification Definitions*. Due to its size, this manual is often on microfilm. The *Classification Definitions* manual contains a written description for every class and subclass used by the PTO. Here we can look up each of our class/subclass numbers and determine their relevance.

Figure 6, below, shows page 116-8 of the *Classification Definitions*, that is, the 8th page for Class 116. About halfway down the left-hand column is the description for subclass 28 (boxed in). Reading the definition, we see that this subclass pertains to signals that are especially adapted for use upon, or in connection with, vehicles.

Below each subclass definition is a "Search Class Cross-Reference." This section contains a listing of additional classes that are related to the subject matter. In the figure, we see that Class 340 is referenced for signal systems used in connection with traffic or vehicles.

Figure 7, below, shows page 116-9 from the *Classification Definitions*. Here, we see that Class 116, subclass 35, relates to "Devices under subclass 28 placed upon a vehicle for indicating to others than the operator, the motion of any change, either actual or intended, in the rate or direction of the motion of the vehicle." This definition tells us that subclass 28 is for signaling devices used only on vehicles and only for the purpose of indicating a change of direction (a turn) or a change in rate of travel (brake lights) to persons other than the driver.

In the search class cross-reference below this definition, we again see a reference to Class 340. Clearly, Class 340, along with the referenced subclass 463, is highly relevant to vehicle turn signals.

116-8 CLASSIFICATION DEFINITIONS June 1997

SEARCH CLASS:
340, Communications: Electrical, subclasses 9ŏ4+ for electrical nautical signaling.

27. Devices under subc!ass 26 includes means for the mechanical production and reception of sound–vibrations transmitted through bodies of water.

(1) Note. The subclass does not include ordinary signals devised for use upon submarine vessels nor electric undersea signal devices.

SEARCH CLASS:
114, Ships, subclasses 327+ for submarine vessels.
367, Communications, Electrical: Acoustic Wave System and Devices, subclasses

28. Signals, indicators, and alarms under the class definition especially adapted by structure for use upon or in connection with vehicles.

and provided for in Class 246, Railway Switches and Signals, are excluded.

SEARCH CLASS:
33, Geometrical Instruments, subclass 264 for vehicle alignment.
200, Electricity: Circuit Makers and Breakers, subclasses 61.27+, 61.54+, and 61.87 to 61.91 for signal type switches used in connection with vehicles.
246, Railway Switches and Signals, (see Note 1).
250, Radiant Energy, subclass 462.1 for self–luminous signaling means.
280, Land Vehicles, subclasses 288.4+ for

340. Communications: Electrical, subclasses 907+ for electrically operated

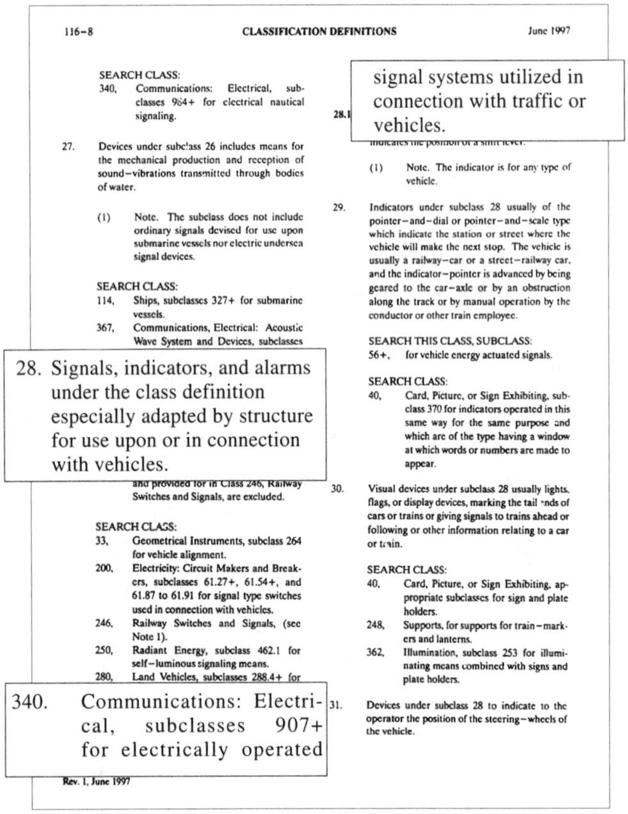

signal systems utilized in connection with traffic or vehicles.

28.1

(1) Note. The indicator is for any type of vehicle.

29. Indicators under subclass 28 usually of the pointer–and–dial or pointer–and–scale type which indicate the station or street where the vehicle will make the next stop. The vehicle is usually a railway–car or a street–railway car, and the indicator–pointer is advanced by being geared to the car–axle or by an obstruction along the track or by manual operation by the conductor or other train employee.

SEARCH THIS CLASS, SUBCLASS:
56+, for vehicle energy actuated signals.

SEARCH CLASS:
40, Card, Picture, or Sign Exhibiting, subclass 370 for indicators operated in this same way for the same purpose and which are of the type having a window at which words or numbers are made to appear.

30. Visual devices under subclass 28 usually lights, flags, or display devices, marking the tail ends of cars or trains or giving signals to trains ahead or following or other information relating to a car or train.

SEARCH CLASS:
40, Card, Picture, or Sign Exhibiting, appropriate subclasses for sign and plate holders.
248, Supports, for supports for train–markers and lanterns.
362, Illumination, subclass 253 for illuminating means combined with signs and plate holders.

31. Devices under subclass 28 to indicate to the operator the position of the steering–wheels of the vehicle.

Rev. 1, June 1997

Figure 6

June 1997 CLASSIFICATION DEFINITIONS 116-9

32. Devices under subclass 28 include license–tags, checks, or other means for identifying a vehicle, with means for automatically dropping or discharging them when the vehicle strikes a person or other object.

(1) Note. The mere presence of indicia upon the checks is not sufficient to exclude the patent from this subclass.

SEARCH CLASS:
221, Article Dispensing, subclass 12 for article dispensers not otherwise provided for, having automatic control of article releasing outlet closures and see also subclass 13 for such dispensers having automatic control of discharge assistant operation.

33. Devices under subclass 28 for indicating or preventing the theft or unauthorized use of a vehicle.

SEARCH THIS CLASS, SUBCLASS:
8, for alarm–locks.
6+ and 77+, for burglar–a
al and other purposes.

SEARCH CLASS:
70, Locks, for locks, per se.
307, Electrical Transmissio
nection Systems, subcl
electrical systems whicl
thorized entry or use of
340, Communications: E
classes 426+ for electr
vehicle burglar alarms.

34. Devices under subclass 28 incl
giving warning when the press
pneumatic tire of an autom
vehicle is either raised above or
the normal pressure, either by puncture, leakage, or otherwise.

SEARCH THIS CLASS, SUBCLASS:
24 and 137+, for signaling devices, per se.

SEARCH CLASS:
73, Measuring and Test:·ɐ, subclasses 146.2+ for a fluid pı ssure gauge combined with a vehicle, tire or tire stem.
200, Electricity: Circuit Makers and Breakers, subclasses 61.22+ for mere circuit–controllers associated with a tire.
340, Communications: Electrical, subclasses 442+ for electrically operated tire deflation alarms.

35. Devices under subclass 28 placed upon a vehicle for indicating to others than the operator the motion or any change, either actual or intended, in the rate or direction of motion of the vehicle.

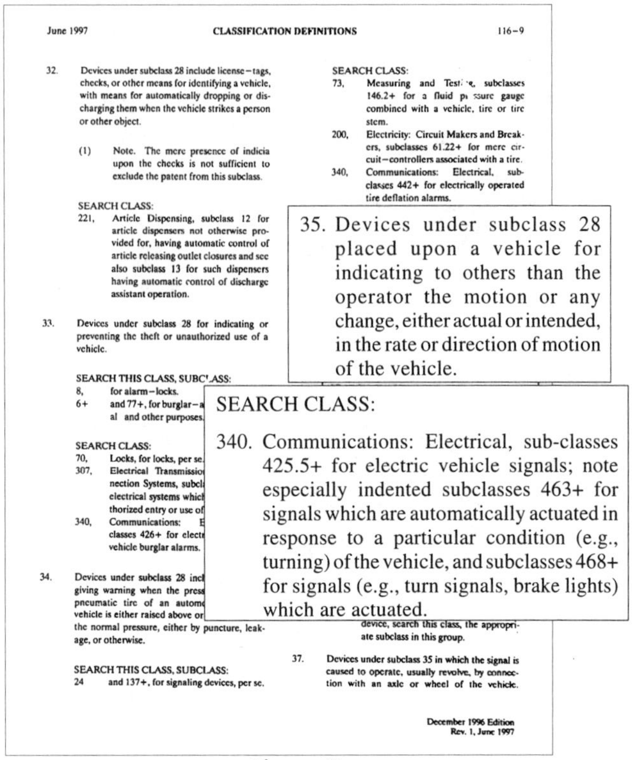

SEARCH CLASS:

340. Communications: Electrical, sub-classes 425.5+ for electric vehicle signals; note especially indented subclasses 463+ for signals which are automatically actuated in response to a particular condition (e.g., turning) of the vehicle, and subclasses 468+ for signals (e.g., turn signals, brake lights) which are actuated.

device, search this class, the appropriate subclass in this group.

37. Devices under subclass 35 in which the signal is caused to operate, usually revolve, by connection with an axle or wheel of the vehicle.

December 1996 Edition
Rev. 1, June 1997

Figure 7

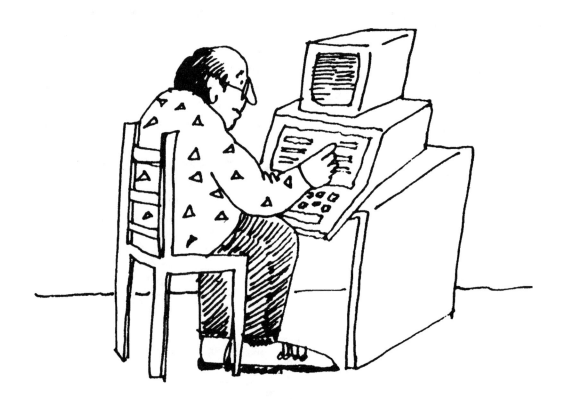

In Figure 8, below, we see page 340-23 from the *Classification Definitions*. Subclass 463 includes signals for turning, braking and backing. However, subclass 465 (shown boxed), "Subject matter under subclass 463 in which the external signal indicates that the vehicle is executing a turning movement," is specifically limited to electronic signals used to indicate vehicle turning.

By using the *Index to the U.S. Patent Classification*, the *Manual of Classification* and the *Classification Definitions*, we have identified Class 340, subclass 465, as a highly likely place to find patents related to turn signals for vehicles. Class/subclass 340/465 is a good place to check to see if our idea for an automatic turn signal canceling device has been anticipated. The process for using the classification manuals is summarized in the flowchart shown in Figure 9, below.

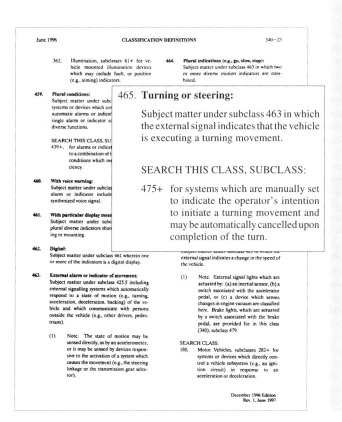

Figure 8

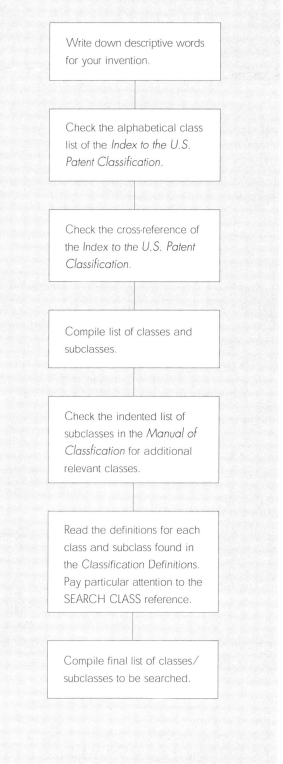

Figure 9

Classification Search Sheet						
A.	B.	C.	D.	E.	F.	G.
Descriptive	Class Nos.	Subclass	Subclass	Get	Search	Get
Words		from Index	from Man.	List	Class	List
			of Class.			
1.Turn Signal	116	28		X	340	
		35		X	340	
2.Vehicle	340	425.5+	465	X	340/475	X

Figure 10

Figure 10 above shows a handy worksheet you can take with you to the PTDL. You'll find a blank worksheet form in Appendix B. We've filled out a portion of the worksheet sample here to show you how it would be used in the context of our turn signal invention. The first column (Column A) is used to list your descriptive words. In the next column, Column B, you record the class numbers of any matching class names you find in the alphabetical listing of classes from the *Index to the U.S. Patent Classification*. Multiple rows are provided in case more than one matching class is found. In our case we have filled in Turn Signal and Vehicle for the first two descriptive terms. The corresponding classes were determined to be 116 (Signals & Indicators) and 340 (Vehicle).

The rest of the worksheet is used to determine the subclasses for which you want to get listings of all issued patents. You might remember from our discussion of how to search through the manuals at the PTDL that to determine this, you would consult the cross-reference list of all known subject areas of invention from the *Index to the U.S. Patent Classification*. In Column C, you would record the subclass of any matching references. For Class 116 in our turn signal example, this turned out to be subclasses 28 and 35. For Class 340, the referenced class was 425.5 (as shown in Figure 2).

Next, you would proceed to the indented list of all the subclasses in the *Manual of Classification*. From our example, it was determined that subclass 465—Turning or Steering—was the most relevant. So we recorded Class 465 under Column D, Subclass from Man. of Class.

From here, you would proceed to the third manual, the *Classification Definitions*. Here you would read the written description for each of your classes and subclasses and decide if you wanted a listing of every patent issued in that classification. For the description of Class 166, subclass 28, we determined that this subclass pertains to signals that are especially adapted for use upon, or in connection with, vehicles. So we marked an "X" in Column E, the "Get List" column next to subclass 28, which reminds us to get a list of patents issued in that class/subclass. The search class cross-reference for subclass 28 (right below the subclass definition—see Figure 7) contained a reference to Class 340. So we note that in the "Search Class" column, Column F.

From the description of Class 340, subclass 465—Turning or Steering—it would appear that this subclass is very relevant to our turn signal canceling invention, so we mark an "X" in Column G (the corresponding "Get List" column). The search class cross-reference for subclass 465 (see Figure

8) contained a reference to subclass 475. So we note that in Column F and mark the Get List column, Column G, for this subclass as well.

The Classification Search Sheet is helpful because as you proceed from left to right, filling out the sheet, you can see exactly where you found your classification information. Also, referencing the search class information (far left column) helps in two ways. First, as discussed previously, it leads you to other places to search. Second, it can give you a feel for the quality of the search results. In the above case, each of our subclass descriptions told us to search Class 340. This is a further indication that we are on the right track.

Finding the correct classification(s) for your invention is the key to a successful patent search. This is because once you have identified a given class, it is a relatively simple matter to obtain a listing of every issued patent within it. As mentioned, this technique is superior to randomly searching the front pages of patents for matching keywords (as explained in Chapter 3, Section A). This is because keyword search results depend entirely on the keywords used. If different words are used to describe similar, patented inventions, you will miss many related patents and never know it.

In fact, relevant prior art is often missed by inexperienced patent searchers, who simply fail to identify the appropriate category(s). Also, this search for patent classification is still dependent upon the words you use to describe your invention. The "Class Finder Tool" is a visual aid to help you with your patent classification search. The Class Finder Tool is shown in Figure 11, below.

The outer circle of the diagram represents the general field or application of the invention. You can think of it as all the relevant factors surrounding your idea. The inner circle represents the invention itself. If the invention is a new application applied to an existing device, then the inner circle is the device that the invention is directly applied to. The blank lines within the inner circle are where you write down the specific attributes of the invention.

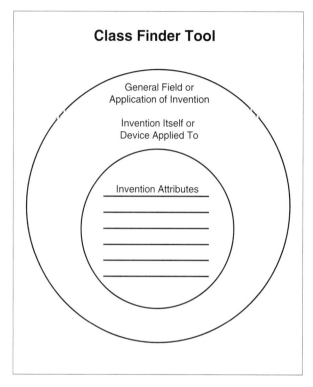

Figure 11

Figure 12 is an example of the class finder tool filled out for our turn signal canceling device. First, we label our inner circle. Since our idea is to cancel a turn signal after a given period of time, our invention is directly applied to a turn signal. This also gives us our most general application of the invention. For example, if we had labeled our inner circle "An astable, multivibrator timer circuit for canceling turn signals," we would be limiting ourselves to just one manifestation of a much wider concept.

Next, we try to find words that will encompass the most general aspects of our invention. Originally, we thought of turn signals applied only to cars. So we write down the word "car" and the word "automobile." However, the circle around the turn signal device reminds us that there are other devices that use turn signals. Examples are such things as boats and bicycles (can you think of

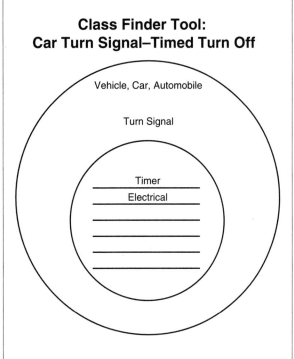

Figure 12

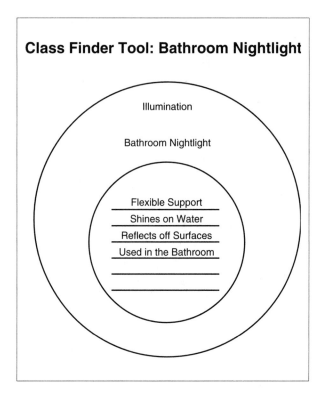

Figure 13

others?). So, we use the general term vehicle to describe bodies in motion that need to signal a change of direction.

Next, we move to the inside of our invention and write down the specific aspects of our idea. In the case of our turn signal, we know that the signal is electrical, as opposed to mechanical, and that a timer is involved to cancel the signal.

As a further example, Figure 13 shows the Class Finder Tool filled out for the bathroom nightlight invention of Chapter 3. Here, the major aspect of the invention is a lamp/nightlight which uses a standard light bulb. Since there are many ways to cast light (for example, fireplaces, arc lamps and reflected sunlight), the general field is illumination. Finally, the specific attributes include a flexible support and use in the bathroom. See Appendix B for a blank Class Finder Tool form.

B. Using CASSIS

In addition to printed format, the PTO publishes a great deal of patent and trademark information on CD-ROM. The PTO has developed a special computer search program to retrieve this information. This program is known as CASSIS (Classification And Search Support Information System). Every PTDL has a least one computer set up to run the CASSIS program. Furthermore, PTDLs have personnel on hand who are willing and able to help you get started on the system. It's a good idea to call ahead and make an appointment.

The CASSIS computer system is based on a series of CD-ROMs. Each CD in the series is devoted to a certain topic. The CD labeled "Patents BIB" contains bibliographical data for utility patents issued from the year 1969 to the present.

This includes the date of issue, state/country of first listed inventor's residence, assignee at time of issue, patent status (withdrawn, expired, etc.), current classifications and patent title.

The CD labeled "Patents CLASS" contains the current classification of all utility, design and plant patents issued from Patent Number 1 to the present.

The CD labeled "Patents ASSIST" contains an electronic version of the manuals used in Section A above, that is, the *Index to the U.S. Patent Classification, Manual of Classification* and the *Classification Definitions*. Other electronic manuals on the Patents ASSIST CD include: the *Classification Orders Index* (provides a list of classifications abolished and established since 1976, with corresponding classification order number and effective date); the *IPC-USPC Concordance* (the *U.S. Patent Classification to International Patent Classification Concordance* is a guide for relating the U.S. Patent Classification System to the Sixth Edition of the *International Patent Classification System*, published by the World Intellectual Property Organization); the *Manual of Patent Examining Procedure* (provides patent examiners and patent applicants with a reference work on the practices and procedures related to prosecution of patent applications in the U.S. Patent and Trademark Office); a listing of attorneys and agents registered to practice before the PTO; and the *Patentee-Assignee Index* (shows ownership at time of issue for utility patents 1969 to present, for other types of patents 1977 to present, and inventors' names from 1975 to present).

The CD labeled "Patents ASSIGN" contains a searchable file of patent assignments recorded at the PTO for patents granted after August 1980.

The CD labeled "Patents SNAP" contains a concordance between U.S. patent numbers and application serial numbers. It includes data for patents with an application date from January 1, 1977, through the date specified on the CD.

The "Patents USAPat" CDs contain facsimile images of U.S. patents from 1994 to the present.

The operative word here is CDs. There are approximately 150 CDs published each year with patent images.

The CD labeled "Patent Abstracts of Japan" contains the English-language translation of abstracts from unexamined Japanese patent applications in Japan, patent applications are published 18 months from the application filing date.

The main menu of the CASSIS computer program is shown in Figure 14 below. Each boxed and arrowed topic refers to a different CD-ROM. By clicking on a topic with the mouse, you load that particular CD-ROM into the CASSIS system.

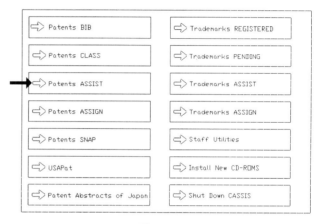

Figure 14

The CASSIS version of the *Index to the U.S. Patent Classification* is found on the "Patents ASSIST" CD-ROM. To access this document, click on the Patents ASSIST topic shown in Figure 14. After a few seconds delay (while the appropriate CD loads) you will see the screen shown in Figure 15 below.

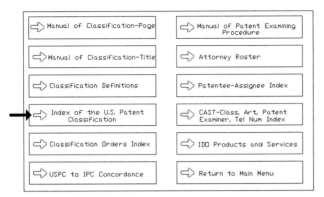

Figure 15

```
F1:Help F2:Browse F3:Display F4:Query F9:Options F10:Quit

   ┌──────────────────────────────────────────┐
   │  United States Department of Commerce     │
   │       Patent and Trademark Office         │
   │                                           │
   │    Index to the US Patent Classification  │
   └──────────────────────────────────────────┘

  Index Term:  _____

  Classification:  _____


     Use the arrow keys to select a search field.
  Touch ENTER to start search or CTRL-BREAK to
  abort search.
```

Figure 16

To select the *Index to the U.S. Patent Classification*, just click on that topic. After another processing delay, you will be presented with the title page for the *Index*. At the bottom of the title page the message "Press Any Key to Continue" will be displayed. To proceed to the search page for the *Index*, you will need to press any key on the keyboard. The "Press Any Key to Continue" prompt is a standard method of halting computer processing so that the user can read a computer screen of information. Usually the ENTER key or the SPACEBAR key are then pressed to continue.

After a key is pressed, the screen shown in Figure 16 will be presented. At this screen we can search for class titles that match our descriptive keywords. For example, to search for an index term that matches the word Vehicle, use the arrow keys to highlight the blank entry field adjacent to the words Index Term and enter the word Vehicle. Then press the ENTER key.

The search results are shown in Figure 17, below. In Figure 17, the number 373 is shown to the far right of the vehicle search term. This means there are 373 occurrences of this term in the *Index*. To review these search results, we need to make use of the special function keys.

```
F1:Help F2:Browse F3:Display F4:Query F9:Options F10:Quit

   ┌──────────────────────────────────────────┐
   │  United States Department of Commerce     │
   │       Patent and Trademark Office         │
   │                                           │
   │    Index to the US Patent Classification  │
   └──────────────────────────────────────────┘

  Index Term:  Vehicle_____  373

  Classification:  _____


     Use the arrow keys to select a search field.
  Touch ENTER to start search or CTRL-BREAK to
  abort search.
```

Figure 17

Across the top of Figure 17, you will see F1:Help, F2:Browse, and so on. This is a description of the functions performed by the various special function keys. Their position on the keyboard is shown in Figure 18, below. In order to review the search results, press the F3:Display special function key.

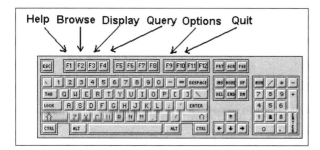

Figure 18

Figure 19

The search results are represented in Figure 19, below. Here, we have our alphabetical cross-reference listing of "invention subject area to search keyword." This is the CASSIS version of the cross-reference list of all known subject areas of invention from the *Index to the U.S. Patent Classification* (as discussed in the preceding section). Again, across the top of the display are the special function key definitions. These key definitions can change depending on which screen you are viewing. In the case of Figure 19, the F2 special function key has changed from a function called Browse to a function called Full.

To see how our search term is referenced in any given invention subject area, we use the arrow keys to highlight the subject area word and then press F2. For example, by using the "page down" key on the keyboard, we can rapidly scroll down our list of 373 subject areas to item 353, "Turn Indicators." To see how the keyword Vehicle is referenced in the "Turn Indicators" subject area, highlight "Turn Indicators," and press the F2 key. The result is shown in Figure 20. Here we see that Class 116, subclass 28R+, is referenced. This is the same result we obtained from our manual search of the *Index*.

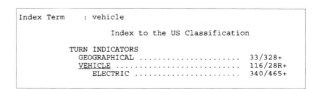

Figure 20

To get a printout of the display shown in Figure 20, select the F4:Actions key. This will give you a popup window with various actions that you can perform. One of these actions is print. To use the print feature, simply highlight the word print and press ENTER. As with any popup window, if you change your mind and want to back out of the operation, just press the ESC key.

After you have searched the *Index* for each of your descriptive terms, you can return to the main Patents ASSIST screen (Figure 15) by selecting the F10:Quit key. After you select this key, you will see a small popup window that displays the message, "Discard current query?" You then have two choices: Proceed or Cancel. To continue the exit to the main Patents ASSIST screen, highlight the word Proceed and press the ENTER key.

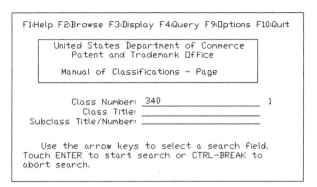

```
F1:Help F2:Browse F3:Display F4:Query F9:Options F10:Quit
  ┌─────────────────────────────────────────────┐
  │   United States Department of Commerce        │
  │        Patent and Trademark Office            │
  │                                               │
  │      Manual of Classifications - Page         │
  └─────────────────────────────────────────────┘

          Class Number: _____
           Class Title: _____
  Subclass Title/Number: _____

    Use the arrow keys to select a search field.
    Touch ENTER to start search or CTRL-BREAK to
    abort search.
```

Figure 21

```
F1:Help F2:Browse F3:Display F4:Query F9:Options F10:Quit
  ┌─────────────────────────────────────────────┐
  │   United States Department of Commerce        │
  │        Patent and Trademark Office            │
  │                                               │
  │      Manual of Classifications - Page         │
  └─────────────────────────────────────────────┘

          Class Number:  340                    1
           Class Title: _____
  Subclass Title/Number: _____

    Use the arrow keys to select a search field.
    Touch ENTER to start search or CTRL-BREAK to
    abort search.
```

Figure 22

From here, we can look at our next reference volume, the *Manual of Classification*. To see a page from this manual click on the "Manual of Classification-Page" box, as shown in the upper left of Figure 15. You will then see the title screen for the *Manual of Classification*. At the bottom of this screen will be the familiar "Press any key to continue" prompt. To proceed, press the spacebar (or any other key on the keyboard).

The next screen is the main search page for the *Manual of Classification*, as shown in Figure 21 above. Here we have three search fields to choose from. We can search for a class number, a class title or a subclass title/number. For example, to obtain the indented list of all the subclasses under Class 340, just enter 340 in the Class Number entry field and press ENTER.

The results are shown in Figure 22. This is very similar to the result screen obtained from the search of the *Index to the U.S. Patent Classification*, as shown in Figure 17. In Figure 17, there were 373 occurrences of the search word Vehicle. For the *Manual of Classification*, the number 1 shown to the far right of the class number 340 indicates that one indented list of subclasses for Class 340 was found. To view the indented list of subclasses under Class 340, select the F3:Display key.

The resulting display is similar to the indented list shown in Figure 3. A printout of a page from the *Manual of Classification* can also be obtained by use of the F4:Actions key. To return to the main Patents ASSIST screen, select the F10:Quit key.

The *Classification Definitions* manual can be accessed by selecting the "Classification Definitions" box, as shown in the left column of Figure 15. You will then see the title screen for the *Classification Definitions* manual. At the bottom of this screen will be the familiar "Press any key to continue" prompt. After proceeding past the title screen, you will see the *Classification Definitions* search screen shown in Figure 23 below.

As shown in the figure, we have five different search fields available. During our search of the *Index to the U.S. Patent Classification* (Figure 20) under the classification "turn indicators—vehicle—electric," we identified the classification 340/465. To obtain the definition for Class 340, subclass 465, we enter 340/465 in the Classification entry field, and then press ENTER. The search results show the number 1 to the far right of the class/subclass combination, 340/465. This indicates that the program has found one class/subclass definition in its search.

```
F1:Help F2:Browse F3:Display F4:Query F9:Options F10:Quit

    ┌─────────────────────────────────────────────┐
    │    United States Department of Commerce      │
    │         Patent and Trademark Office          │
    │                                              │
    │           Classification Definitions         │
    └─────────────────────────────────────────────┘
      Classification:  340/465 _____  1
          Class title: _____
      Class Definition: _____
    Subclass Definition: _____
          All Fields: _____

      Use the arrow keys to select a search field.
    Touch ENTER to start search or CTRL-BREAK to
    abort search.
```

Figure 23

Class 340, Subclass 465.

Turning or steering:

Subject matter under subclass 463 in which the external signal indicates that the vehicle is executing a turning movement.

SEARCH THIS CLASS, SUBCLASS:

475+, for systems which are manually set to indicate the operator's intention to initiate a turning movement and may be automatically canceled upon completion of the turn.

Figure 24

To access the Patents CLASS CD-ROM, click on the Patents CLASS topic. After a few seconds delay, you will be presented with the three selections shown in Figure 25, below. To search for all the patents issued within a particular subclass, click on the "Classification by Subclass" box. After proceeding past the usual title screen, you will see the Classification by Subclass search screen shown in Figure 26. This screen has only one entry field. To search for all the patents issued in Class 340, subclass 465, type in "340/465" and press ENTER. The search result will then show the number 1 to the far right of the class/subclass combination, indicating that the search is complete.

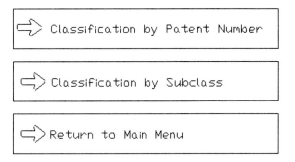

Figure 25

To view the class/subclass definition, select the F3:Display key. The resulting display is shown in Figure 24, above. As with the other manuals, a printout of this definition can be obtained by using the F4:Actions key. To return to the main Patents ASSIST screen, select the F10:Quit key.

Another feature of the CASSIS system is the ability to obtain a listing of all the patents issued within a given class/subclass. To explore this feature, we must exit from the Patents ASSIST CD-ROM and load the Patents CLASS CD-ROM. To quit the Patents ASSIST CD-ROM, click on the "Return to Main Menu" box at the bottom of the right-hand column shown in Figure 15. You will then return to the main menu of the CASSIS program, as shown in Figure 14.

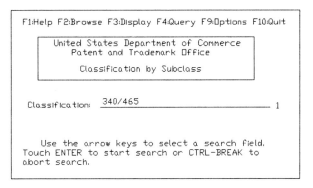

Figure 26

To view the list of issued patents, select the F3:Display key. The resulting display is shown in Figure 27, below. As with the other CASSIS functions, a printout of this display can be obtained by using the F4 key. To return to the main Patents CLASS screen, select the F10 key.

Original and Cross-Reference Classification

Patents are issued with an original classification pertaining to subject matter, and usually one or more related cross-reference classifications. To the right of each patent number in Figure 27 is an "X" or an "O." This means that the patent was either originally classified (O) in class/subclass 340/465 or cross referenced (X) to it. The total number of Original Classifications (OR's) and cross-reference classifications (XR's) are summarized at the top of the figure.

```
Classification: 340/465      ORs: 61        XRs: 56         Total: 117

5696484 X 5689232 X 5682138 X 5677671 X 5663708 O 5619182 X 5610577 O
5594415 X 5463370 X 5424715 X 5416465 O 5309143 X 5281950 X 5253115 X
5198798 X 5097917 X 5086289 X 5023592 X 4996657 X 4994786 X 4868541 O
4853672 O 4760372 X 4638295 O 4559516 X 4325052 X 4122318 X 3784974 X
2934744 X 2784269 X 2674667 X 2667545 X 2432388 O 2302098 X 2248760 O
2201795 X 2188058 X 2186766 U 2180894 X 2180688 O 2178073 X 2175848 O
2168480 O 2148428 O 2133000 O 2126940 O 2114731 O 2111931 O 2109408 O
2108454 O 2089183 X 2064735 O 2061401 O 2027821 O 2010454 X 1995236 O
1977887 O 1973299 O 1968749 O 1923162 O 1910257 O 1908124 O 1896905 X
1890677 O 1832326 O 1831814 O 1802647 X 1779799 O 1774273 X 1770415 X
1768717 O 1763465 O 1752289 O 1750738 X 1749169 O 1749168 O 1707305 X
1695712 O 1683818 O 1670744 X 1664791 O 1663971 O 1651540 O 1625565 O
1623219 O 1610901 X 1600560 X 1598358 O 1593574 X 1582069 X 1575445 O
1542431 O 1532221 X 1506597 X 1482540 O 1468830 O 1341932 X 1331158 X
1320566 O 1270714 X 1248937 X 1240458 X 1227226 O 1215155 O 1210283 O
1198495 O 1194537 X 1191830 X 1179306 X 1164832 X 1158355 X 1140229 X
1138834 O 1120589 O 1112278 O 1106982 O 1033208 O
```

Figure 27

The various options and features of the CASSIS system can be confusing for new users. Fortunately, context-sensitive help is available. By pressing the F1:Help key, a popup window with detailed explanations of CASSIS features is displayed. The contents of this help window will change depending on where you are within the program. The help screen is removed by pressing the ESC key.

You can actually practice using the CASSIS system in the comfort of your own home by order-

ing the *CASSIS Sampler* (ordering information at the end of this section). The PTO provides this demonstration CD-ROM free of charge. The *CASSIS Sampler* includes small samples of most of the products currently available in the CASSIS CD-ROM series.

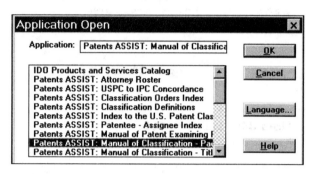

Figure 28

The *CASSIS Sampler* comes with complete installation instructions. When the program is started, you will see a startup logo for the Patent and Trademark Office, followed by the main selection menu shown in Figure 28. To select a product, just use the mouse to highlight the item and click once. For example, in Figure 28 we have selected a sample from the Patents ASSIST CD, namely, a page from the *Manual of Classification*.

After a few seconds delay, you will see the *Manual of Classification* search screen shown in Figure 29. To search for a class number, just type in the numeric value in the Class Number entry field and press ENTER. In Figure 29, we have entered class number 2.

After you press the enter key, the CASSIS Sampler program will search for the specified class. If the class is found, a 1 will be entered to the far right, adjacent to the class number field (Figure 29). If the class is not found, a zero will be indicated in this location. Remember, the *CASSIS Sampler* contains only a small fraction of the available patent classification data. So the class you are looking for may not be present. Figure 30 lists the available classes in the *CASSIS Sampler*.

```
CD Answer - [ Patents ASSIST: Manual of Cla:Search]
 File   Edit   Options   Browse   Data   Window   Help
```

United States Department of Commerce
Patent and Trademark Office

Cassis Sampler: Manual of Classification - Page

For the complete Manual of Classification - Page data, order Patents ASSIST.

Class Number: 2   1
Class Title:
Subclass Title/Number:

Use the arrow keys to highlight search field.
Touch ENTER to start search, CTRL-BREAK to abort search.

Figure 29

```
Cassis Sampler:  Search results may be neither complete nor accurate.
  Class
  Number  Class Title (may be truncated; see Full Display)
  -------  ------------------------------------------------------------------
  2        APPAREL
  27       UNDERTAKING
  42       FIREARMS
  60       POWER PLANTS
  84       MUSIC
  123      INTERNAL-COMBUSTION ENGINES
  244      AERONAUTICS
  296      LAND VEHICLES: BODIES AND TOPS
  354      PHOTOGRAPHY
  379      TELEPHONIC COMMUNICATIONS
  424      DRUG, BIO-AFFECTING AND BODY TREATING COMPOSITIONS
  426      FOOD OR EDIBLE MATERIAL: PROCESSES, COMPOSITIONS, AND PRODUCTS
  436      CHEMISTRY: ANALYTICAL AND IMMUNOLOGICAL TESTING
  446      AMUSEMENT DEVICES: TOYS
  450      FOUNDATION GARMENTS
  552      ORGANIC COMPOUNDS -- PART OF THE CLASS 532-570 SERIES
  D02      APPAREL AND HABERDASHERY
  D03      TRAVEL GOODS AND PERSONAL BELONGINGS
```

Figure 30

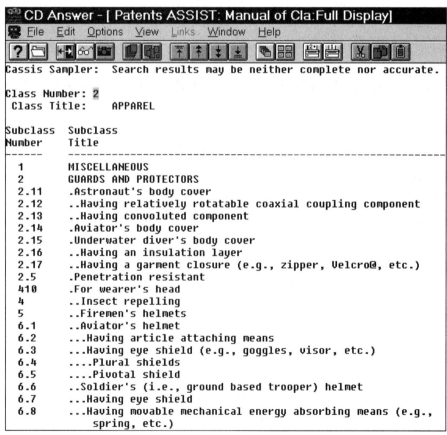

Figure 31

Figure 32

If the class data are available, you can view the information by selecting the Display choice under the Data menu, as shown in Figure 31. You will then be presented with the *Manual of Classification* page for that class (in this case, class number 2— Apparel), as shown in Figure 32, above.

Although the search software included on the *CASSIS Sampler* is fully functional, searches performed on the small sample data are for demonstration purposes only, and should in no way be considered a complete or accurate search. Also, some of the screens and menus of the *CASSIS Sampler* are slightly different from the fully functional version at your local PTDL.

You can order the *CASSIS Sampler* CD by mail, fax or phone. To order, specify:

CASSIS Sampler (GIS-5000G-CD)

Mail to:
U.S. Patent and Trademark Office
General Information Services Division
Crystal Plaza 3, Room 2C02
Washington, DC 20231
Fax: 703-305-7786
Phone Order: 800-786-9199
To record your order: 703-308-4357

C. Using the Automated Patent System (APS)

The APS (Automated Patent System) text search program allows access to several patent text data files. The interface to the APS computer system is different from the Internet search systems discussed in Chapters 3 and 4, and the CASSIS system discussed above. Those systems have what is known as a Graphical User Interface (or GUI— pronounced "gooey" in computer-speak). A computer system with a GUI has images of buttons and menu boxes that can be selected with a mouse click. The APS system is a text-based system. This means that no graphical images are used. All operator input is through the keyboard and the mouse is not used. This makes working with the

APS a bit more difficult, but the results are very much worth the effort.

Before you can use the system, you will need to have a library assistant log in for you. After the assistant enters her login ID and password, you will see the main text search window shown in Figure 33, below.

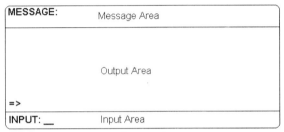

Figure 33

The text search window is divided into three areas: the Message Area, the Output Area and the Input Area. The message area displays system status messages, such as "text search in progress," and provides a list of available special functions. The output area is the large middle portion of the computer display shown in Figure 33. The system response to your keyboard input is displayed here. The input area is where you enter your keyboard commands.

The first thing you need to do is select which data file to search. The USPAT file contains most patents issued from 1971 to the present. A new data file called USOCR contains approximately 100,000 additional patents. These are patents issued in 1970 and patents issued from 1971 through 1975 that were not included in the USPAT file. Both data files can be accessed by selecting the ALLUS data file. ALLUS means all the U.S. patents in the database. To select the ALLUS data file, you use the FILE command as shown below.

Using the keyboard, type in: FILE ALLUS and press ENTER. Commands typed into the input area are copied to the output area. After the enter key is pressed, the main display area will look like the display area shown in Figure 34. The FILE ALLUS command that you entered is copied to the main display area. The command is preceded by the => characters.

```
=> FILE ALLUS
```

Figure 34

To see a list of all the available commands, just type HELP COMMANDS as shown in Figure 35.

```
=> HELP COMMANDS
```

Figure 35

The system will then respond with the information shown in Figure 36.

```
Enter one of these commands at the arrow prompt (=>).

ACTIVATE ------- Assign L#s to saved query or answer set.
DELETE --------- Delete saved or current session items.
DISPLAY -------- Display saved or current session items.
EDIT ------------ Modify the text of an E-number entry.
EXPAND -------- Look at the index around a term.
FILE ------------ Specify the search and display file.
FOCUS --------- Rank answers in order of relevancy.
HELP ----------- For help on how to use the system.
LOGOFF ------- End the online session.
NEWS ---------- Display current news about the system.
SAVE ----------- Save an L-numbered query or answer set.
SEARCH ------- Perform a search.
SELECT -------- Build expand terms from answer fields.
SET ------------ Set terminal and interaction options.
SORT ---------- Sort Answers of an L-number list
TABULATE ---- Analyze SmartSELECT L-number data.
? ---------------- The same as HELP.
For more detailed information about a command, enter HELP and
the name of the command.

    Example: => HELP SEARCH  (For help with the SEARCH
command).
```

Figure 36

Each individual command has its own help description. This is a quick way to learn how to use the APS commands. For example, the bottom of Figure 36 shows you how to get help for the SEARCH command by typing in HELP SEARCH.

In Section A of this chapter, we proposed a turn signal canceling invention. With the APS program, we can perform a word search of the entire text of issued patents since 1971 for keywords related to this idea. If you reviewed the material in Chapters 3 and 4, you may recall that we were only able to search the entire text of patents issued since 1976, at the PTO's website. At the IBM website, we could search back to 1971, but we were limited to the front page plus the claims section of the issued patents.

This process of keyword searching relies on Boolean logic, which was covered in Chapter 1. So if you haven't read Chapter 1 yet, you should do so now and then return here.

To search for the terms TURN and SIGNAL, we simply type in the command:

SEARCH TURN AND SIGNAL

Here we have used the command SEARCH and the Boolean AND operator to connect the words Turn and Signal. The system will then search through the text of all the patents in the data files USPAT and USOCR, for the words Turn and Signal. The system response is shown in Figure 37, below.

```
=> SEARCH TURN AND SIGNAL

FILE 'USPAT'

        658193 TURN
        543888 SIGNAL

   L1  243216 TURN AND SIGNAL

FILE  'USOCR'

        32410 TURN
        16724 SIGNAL
   L2  8114 TURN AND SIGNAL

TOTAL FOR ALL FILES

   L3  251330 TURN AND SIGNAL
```

Figure 37

There were 658,193 patents that contained the word Turn in the USPAT file and 543,888 patents that contained the word Signal. The words Turn and Signal together occurred in 243,216 patents. This group of 243,216 patents makes up what is called an "answer set." To the left of our answer set is the "answer set L number." The answer set L number is a numbered label that is applied to each search that we perform. In this case, the answer set L number is "L1." The L numbers increase sequentially for each new search.

The L2 answer set label refers to patents in the much smaller USOCR data file that contains our search words. Because this data file covers only approximately 100,000 patents, there were only 8,114 matches for the words Turn and Signal together.

The L3 answer set label simply combines the results from both the USPAT and USOCR patent data files. In this case, 243,216 (L1) plus 8,114 (L2) occurrences of our search words are combined into a result of 251,330 (L3) matching patents.

Before you can view the patents contained within these search results, you must decide three things:

- Which answer set do you wish to look at?
- Which patents do you wish to see within the answer set?
- Which part of the patents do you wish to read?

These three items are specified by using the DISPLAY command. If you type in just the word DISPLAY, the system will prompt you for the needed information. This is shown in Figure 38, below. Directly below the word "display," the system responds by asking for an L number, an answer number or range and a display format.

The APS program will supply default values for each answer. The system defaults are enclosed within parentheses. The default answer for the L number is just the L number for the last search performed. In our case, this L number is L3. The default answer for the answer number or range is 1. This corresponds to the most recently issued patent that contains our search terms. The patents are always stored chronologically within the answer set. The default display format is the CIT format. This will determine how much of our patent information will be displayed on screen. The CIT format stands for the "Citation" format. It includes the patent number, issue date, title, first inventor and class/subclass.

```
=> DISPLAY

ENTER (L3), L# OR ?:

ENTER ANSWER NUMBER OR RANGE (1):
    ENTER DISPLAY FORMAT (CIT):
```

Figure 38

To accept the default, you can do one of three things:

1. Press the space bar on the keyboard, then press ENTER.
2. Type in a period (.), then press ENTER.
3. Type in the value shown in parentheses, then press ENTER.

You can also type a question mark (?) or the word Help to display help information about the display prompt.

```
=> DISPLAY

ENTER (L3), L# OR ?:L1

ENTER ANSWER NUMBER OR RANGE (1):1
    ENTER DISPLAY FORMAT (CIT):CIT
```

Figure 39

In Figure 39 above, we have entered the L1 label for our answer set and accepted the defaults of 1 and CIT for our answer number and display format, respectively. The resulting system response is shown in Figure 40.

---

1. 5,717,985, Feb. 10, 1998, Sintered metal fiber core blotter roll and method of making same; Richard G. Labombard, et al., 399/249, 237, 248 [IMAGE AVAILABLE]

Figure 40

As you can see, the returned information corresponds to our CIT format. The patent number, issue date, title, first inventor and class/subclass information is returned. It is also obvious that this patent has nothing to do with turn signals. So, why was it included in the answer set?

The large number of matching patents (251,330) in the search results of Figure 37 illustrates, again, the fact that when you execute a simple search command with the APS, you are searching through the words of the entire patent. Therefore any occurrence of your search terms in the patent title, abstract, specifications or claims will be returned by the APS program as a match.

The APS search results differ in both form and content from the results obtained over the Internet. After performing a search with the PTO and IBM Internet sites, the matching patent titles are displayed. By clicking on these titles, the searcher can then display the text and graphic images of each page of the patent.

The APS system, on the other hand, uses L-numbered labels to reference its search results. The actual patent data is then displayed according to the form of the display command issued. Because you are searching through the words of the entire text of patents issued since 1971 with the APS, the results obtained are more comprehensive than those gathered over the Internet.

In Section A of this chapter, we spoke at length about the process of identifying the class and subclass of your invention. In Section B, we described

how to find a list of all the patents issued within a class/subclass. Obviously, it isn't possible or efficient to read over 251,330 patents, looking for an invention that is similar to yours. So what you want to do is first identify the class and subclass in the field of your invention, and then get a listing of all the patents issued within that class/subclass.

In order to do this with the APS, you have to limit your search to certain sections of the patent. We accomplish that with the use of a "Search Index" added to the end of our search command. The search index is a slash (/), followed by a group of characters that limit the scope of the search to selected subsections of the patent.

For example, in Section A of this chapter, we identified Class 340, subclass 465, as a highly likely place to find patents related to turn signals for vehicles. To search for all of the patents found in class/subclass 340/465, we use the search command shown in Figure 41 with the /CCLS search index. CCLS is the PTO's designation for Current Patent Class and Subclass.

=> SEARCH 340/465 /CCLS

Figure 41

This command will return the results shown in Figure 42.

FILE 'USPAT'
L4   118 340/465 /CCLS

Figure 42

As you can see, the number of patents returned has been drastically reduced to 118 in the L4 answer set. A list of other commonly used patent search indexes is shown in Table 3 below.

USPAT Search Index Characters	
Patent Abstract	/AB
Patent Claims	/CLM
Current Patent Class and Subclass	/CCL3
Inventor Name	/IN
Patent Number	/PN

Table 3

To see the first patent in the L4 answer set, we enter the display command as shown in Figure 43.

```
=> D L4
```

Figure 43

Here, we have used the short (or expert) form of the display command. This form comes in handy once you are familiar with the various command words. By using the letter D, followed by the term L4, the APS program accepts the display command and takes L4 as the answer to its first requirement, namely, which L numbered answer set to use. The default values for the next two requirements are then used. This results in the display of the most recent patent of our answer set, shown in Figure 44.

```
1. 5,712,618, Jan. 27, 1998, Method and
apparatus for an automatic signaling device;
Michael R. McKenna, 340/475, 463, 465,468; 362/
80 [IMAGE AVAILABLE]
```

Figure 44

To display the abstract of Patent Number 5,712,518, we need to change from the CIT display format to the AB (short for abstract) display format. We do this by typing in the command shown in Figure 45, below.

```
=> D AB
```

Figure 45

This command accepts L4 as our answer set, selects the first patent in the set and displays its abstract. The result is shown in Figure 46. A quick reading of the abstract indicates that this patent is highly relevant to our invention idea.

```
US PAT NO: 5,712,618 [IMAGE AVAILABLE]
L4: 1 OF 118

ABSTRACT:

An automatic signaling device for a vehicle
which automatically initiates a warning signal to
pedestrians and to other vehicles in connection
with lane changes and upon turns. The present
invention is activated and deactivated
automatically providing significant safety
advantages for all of those using the roads and
highways.
```

Figure 46

To display the entire text of Patent Number 5,712,618, simply enter the command D, followed by the word ALL. The command, as well as the first page of the APS response, is shown in Figure 47, below.

```
=> D ALL

5,712,618 [IMAGE AVAILABLE]  Jan. 27, 1998        L4: 1 of 118

        Method and apparatus for an automatic signaling device

INVENTOR:      Michael R. McKenna, 1122 W. Morse Ave.,
               Chicago, IL 60626
APPL-NO:       08/520,537
DATE FILED:    Aug. 29, 1995
INT-CL:        [6] B60Q 1/34
US-CL-ISSUED:  340/475, 463, 465, 468; 364/424.01, 424.05,
               426.02; 362/80
US-CL-CURRENT: 340/475, 463, 465, 468; 362/80
SEARCH-FLD:    340/463, 465, 468, 436, 671, 475; 364/424.01,
               426.02, 424.05; 362/80, 36
REF-CITED:
                  U.S. PATENT DOCUMENTS
      3,784,974  1/1974  Hamashige              340/465
      3,895,683  7/1975  Lang et al.         180/103
      4,123,116  10/1978 Holtzman et al.        340/73
      4,942,529  7/1990  Avitan et al.       364/424.01
      4,996,657  2/1991  Shiraishi et al.    364/424.05
      5,079,708  1/1992  Brown               364/424.05
      5,335,176  8/1994  Nakamura            364/424.05
      5,345,385  9/1994  Zomotor et al.         364/424.05
      5,428,512  6/1995  Mouzas              362/80
      5,467,072  11/1995 Michael             340/436
ART-UNIT:      267
PRIM-EXMR:     Jeffery Hofsass
ASST-EXMR:     Timothy Edwards, Jr.
LEGAL-REP:     Michael R. McKenna
ABSTRACT:
An automatic signaling device for a vehicle which automatically
initiates a Method and apparatus for an automatic signaling
device warning signal to pedestrians and to other vehicles in
connection with lane changes and upon turns. The present
invention is activated and de-activated automatically providing
significant safety advantages for all of those using the roads
and highways.

          15 Claims, 2 Drawing Figures
```

Figure 47

At the bottom of Figure 47, two drawing figures are listed for Patent Number 5,712,618. These can't be displayed with the APS system. However, in the following section we will show you how these drawings can be reviewed using the microfilm patent records.

A list of commonly used patent display formats is shown in Table 4, below.

USPAT Display Format	Characters
Display Entire Text of Patent	ALL
Display Abstract	AB
Display Patent Number, Issue Date, Title, First Inventor, Current Classifications	CIT (Default)
Display Inventor Information	IN
Display Patent Title	TI

Table 4

One problem with the APS is that if you display more results than will fit on one full screen, some of the information will scroll out of view. To prevent this from happening, make use of the Hold/ Resume special function keys. This corresponds to F4 on the standard APS keyboard and is shown in Figure 48, below.

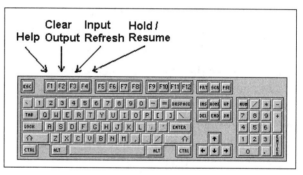

Figure 48

By pressing the F4 key once while the main display area of the APS is being updated, you can prevent information from scrolling off the top of the display. By pressing the F4 key a second time, the display will resume updating.

Two other very useful special function keys are the Continuous Print and the Save to Disk keys. These keys are shown in Figure 49.

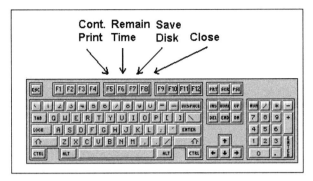

Figure 49

If there is a printer attached to the APS terminal that you are using, you can get a continuous print-out of everything displayed in the main display area by pressing F5. By pressing F7, the entire contents of your APS session (all your input commands and search results, for example) can be saved to a floppy disk.

To get a quick printout of only the contents of the current screen display, you can use the F10 special function key shown in Figure 50 below.

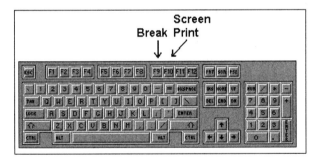

Figure 50

D. Searching Pre-1971 Patents

We have focused on recently issued patents so far in this book. That is, patents that have been issued since 1971. This is because recent patent information has been published in electronic form. This

facilitates the use of powerful computer search tools such as the Internet sites, APS and CASSIS. However, the bulk of U.S. patent information available for searching is in the form of microfilm found only in the PTDLs (and in the form of actual print copies at the PTO's office in Virginia).

At a minimum, all PTDLs maintain a 25-year backfile of issued patents on microfilm. Additionally, some PTDLs have complete microfilm records of all patents issued in the United States. These records will contain facsimile images of every page of every patent within their collection. There are two situations when you will need to reference this collection.

1. When the listing of patents issued to a particular class includes patents older than 1971.
2. When you uncover a patent that is relevant to your invention and the referenced patents (on the front page) are older than 1971.

As an example of the first case situation, let's return to our turn signal canceling device. Previously we determined that class/subclass 340/465 was highly relevant to our invention idea. There are several ways to obtain a listing of all the patents issued in this class/subclass:

1. Output from the APS system.
2. Output from the CASSIS program.
3. Output from Internet patent search resources.

Let's take a look at the output from the CASSIS program for class/subclass 340/465. This is shown in Figure 51, below. Here, starting with Patent Number 5,696,484, the patents are listed in reducing numerical order, from left to right. To get a rough idea of the relationship between patent number and issue date, patent number 3,500,000 was issued in the year 1970. Therefore, for references to patent numbers less than 3,500,000 you will need to reference the microfilm collection. Since the idea of a turn signaling device predates 1970 by many years, it is no surprise that Figure 51 contains many references to older patents.

```
Classification: 340/465      ORs: 61      XRs: 56      Total: 117

5696484 X 5689232 X 5682138 X 5677671 X 5663708 O 5619182 X 5610577 O
5594415 X 5463370 X 5424715 X 5416465 O 5309143 X 5281950 X 5253115 X
5198798 X 5097917 X 5086289 X 5023592 X 4996657 X 4994786 X 4868541 O
4853672 O 4760372 X 4638295 O 4559516 X 4325052 X 4122318 X 3784974 X
2934744 X 2784269 X 2674667 X 2667545 X 2432388 O 2302098 X 2248760 O
2201795 X 2188058 X 2186766 O 2180894 X 2180688 O 2178073 X 2175848 O
2168480 O 2148428 O 2133000 O 2126940 O 2114731 O 2111931 O 2109408 O
2108454 O 2089183 O 2064735 O 2061401 O 2027821 O 2010454 X 1995236 O
1977887 O 1973299 O 1968749 O 1923162 O 1910257 O 1908124 O 1896905 X
1890677 O 1832326 O 1831814 O 1802647 X 1779799 O 1774273 X 1770415 X
1768717 O 1763465 O 1752289 O 1750738 X 1749169 O 1749168 O 1707305 X
1695712 O 1683818 O 1670744 X 1664791 O 1663971 O 1651540 O 1625565 O
1623219 O 1610901 X 1600560 X 1598358 O 1593574 O 1582069 X 1575445 O
1542431 O 1532221 X 1506597 X 1482540 O 1468830 O 1341932 X 1331158 O
1320566 O 1270714 X 1248937 X 1240458 X 1227226 O 1215155 O 1210283 O
1198495 O 1194537 O 1191638 O 1179306 X 1164832 X 1158355 X 1140229 X
1138834 O 1120589 O 1112278 O 1106982 O 1033208 O
```

Figure 51

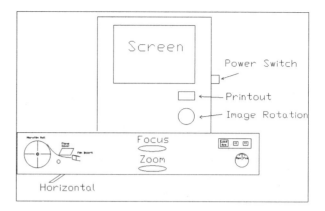

Figure 52

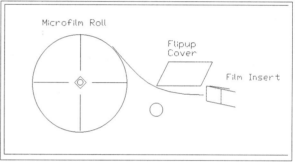

Figure 53

For example, in Figure 51, patent number 2,432,388 is shown boxed. Since this patent number predates patent 3,500,000 by a large margin, it was issued before 1970 by many years. To view this patent, we need to get the appropriate roll of microfilm. Each roll of microfilm is labeled with the first and last patent number contained on that roll. Rolls are stored sequentially, so you just need to look for the range of numbers that contains the patent you seek. A PTDL assistant can help you get started.

Figure 52 shows a sketch of the typical microfilm reader used at the PTDL. Turn the reader on using the power switch on the right-hand side. Figure 53 is a close-up view of the lower left portion of the reader, where the microfilm rolls are loaded. When you take the roll of microfilm out of its box, it will usually have a rubber band wrapped around it to keep the film from unraveling. Remove the rubber band and insert the roll on the protruding rod at the left of Figure 53. Make sure that you rotate the roll of film so that the square section at the base of the rod is inserted into the film roll. This helps lock it into place.

Unroll the clear section of microfilm at the beginning of the roll and feed it under the flipup cover as shown in the figure. There is a small push button which flips up the cover. Next, feed the film into the film insert until the first images appear on the screen of the viewer. Press the flipup cover down and lock it into place. Then press the load button on the lower right of the viewer. A close-up view of this section of the viewer is shown in Figure 54. The load button is actually a toggle button. The first time you press it, it loads the microfilm. The second time you press it, when you are finished, it rewinds the microfilm.

Once you have loaded the film, you need to forward the reel to the position of your patent. The forward and rewind knob is shown in Figure 54. To move slowly forward, move the knob slightly to the right; to move forward quickly move the knob further to the right (up to a quarter turn). The rewind or reverse direction works the same way, with increasing rewind speed as you rotate the knob further to the left. With a little practice, you will get the hang of it.

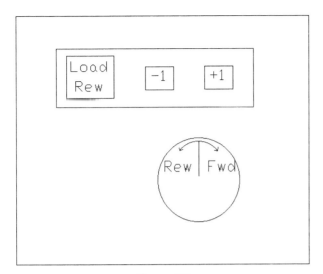

Figure 54

In Figure 55, we show a typical section of microfilm. Each page of the patent is separated by a black space where the patent number is written. The patent number is written to the left of each page of the patent. In Figure 55, we see the last page of patent number 2,432,387 followed by the patent we wish to review, patent number 2,432,388.

Figure 56 shows the first page of patent number 2,432,388, which is the drawing page. Figure 57 shows the first page of the patent text. From here we can see that patent number 2,432,388, Directional Signal System For Vehicles, was issued on December 9, 1947.

Older patents have a slightly different format than their modern counterparts. For example, the referenced patents section is not listed until the last page.

To obtain a printout of what is displayed on the microfilm reader, use the zoom and focus wheels shown in Figure 52 to position the page of text as shown in Figure 58. A printout machine is usually located directly below the reader. The cost is usually ten cents a page. Just insert a dime into the machine, align the page with the markers and press the print button shown in Figure 52, above.

Ordering Copies

If you are not too pressed for time, you can also order high-quality copies of patents discovered in the course of a search. This is done via the library duplication department. Costs are around $5 per patent, with a one-week turnaround time.

When you are finished, be sure to press the rewind button and wait for the roll of microfilm to completely rewind. Then replace it in its box and return the box to the proper sequence position with the other microfilm rolls.

Figure 55

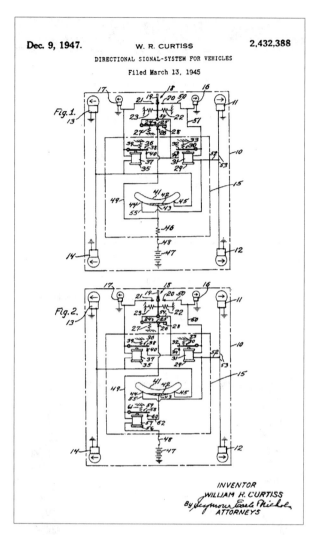

Figure 56

Patented Dec. 9, 1947   2,432,388

UNITED STATES PATENT OFFICE

2,432,388

DIRECTIONAL SIGNAL SYSTEM FOR VEHICLES

William R. Curtiss, Meriden, Conn., assignor to
Great American Industries. Inc., Meriden,
Conn., a corporation of Delaware

Application March 13, 1945. Serial No. 582,465

6 Claims. (Cl. 177—339)

This invention relates to improvements in directional or direction indicating signal systems for vehicles for properly indicating right and left turns.

One object of this invention is to provide an improved directional signal system for vehicles in which control means is automatically operable by centrifugal force while the vehicle is making a turn, to properly actuate the directional signal means, and when the vehicle completes the turn, the absence of action by centrifugal force automatically causes the control means to shut off the directional signal means.

Another object of this invention is to provide an improved directional signal system for vehicles in which control means including a primary switch which is optionally closable by the operator of the vehicle in either of two ways, to initially actuate the one or other of the right and left-directional signal means, after which automatically operable centrifugal switch means takes over and continues the actuation of the signal means which has first been operated by the primary switch means and then after completion of the turn, automatically causes cessation of operation of such signal means.

With the above and other objects in view, as will appear to those skilled in the art from the present disclosure, this invention includes all features in the said disclosure which are novel over the prior art.

In the description and claims, the various parts and steps are identified by specific terms for convenience, but they are intended to be as generic in their application as the prior art will permit.

In the accompanying drawings forming part of this disclosure, in which certain ways of carrying out the invention are shown for illustrative purposes:

Fig. 1 is a schematic view illustrating one way of carrying out the invention; and

Fig. 2 is a schematic view of another way of carrying out the invention.

Referring to Fig. 1 of the drawings, the broken line outline or enclosure 10 indicates an automobile or other vehicle, provided with respectively front and rear right-directional signal means or direction indicators in the form of signal lamps 11 and 12 and with respectively front and rear left-directional signal means or signal indicators or direction indicators in the form of signal lamps 13 and 14. A broken line outline or enclosure 15 indicates a box or other container in which may be placed, if so desired, all of the mechanisms illustrated

within the broken line enclosure 15. It will be seen that the mechanisms located in the box 15 have no operational connection with any of the other mechanisms of the signal-system other than electric wire connections, and that, therefore, the box 15 can be placed in any desired location in or on the vehicle.

16 is a right-directional pilot lamp and 17 is a left-directional pilot lamp which two pilot lamps 16 and 17 will preferably be located within the view of the operator of the vehicle. Each pilot lamp could be as small as two candle power, and each signal lamp could be fifteen candle power or more or less.

18 is a primary or initiating single-pole double-throw switch, the switch arm 19 of which is normally held in open intermediate position between two switch contacts 20 and 21 by any suitable yielding means, such for example, as the springs 22 and 23, so that if the switch arm 19 is moved into contact with either of contacts 20 or 21 and then released, the switch arm 19 is automatically returned by the springs 22 and 23 to its central open position shown in Fig. 1. A release switch 24 has its switch arm 25 normally yieldingly held closed against the switch contact 26, by any suitable means such as the spring 27 and may, if desired, have the switch arm provided with a press button 28 for convenience. Both of the switches 18 and 24 would ordinarily be located within easy reach of the operator of the vehicle.

29 is a right directional relay which has what is known in the art as a lock-in switch 30, although it is pulled to and held in its closed-circuit position solely by the electromagnetic action of the current passing through the coil of the relay. When suitable electric current passes through the coil 31 of relay 29, the switch arm 32 of switch 30 is pulled down against action of the spring 33 and into contact with the switch contact 34, in the lock-in or hold-in position. Similarly, the left-directional relay 35 has a lock-in switch 36. When suitable electric current passes through the coil 37 of relay 35, the switch arm 38 of switch 36 is pulled down against action of the spring 39 and into contact with the switch contact 40 in the lock-in position.

41 is a single-pole double-throw centrifugal switch, in the form shown being a mercury switch which will be arranged to extend transversely of the vehicle. Mercury 42 is normally in contact with the central contact 43 of the switch 41, and when the vehicle makes a right turn, for example, the centrifugal force set up by the turning action of the vehicle, will cause the mercury 42 to flow

Figure 57

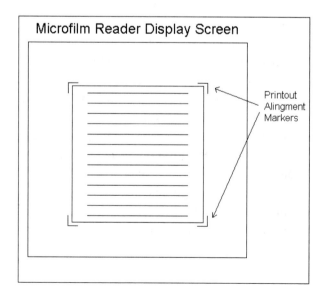

Figure 58

E. Summary and Comparison of PTDL Resources

The following table summarizes the various resources available at the PTDL. Only the most common patent search resources are listed and it is by no means an exhaustive listing.

As you can see, there is some overlap in the use of the various resources.

PTDL Resources	Use
Index to the U.S. Patent Classification	Find class and subclass names that correspond with descriptive words for your invention.
The Manual of Classification	Find further subclasses that may be related to your invention.
The Classification Definitions	Review the descriptions of classes and subclasses to determine which apply to your invention.
CASSIS	Search electronic versions of classification manuals. Extract list of patent numbers issued in a given class/subclass.
APS	Extract the text of patents issued in a given class/subclass. Review selected text of issued patents since 1970. Perform keyword searches of all patents issued since 1970.
Microfilm	Search images of patents prior to 1970

To briefly summarize the patent search process at the PTDL:

Use the classification manuals or CASSIS to determine the appropriate class/subclass(es) for your invention.

Use CASSIS or APS to obtain a listing of the patents issued within those class/subclass(es).

Use APS to review each patent within the selected class/subclass(es) to determine relevance. To review the drawings of relevant patents, use the microfilm readers.

Use microfilm readers to review pre-1971 patents.

An alternative method would be to perform keyword searches of the patents first. Then, after locating a patent that is related to your invention, you can search the class/subclass(es) of that patent. This is not the most efficient way of searching the patent database, but can come in handy if you are really stumped when trying to find relevant classes.

Summary

Hitting the Books

- Use the *Index to the U.S. Patent Classification* to find class and subclass names that correspond with descriptive words for your invention.
- Use the *Manual of Classification* to find further subclasses that may be related to your invention.
- Use the *Classification Definitions* to review the descriptions of classes and subclasses and determine which apply to your invention.

Using CASSIS

- Search electronic versions of the classification manuals.
- Extract a list of patent numbers issued in a given class/subclass.

Using APS

- Extract the text of patents issued in a given class/subclass.
- Perform keyword searches of all patents issued since 1970.
- Review selected text of issued patents since 1970.

Searching Pre-1971 Patents

- Use microfilm readers to search patents issued before 1971 (patent numbers under 3,500,000).

■

Part 3

Maximum Performance

n Part 3, we will further develop the patent searching tools and techniques discussed in Part 2. These advanced patent searching techniques are essential for going beyond a preliminary search to produce comprehensive search results.

In Chapter 6, we build upon the techniques learned in Chapters 3 and 4. We return to the world of the Internet and compose complex Boolean expressions at the PTO and IBM websites. These advanced commands will allow you to produce highly effective search results.

In Chapter 7, we build upon the material covered in Chapter 5 and explore the advanced use of the APS system at your local PTDL. Chapter 7 will also introduce you to the searchable Japanese and European patent abstracts files at the PTDL.

In Chapter 8, we go beyond the PTO and IBM websites and investigate some additional Internet patent search resources. Some of these resources are available at no cost; others will charge a fee.

In Chapter 9, we move beyond patents and explore other sources of prior art.

Finally, in Chapter 10, we provide some tips for evaluating your search results.

CHAPTER

6

Advanced Internet Patent Searching

This chapter introduces you to advanced Boolean search commands at the PTO Internet site. Before attempting these techniques, it is necessary to have a good understanding of basic Boolean logic (Chapter 1). Also, before starting this section, you will be best served by understanding the basic keyword searching methods used at the PTO (Chapter 3) and the IBM (Chapter 4) websites.

A. Advanced Patent Searching at the PTO Website

In Chapters 1 and 3, we explained the basics of Boolean searching and using the PTO website to search for post-1976 patents. That information was enough to get you started. Now that you grasp the basics, it's time to improve your searching skills.

1. Using Multiple Boolean Operators

Simple Boolean expressions are generally understood to mean the use of two keywords connected by a single Boolean operator. For example:

> Fire AND Protection
> or
> Building OR Structure

The first query would return all of the patents that contained both of the words Fire and Protection. By requiring both of the keywords to be present, we reduce the size of our search results. The second query would return all of the patents that contained the word Building or the word Structure. By requiring only one of the keywords to be present, we enlarge the size of our search results.

An advanced Boolean query involves the use of more than one operator and sometimes the use of parentheses. For example:

> Fire AND Protection AND (Building OR Structure)

This Boolean search command would return only patents that contained the words Fire, Protection and the word Building or the word Structure. The first two keywords use a logical AND operation to narrow the search results. Then the logical AND operation is applied to the expression contained within the parentheses. The use of the parentheses around the keywords "Building OR Structure" means that patents are searched for either of these words (this widens the size of the search results, because either keyword can cause a hit). However, the result of the search for the keywords "Building OR Structure" is then further narrowed because these two words must occur in combination with the words Fire and Protection. The flowchart of Figure 1 illustrates this process. The correct placement of parentheses is important because this determines how the keywords are combined.

Let's try some advanced search commands at the PTO website and examine the results. As shown in Chapter 3, to get to the PTO patent search website, you need to use the following address (you can also get to the patent search site through the PTO's homepage at www.uspto.gov):

> http://www.uspto.gov/patft

Towards the bottom of the PTO main Web page are the hypertext links shown in Figure 2 below. To get to the advanced search page, click on the Advanced Search link, located under the Bibliographic Database title.

The advanced search page is shown in Figure 3 below. There are several similarities to the Boolean search page discussed in Chapter 3. The Select Database radio buttons allow you to specify the range of years that you wish to search. You can search through the entire patent database from 1976 to the present by selecting the All button. By selecting the Specify button, you can limit your search to patents issued within the specified years.

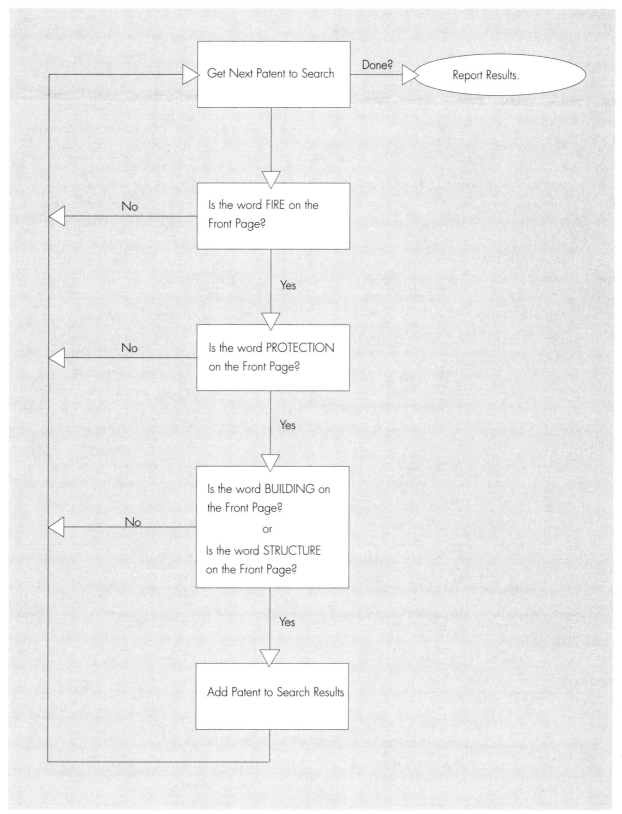

Figure 1

Figure 2

For this example, we will select Specify and set the year range to 91-95.

The Rank Results radio button is also the same as in the Boolean search page. For this example, we will accept the default setting of Chronologically.

The Query box of the advanced search page is quite different from the Boolean search page. We no longer have the two keyword entry fields separated by a Boolean operator field, as shown in Chapter 3, Figure 9. Instead, we are faced only with a challenging blank box. It is here that we enter our advanced Boolean expressions. Let's type in the search command "Fire AND Protection AND (Building OR Structure)," as shown in the figure. To start the search, just click on the Search button shown in the lower right of Figure 3.

First note in the Search Summary section in Figure 4, below, that your query was modified slightly by the search engine to enclose your first two search terms in parentheses. It also enclosed your entire query in parentheses. Below, we explain what these parentheses mean and when you can use the same approach to perform your search.

In Chapter 3, we executed the simple Boolean search command "Fire AND Protection" for patents issued in the years 1991 through 1995. The results we obtained (Figure 10 of Chapter 3) show that 132 hits were found. Now, by using a more complex Boolean expression, we were able to add the requirement for the keywords Building or Structure. The results of our new search are shown in Figure 4 below. From the figure, you can see that the number of matching patents has been reduced from 132 to 26.

The Query entry box of the advanced search page allows you to type in any valid Boolean search command. This provides you with the ability to precisely define your search requirements. It means that your search results will be more relevant and that there will be less material to read over. Of course, the down side to the advanced query box is that if you are too narrow in your search requirements, you may overlook patents that are relevant. For example, instead of

---

U.S. Patent Advanced Search Page

This page provides an interface for advanced, multi-term searching of the U.S. Patent Database. Help on formulating queries is available.

Select Database:
○ All ● Specify: 91-95 ▾ [Database Contents]

Query:

```
fire AND protection AND (building OR structure)
```

Example: **ttl/needle or ttl/syringe andnot (sew* or thread)**

Rank Results
● Chronologically
○ By Relevance

Search   Reset

Data current through: 2/24/98

Figure 3

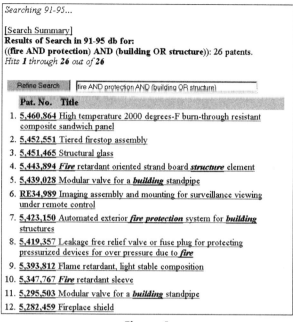

Searching 91-95...

[Search Summary]
Results of Search in 91-95 db for:
((fire AND protection) AND (building OR structure)): 26 patents.
Hits 1 through 26 out of 26

Refine Search | fire AND protection AND (building OR structure)

Pat. No. Title

1. **5,460,864** High temperature 2000 degrees-F burn-through resistant composite sandwich panel
2. **5,452,551** Tiered firestop assembly
3. **5,451,465** Structural glass
4. **5,443,894** *Fire* retardant oriented strand board *structure* element
5. **5,439,028** Modular valve for a *building* standpipe
6. **RE34,989** Imaging assembly and mounting for surveillance viewing under remote control
7. **5,423,150** Automated exterior *fire protection* system for *building* structures
8. **5,419,357** Leakage free relief valve or fuse plug for protecting pressurized devices for over pressure due to *fire*
9. **5,393,812** Flame retardant, light stable composition
10. **5,347,767** *Fire* retardant sleeve
11. **5,295,503** Modular valve for a *building* standpipe
12. **5,282,459** Fireplace shield

Figure 4

the words Building or Structure, a relevant patent may contain the words edifice, palace or skyscraper.

As always, to read the front page of any patent reported as a hit, just click on the patent number. To return to the advanced search page, just click on the back arrow of your browser.

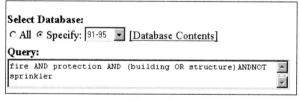

Select Database:
○ All ⊙ Specify: 91-95 ▼ [Database Contents]
Query:
fire AND protection AND (building OR structure) ANDNOT sprinkler

Figure 5

As explained in Chapter 1, another important Boolean operator is the ANDNOT operator. As you may recall, the ANDNOT operator allows you to exclude certain keywords from the search results. Let's suppose that our invention is a fire protective device used in various buildings, but does not

involve sprinklers. To exclude sprinklers from the search results, we add "ANDNOT sprinkler" to our search command and compose the following query (shown in Figure 5):

> Fire AND Protection AND (Building OR Structure) ANDNOT Sprinkler

2. Using Parentheses to Organize Your Search Query

When using multiple Boolean operators, it's important to keep in mind which terms are evaluated first. Proceeding from left to right in the above command, the AND operator will first be used to combine the two terms Fire AND Protection. The next term encountered is the word Building. But this word is enclosed in parentheses with the OR operator and the word Structure. This forces the expression within the parentheses (Building OR Structure) to be evaluated first. Then the AND operator is used to combine the result with the first two words. Finally, the ANDNOT operator will be used to exclude the term Sprinkler.

If you are in doubt about the order of evaluation of a complex Boolean expression, you can always add more parentheses. For example, in the expression shown below:

> ((Fire AND Protection) AND (Building OR Structure))

First, the inner parentheses around Fire AND Protection causes these two terms to be AND'ed together. Then, the parentheses around Building OR Structure causes these two terms to be OR'ed together. Finally, the outer parentheses causes the results of both operations to be AND'ed together.

In fact, the PTO's patent server will automatically add parentheses to your search command and display it at the top of your search results. In this way, you can check to see that the executed search command matches what you intended.

Figure 6 shows the results of our search that excludes Sprinklers. Notice that the executed search command is displayed at the top of the search results. Namely:

(((Fire AND Protection) AND (Building OR Structure)) ANDNOT Sprinkler)

Here, we can see that Fire AND Protection will be evaluated first. Then Building will be OR'ed with Structure. Then the results of these two operations will be AND'ed together. Finally, the ANDNOT Sprinkler operation will be applied to all of the above.

Searcher's Secret Number 9

When in doubt about the order of evaluation in complex patent search commands, use parentheses to explicitly set the order. Then check the output command at the top of the results report.

In Figure 6, the total number of resulting hits has been further reduced from 26 to 22. Also note that patent numbers 5,439,028 and 5,295,503 (items 5 and 11) from Figure 4 have been eliminated from Figure 6. Obviously the word sprinkler was used on the front page of these patents.

3. Using Field Codes to Narrow Your Search

So far, we have been searching the entire front page of issued patents with the advanced search mode of the PTO's Bibliographic database. We can, however, limit our searches to certain sections of the front page through the use of Field Codes. Why limit your search to only selected sections? Why not always search through the maximum amount of patent text available? In fact, why use the Bibliographic database and not the Full-Text database? The answer is that by always searching through the maximum amount of patent text, you will often get thousands of matching patents that don't really have any bearing on your invention. Selected keywords like Fire and Protection can occur in many contexts. They are used in literally thousands of different types of inventions. Constructing queries that blindly look for any use of these keywords will often return many irrelevant hits.

Searching 91-95...

[Search Summary]
Results of Search in 91-95 db for:
(((fire AND protection) AND (building OR structure)) ANDNOT sprinkler): 22 patents.
Hits 1 through 22 out of 22

| Refine Search | fire AND protection AND (building OR structure)ANDNOT sp |

Pat. No. Title

1. **5,460,864** High temperature 2000 degrees-F burn-through resistant composite sandwich panel
2. **5,452,551** Tiered firestop assembly
3. **5,451,465** Structural glass
4. **5,443,894** *Fire* retardant oriented strand board *structure* element
5. **RE34,989** Imaging assembly and mounting for surveillance viewing under remote control
6. **5,423,150** Automated exterior *fire protection* system for *building* structures
7. **5,419,357** Leakage free relief valve or fuse plug for protecting pressurized devices for over pressure due to *fire*
8. **5,393,812** Flame retardant, light stable composition
9. **5,347,767** *Fire* retardant sleeve
10. **5,282,459** Fireplace shield
11. **5,261,555** Insulated *structure*
12. **5,230,954** *Fire-protection* and safety composite glass panel

Figure 6

US Patent Field Codes			
Field Code	**Field Name**	**Field Code**	**Field Name**
TTL	Title	IN	Inventor Name
ABST	Patent Abstract	IC	Inventor City
ISD	Issue Date	IS	Inventor State
PN	Patent Number	ICN	Inventor Country
APD	Application Date	GOVT	Government Interest
APN	Application Number	LREP	Legal Rep.
AN	Assignee Name	PCT	PCT Information
AC	Assignee City	PRIR	Foreign Priority
AS	Assignee State	REIS	Reissue Data
ACN	Assignee Country	RLAP	Related U.S. App. Data
ICL	Int. Class	REF	U.S. References
CCL	Current U.S. Class	FREF	Foreign References
EXP	Primary Examiner	OREF	Other References
EXA	Assistant Examiner		

Figure 7

At the bottom of the advanced search page is a table showing all the available field codes. This is shown in Figure 7 above. Next to the field codes is the name of the field. You may recognize by now that this field name is actually a hypertext link. To get a further description of any particular field code, just select it's name. For example, to read a description of the inventor name field code (IN) just click on inventor name at the top of the right-most column of Figure 7. The resulting description is shown in Figure 8.

As a learning exercise in the use of field codes, let's suppose we wish to limit our patent search to the patent title only. This comes in handy when your descriptive keywords succinctly describe the invention, and are therefore very likely to appear

in the patent title. Note that this type of restricted search is far too narrow in scope to produce a comprehensive search result, except as a quick check for the most obvious prior art patents.

We would then use the TTL field code shown at the upper left of Figure 7. Let's further suppose that we wish to search for the words Fire and Protection, or the words Safety and Glass, in the titles of issued patents. We would then compose the query shown in Figure 9 above.

> (TTL/Fire AND TTL/Protection) OR (TTL/Safety AND TTL/Glass)

Notice how each keyword is preceded by the characters "ttl/." This tells the patent search

---

Inventor Name (IN)
    Definition: The inventor(s) of patented item.
    Tips: If you want to search for the full name of the inventor, you have to format your query like: "last_name; first_name initial". The quotes are essential, since this is a phrase search. For example, to search for patent invented by John E. Doe, search for IN/"Doe; John E." instead. If the inventor were John E. Doe III, you'd search for IN/"Doe III; John E.".

▲

Figure 8

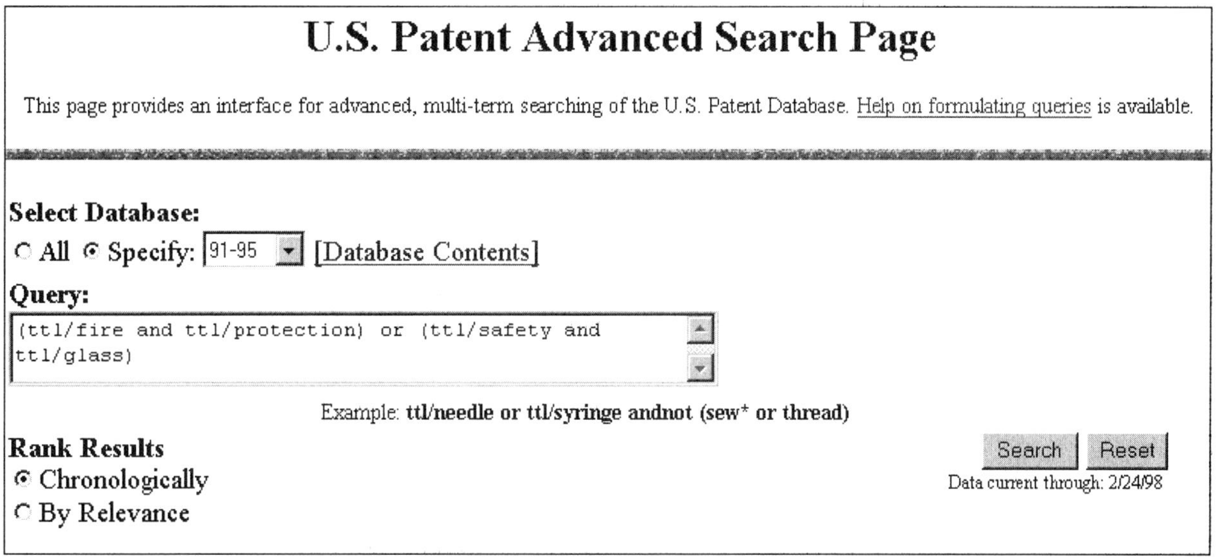

U.S. Patent Advanced Search Page

This page provides an interface for advanced, multi-term searching of the U.S. Patent Database. Help on formulating queries is available.

Select Database:
○ All ◉ Specify: [91-95 ▾] [Database Contents]

Query:
```
(ttl/fire and ttl/protection) or (ttl/safety and
ttl/glass)
```
Example: **ttl/needle or ttl/syringe andnot (sew* or thread)**

Rank Results   [Search] [Reset]
◉ Chronologically   Data current through: 2/24/98
○ By Relevance

Figure 9

program to look for that keyword in the patent title only. You might think that you could place the characters "ttl/" outside the parentheses, hoping that the patent search program would apply the contained expression to the title search. However, the program does not work this way and the field code must precede each keyword with which it is used.

The results of our patent title search are shown in Figure 10 below. You can see there were 43 hits for the words Fire and Protection, or Safety and Glass. A close look at Figure 10 shows that each of these patents has at least one of these pairs of keywords in their respective titles. If the Identifying name selected for the title of an issued patent matches one of your descriptive keywords, you should certainly examine that patent closely for relevance to your idea.

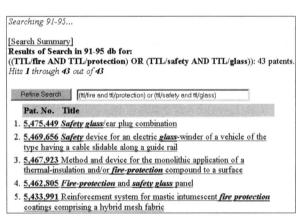

Figure 10

4. Using the XOR Boolean Operator

Another Boolean operator that is available at the PTO website is the XOR operator. To see how this works, we can change the OR condition of our previous query to XOR (as shown in Figure 11 below).

Using the Refine Search Feature

In Figure 11, we have actually skipped a step. Here we have taken advantage of the refine search box. This is the entry box shown in the center of Figure 11. For each search results listing, the PTO patent server program copies your input query into this entry box. If you want to make a slight change to the query and resubmit it, you can do it right from the results Web page. Instead of using the back arrow to return to the advanced search page, just type your changes into this box and click on Refine Search.

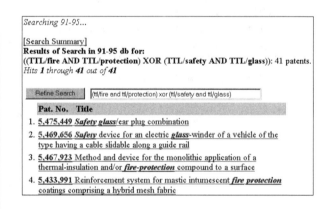

Figure 11

Notice that in Figure 10, patent number 5,462,805 (item #4 on the list) has both groups of keywords, "fire and protection" and "safety and glass," in the title. This is because of the OR condition that was used to conduct the search. With the use of the XOR condition, patent number 5,462,805 has been removed from the results shown in Figure 11. Recall from Chapter 1 that with the XOR condition only one group of keywords can be present in the result.

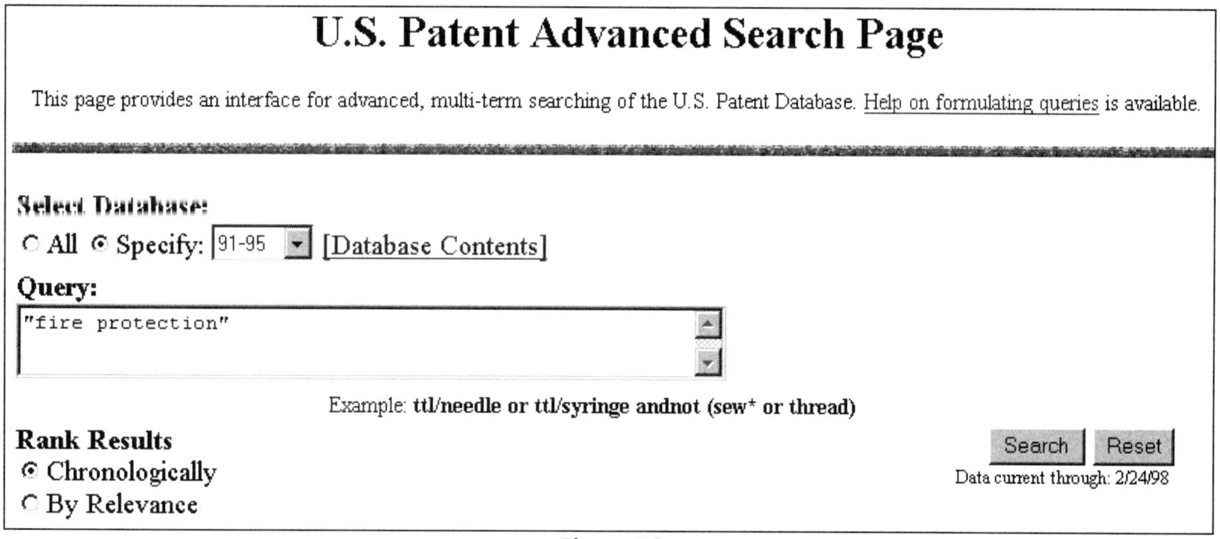

U.S. Patent Advanced Search Page

This page provides an interface for advanced, multi-term searching of the U.S. Patent Database. Help on formulating queries is available.

Select Database:
○ All ● Specify: 91-95 ▼ [Database Contents]

Query:

    "fire protection"

Example: **ttl/needle or ttl/syringe andnot (sew* or thread)**

Rank Results
● Chronologically
○ By Relevance

Search Reset

Data current through: 2/24/98

Figure 12

5. Searching for a Phrase

Another way that we can use the advanced search page is through the use of a quoted phrase. In Chapter 3, we searched for the words fire and protection connected with the Boolean AND operator. However, these words are often adjacent to each other. To search for the phrase "fire protection," just enclose the words in double quotes as shown in Figure 12 above. Then select the Search button. The results are shown in Figure 13 below.

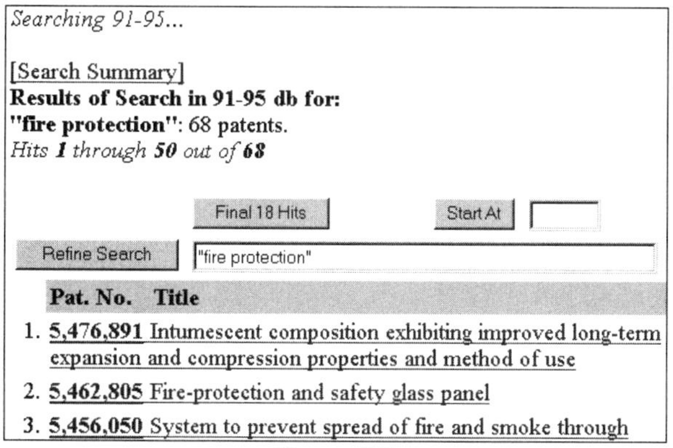

Searching 91-95...

[Search Summary]
Results of Search in 91-95 db for:
"fire protection": 68 patents.
Hits 1 through 50 out of 68

Final 18 Hits   Start At [   ]

Refine Search   "fire protection"

Pat. No. Title
1. **5,476,891** Intumescent composition exhibiting improved long-term expansion and compression properties and method of use
2. **5,462,805** Fire-protection and safety glass panel
3. **5,456,050** System to prevent spread of fire and smoke through

Figure 13

Here we see that there are 68 patents (front page), issued in the years 1991 through 1995, that have the phrase "fire protection" in them. This is a lot less than the 132 patents obtained with the "Fire AND Protection" query of Chapter 3. Care should be exercised with the use of phrases. If the sequence of words does not exactly match their use in the patent text to be searched, you won't get a match and you could miss a relevant prior art patent. As a general rule you should only use two- or three-word phrases that are highly likely to be used in that exact form.

6. Combining a Phrase Search With Field Codes

The use of double quotes can also be combined with field codes to produce highly specific and powerful searches. These searches are powerful and specific because you can search through years of patent text to find the exact phrase you expect to find in the exact field where you expect to find it.

For example, suppose you have discovered a particular inventor who works in the same field as yourself. It might be very helpful to find all the patents that have been issued to this person. To search for all of the patents issued to a particular inventor, enclose the inventor's name in quotes and precede it with the IN field code.

For example, one of the most interesting inventors that I have ever met is a man named Dr. Robert L. Forward. Dr. Forward has a Ph.D. in gravity physics and worked at Hughes Research Labs for over 30 years. During his time at Hughes and since recently retiring, Dr. Forward has been granted several patents. To search for all of the patents issued to Dr. Forward since 1976, we compose the following query:

IN/"Forward,Robert L."

Here we have used the inventor name field code IN, followed by the name of the inventor, last name first. Also note the placement of a comma between the last and first name. This search command is shown in Figure 14 below. We have also selected the All radio button under the Select Database heading. This will change the range of years to be searched from 1991–1995 to the entire patent database.

The results of our search are shown in Figure 15 below. Here we see a list of patents issued to Dr. Forward since 1976. To see the front page of the first patent, just click on it with the mouse. This is shown in Figure 16.

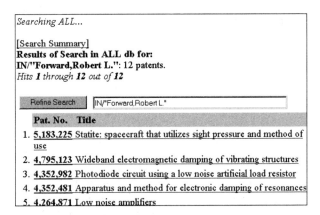

Figure 15

Figure 14

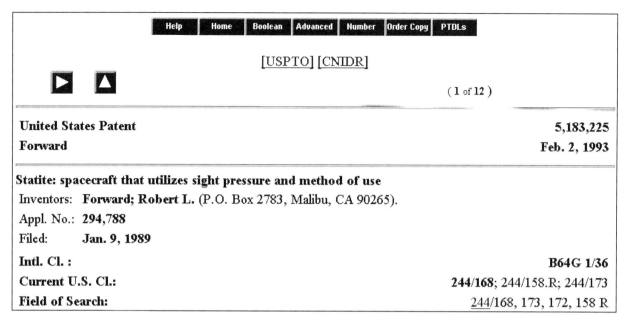

| Help | Home | Boolean | Advanced | Number | Order Copy | PTDLs |

[USPTO] [CNIDR]

(1 of 12)

| United States Patent | 5,183,225 |
| Forward | Feb. 2, 1993 |

Statite: spacecraft that utilizes sight pressure and method of use
Inventors: **Forward; Robert L.** (P.O. Box 2783, Malibu, CA 90265).
Appl. No.: **294,788**
Filed: **Jan. 9, 1989**

Intl. Cl. :	B64G 1/36
Current U.S. Cl.:	244/168; 244/158.R; 244/173
Field of Search:	244/168, 173, 172, 158 R

Figure 16

Navigating Search Results

At the upper left of Figure 16, there are two buttons with arrows on them. These buttons allow you to quickly navigate through a list of patents. To the right of these buttons, you will see "(1 of 12)." This means that you are currently looking at patent number 1 in a list of 12 patents. After you have finished reading the front page of patent number 5,183,225, you can immediately jump to the next patent on the list by clicking on the right (or forward) pointing arrow. This saves you the extra step involved in going back to the patent list and then selecting another patent title. Remember that the patents are listed chronologically, from the most recent patent to the oldest patent in the list.

After clicking on the forward arrow, you are presented with patent number 4,795,123, as shown in Figure 17. Now an extra directional button has appeared at the upper left. This button (having a left or reverse pointing arrow) will allow you to immediately jump to the previous patent on the list. These forward and reverse buttons can save you a lot of time when reading through long lists of patent results. By selecting the button with the upward pointing arrow, you can jump from any individual patent front page to the patent title list.

Help | Home | Boolean | Advanced | Number | Order Copy | PTDLs

[USPTO] [CNIDR]

(2 of 12)

United States Patent **4,795,123**
Forward, et. al. **Jan. 3, 1989**

Wideband electromagnetic damping of vibrating structures

Inventors: **Forward; Robert L.** (Oxnard, CA); **Griffin; William S.** (Manhattan Beach, CA).
Assignee: **The United States of America as represented by the Secretary of the Air Force** (Washington, DC).
Appl. No.: **49,358**
Filed: **May 14, 1987**

Intl. Cl. : **F16M 13/00**
Current U.S. Cl.: **248/550**; 188/378; 73/668
Field of Search: 248/550, 648, 562, 636, 630; 318/460, 605, 649, 651, 648; 188/378; 267/136; 73/668; 74/574

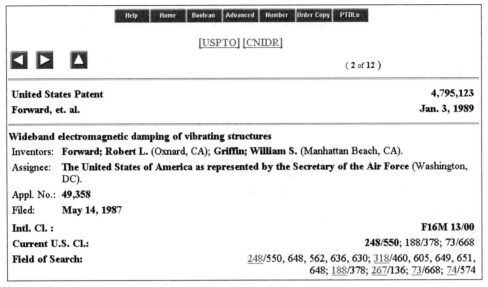

Figure 17

7. Using Wildcards in Your Advanced Patent Search

Wildcards can also be used for advanced patent searches. Let's suppose that you constructed the query: (Fireproof OR Firestop) AND Building. The results for searching the front pages of patents, from the years 1991 through 1995, are shown in Figure 18 below. As you can see, there were 13 hits or occurrences of our search query. To widen the scope of our search to include words like fireplace, firewall and firetrap, we could use a series of [OR] statements like the following:

(Fireproof OR Firestop OR Fireplace OR Firewall OR Firetrap) AND Building

But a more thorough and efficient approach would be to use the asterisk wildcard (*) to substitute for any characters occurring after the word Fire. Now, our search command looks like:

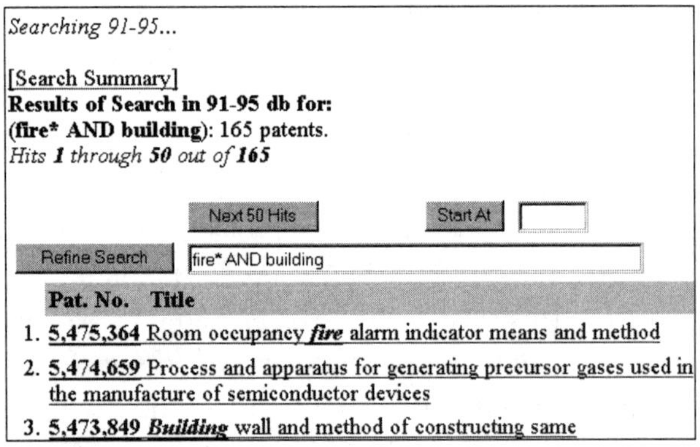

(Fire* AND Building)

The results of this query are shown in Figure 19 below. Now, there are 165 hits, as opposed to 13 hits for our previous search.

Searching 91-95...

[Search Summary]
Results of Search in 91-95 db for:
((fireproof OR firestop) AND building): 13 patents.
*Hits **1** through **13** out of **13***

Refine Search | (fireproof or firestop) AND building

Pat. No. Title
1. 5,452,551 Tiered ***firestop*** assembly
2. 5,426,908 Method of construction using corrugated material
3. 5,425,207 Method of constructing buildings and other structures using corrugated material

Figure 18

Searching 91-95...

[Search Summary]
Results of Search in 91-95 db for:
(fire* AND building): 165 patents.
*Hits **1** through **50** out of **165***

Next 50 Hits | Start At

Refine Search | fire* AND building

Pat. No. Title
1. 5,475,364 Room occupancy ***fire*** alarm indicator means and method
2. 5,474,659 Process and apparatus for generating precursor gases used in the manufacture of semiconductor devices
3. 5,473,849 ***Building*** wall and method of constructing same

Figure 19

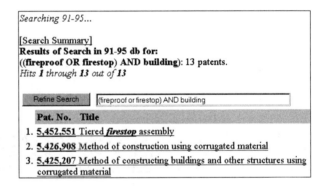

B. Advanced Patent Searching at the IBM Website

Let's try some advanced search commands at the IBM website and examine the results. As shown in Chapter 4, you will need to use the following address to get to the IBM website:

http://www.patents.ibm.com

Towards the bottom of the Web page are the hypertext links shown in Figure 20 below. To get to the advanced search page, click on the Advanced Text Search link.

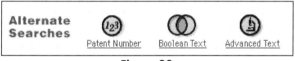

Figure 20

1. Understanding the IBM Advanced Text Search Page

The IBM advanced text search page is shown in Figure 21. As in the simple Boolean text search page of Chapter 4, we have two boxes to specify the range of search years. However, the entry boxes for our search queries are quite different from the Boolean text search page. Instead of having two keyword entry fields separated by a Boolean operator field, we have multiple entry boxes.

Here is a major design difference between the IBM advanced search page and the PTO advanced search page. At the PTO website, there is just one entry box and it is up to the user to type in the required field codes for each search term. At the IBM site, the need for field codes has been eliminated. Instead, we have multiple entry boxes for previously defined fields. All the user has to do is select which fields or sections of the patent to search and which keywords to search for in those sections. To

search the titles of patents, the user fills out the entry box adjacent to the title field. To search the claims of patents, the user fills out the entry box adjacent to the claims field. To search all of the available fields of the patent, enter your keywords in the Any Field entry box.

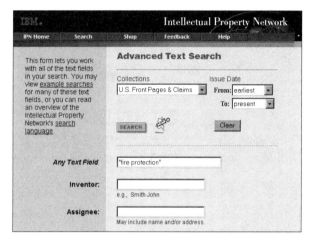

Figure 21

Each entry box will accept individual keywords, Boolean expressions, phrases and wildcards. For example, in Figure 21 we have entered the phrase "fire protection." To start the search process, just click the Search button shown at the center of the figure. The results are shown in Figure 22 below. There were 475 hits from our search. The large number of hits is due to two factors:

1. We searched through the entire patent database from 1971 to the present.
2. When we search all fields at the IBM site, we are not only searching the front page of the patent, but the claims as well.

2. Proximity Operators

In addition to the usual Boolean operators, the IBM system allows you to use a series of *proximity operators*. Proximity operators come in very handy when we want to look for two or more words that should be found near each other. In other words, instead of specifying the exact sequence of words, as in the phrase "fire protection," we can look for "fire" and "protection" occurring in any order within a sentence or a paragraph.

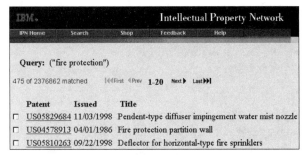

Figure 22

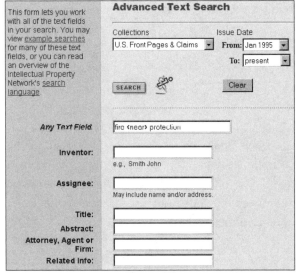

Figure 23

In Figure 23, we have replaced the phrase "fire protection" with the query "fire <near> protection." When we click the search button, the IBM program will look for any occurrence of the words Fire and Protection within 256 words of each other. Since we will be getting a lot more hits, we have changed the range of years to be searched to 1995 through the present. The results of our proximity

search are shown in Figure 24 below. There were 435 occurrences of the word Fire near the word Protection.

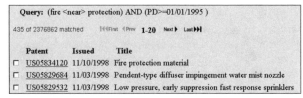

Figure 24

Proximity operators can be used in any query box. Let's suppose that our fire protection invention involves safety glass that can provide a measure of thermal insulation. We may reason that a similar patented invention would discuss safety glass and fire within its abstract. Of course, we don't know the exact order in which these words may occur, so we construct the generalized query shown in Figure 25. The results from this search are shown in Figure 26. By confining our search to the abstract of the patent, we have reduced the number of hits from 435 to 47.

Advanced Text Search

This form lets you work with all of the text fields in your search. You may view example searches for many of these text fields, or you can read an overview of the Intellectual Property Network's search language.

Collections: U.S. Front Pages & Claims

Issue Date: From: Jan 1995 To: present

SEARCH   Clear

Any Text Field:

Inventor:
e.g., Smith John

Assignee:
May include name and/or address.

Title:

Abstract: glass <near> fire

Attorney, Agent or Firm:

Related Info:

Figure 25

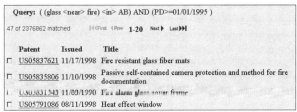

Figure 26

Figure 28

Advanced Text Search

This form lets you work with all of the text fields in your search. You may view example searches for many of these text fields, or you can read an overview of the Intellectual Property Network's search language.

Collections
U.S. Front Pages & Claims

Issue Date
From: Jan 1995
To: present

SEARCH   Clear

Any Text Field:

Inventor:
e.g., Smith John

Assignee:
May include name and/or address.

Title:

Abstract: glass <near/5> fire

Attorney, Agent or Firm:

Related Info:

Figure 27

In addition to the default <near> value of 256, the IBM system uses two other predefined <near> values. By replacing the <near> operator with the <paragraph> operator, you require two keywords to be within 100 words of each other. Similarly, by using the operator <sentence>, you require two keywords to be within 15 words of each other. These values are summarized in Table 1 below.

Operator	Proximity Required (in words)
<near>	256
<near/n>	n is any integer from 1 to 1,024
<paragraph>	100
<sentence>	15

Table 1

3. Specifying Degree of Nearness

With the Near operator, you can actually specify the degree of "nearness" that one keyword must be to another. For example, to specify that the word "glass" must be separated from the word "fire" by no more than five words, we use the search command:

glass <near/5> fire

Any value from 1 to 1,024 may be used with the word "near." In Figure 27, we specify that "glass" and "fire" must be within five words of each other in the patent abstract in order to record a hit. The results in Figure 28 show that this requirement has further reduced the number of matching patents to 17.

Advanced Text Search

This form lets you work with all of the text fields in your search. You may view example searches for many of these text fields, or you can read an overview of the Intellectual Property Network's search language.

Collections
U.S. Front Pages & Claims

Issue Date
From: Jan 1995
To: present

SEARCH   Clear

Any Text Field: building OR structure

Inventor:
e.g., Smith John

Assignee:
May include name and/or address.

Title:

Abstract: glass <near> fire

Attorney, Agent or Firm:

Related Info:

Figure 29

4. Multiple Field Searching

More than one field at a time can be used on the advanced search page. For instance, note that in Figure 29 we have added the requirement that the word "building" or the word "structure" must occur somewhere in the patent. When more than one search field is used, all of the fields are AND'ed together to produce the final search command. When you fill out the search entry boxes as shown above, the IBM system will compose the following search command:

(Building OR Structure) AND ((glass <near> fire) <in> ABSTRACT)

The "Building OR Structure" part of the query has been connected to the "glass <near> fire" part by the Boolean AND operator. The results of this search are shown in Figure 30. Since we have added the additional requirement for "Building OR Structure" to be present somewhere in the patent, the number of matching patents has been reduced to 25. Also notice that under the Query, our exact search command has been reproduced.

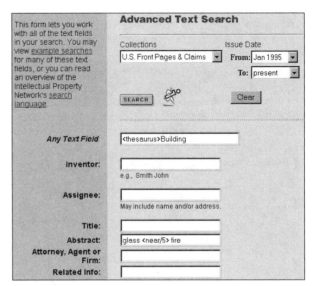

Figure 31

5. The Thesaurus Feature

The IBM patent search program also has a built-in thesaurus operator. The thesaurus operator is used to search for the specified keyword and any of its synonyms. In Figure 31, we have replaced the "Building OR Structure" query in the Any Field entry box with "<thesaurus> Building." We have also changed the "degree of nearness" for the words

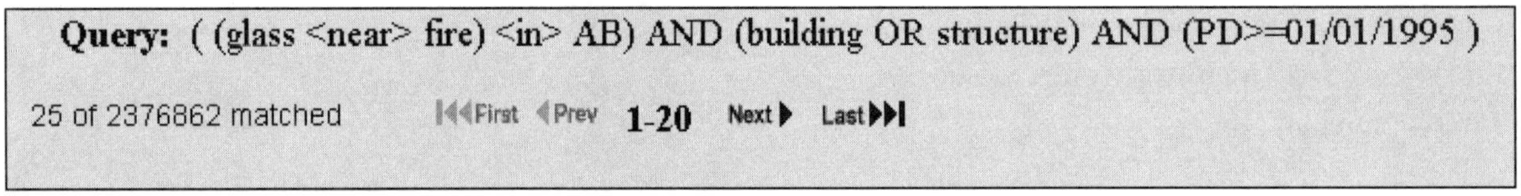

Query: ((glass <near> fire) <in> AB) AND (building OR structure) AND (PD>=01/01/1995)

25 of 2376862 matched   ◄◄First ◄Prev **1-20** Next▶ Last▶▶|

Figure 30

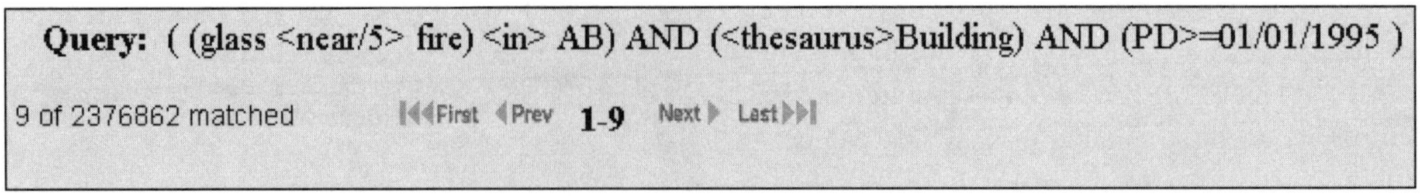

Query: ((glass <near/5> fire) <in> AB) AND (<thesaurus>Building) AND (PD>=01/01/1995)

9 of 2376862 matched   ◄◄First ◄Prev **1-9** Next▶ Last▶▶|

Figure 32

glass and fire from the default value of 256 to 5. The results of our search are shown in Figure 32.

The abstract from one of the matching patents (5,711,120) is shown in Figure 33. Here, the thesaurus operator has found the word "building" (underlined). Patent number 5,425,901 is shown in Figure 34 and the word "constructions" (underlined) was found in the patent abstract. Here, the thesaurus operator has substituted the requirement for the word "building" with the word "constructions."

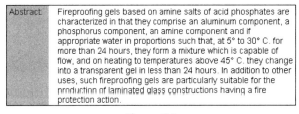

Abstract Fireproofing gels based on amine salts of acid phosphates are characterized in that they comprise an aluminum component, a phosphorus component, an amine component and if appropriate water in proportions such that, at 5° to 30° C. for more than 24 hours, they form a mixture which is capable of flow, and on heating to temperatures above 45° C. they change into a transparent gel in less than 24 hours. In addition to other uses, such fireproofing gels are particularly suitable for the production of laminated glass constructions having a fire protection action.

Figure 34

6. The IBM NOT BooleanOperator

To exclude a particular word from the search results, we use the NOT Boolean operator. The Boolean operators AND and NOT are combined into a single operator called ANDNOT at the PTO's website. This is not the case for the IBM system. Here, the user must combine the NOT operator with either the operator AND or the operator OR. Figure 35, below, shows the results obtained when we use the NOT operator combined with the AND operator to exclude the word "door" from our search of the patent abstract field.

Abstract A non-operable window frame assembly comprising two frame sections, each of which slips into a rectangular hole in a wall from opposite sides of the wall; the wire glass or fire resistant glazing material is held in place by means of four pieces of square sugar molding screwed in from the top of the molding; the screws go through both sections of the window frame assembly; holding the entire assemblage in place without the need for anchor clips, making the window frame assembly self anchoring. The size of the glazing material is up to 36"×36". The height of the square molding is a minimum of one inch, making the maximum size of the exposed glazing material 34"×34". The entire assemblage comprising the window frame assembly and wire glass or fire resistant glazing material meets Underwriters Laboratories standards with a fire rating "C" label (45 minutes). The miters of the two from sections are continuously welded at the corners. The window frame assembly can be used for both interior and exterior walls of varying widths. For installations in an exterior wall, the glazing material can be replaced if it is broken from the inside of the building without the need for scaffolding or ladders on the exterior of the structure. The window frame assembly can be manufactured with or without a drywall return.

Figure 33

Query: ((glass <near/5> fire AND NOT door) <in> AB) AND (<thesaurus>Building) AND (PD>=01/01/1995)

8 of 2376862 matched ⊩◄First ◄Prev **1-8** Next▶ Last▶▶|

Figure 35

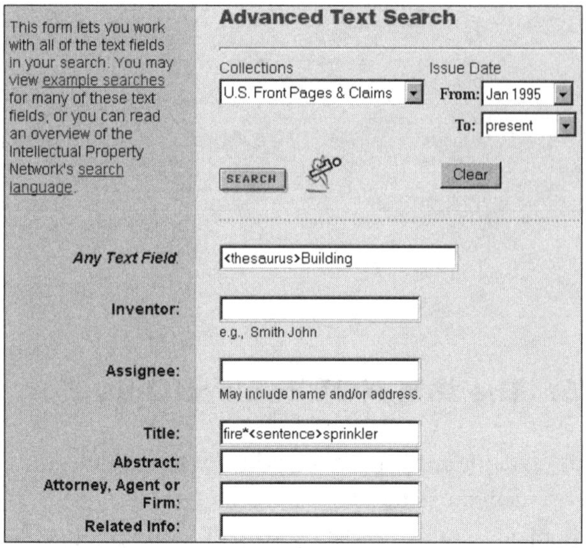

This form lets you work with all of the text fields in your search. You may view example searches for many of these text fields, or you can read an overview of the Intellectual Property Network's search language.

Advanced Text Search

Collections   Issue Date
U.S. Front Pages & Claims ▼   From: Jan 1995 ▼
                                 To: present ▼

[SEARCH]   [Clear]

Any Text Field: <thesaurus>Building

Inventor:
e.g., Smith John

Assignee:
May include name and/or address.

Title: fire*<sentence>sprinkler

Abstract:

Attorney, Agent or Firm:

Related Info:

Figure 36

7. Using Wildcards

The IBM patent search language also allows for the use of wildcards. In Figure 36, we have combined the asterisk wildcard (*) with the keyword Fire in the patent title search box. This will find occurrences of the word Fire, Fires, Fireman, etc. By also using the proximity operator <sentence>, we require that both Sprinkler and the word stem Fire be in the patent title. In Figure 36, we have also used the <thesaurus> operator to find the word Building and all of its synonyms. The results are shown in Figure 37.

C. Summary and Comparison of the PTO and IBM Websites

Table 2 shows a comparison of the various advanced search features present on the PTO and IBM websites. Both systems allow the combination of multiple Boolean operators with wildcards and search phrases.

Functions	PTO	IBM
Combine Multiple Boolean Operators	Yes	Yes
Search Phrases	Yes	Yes
Proximity Operators	No	Yes
Online Thesaurus	No	Yes

Table 2

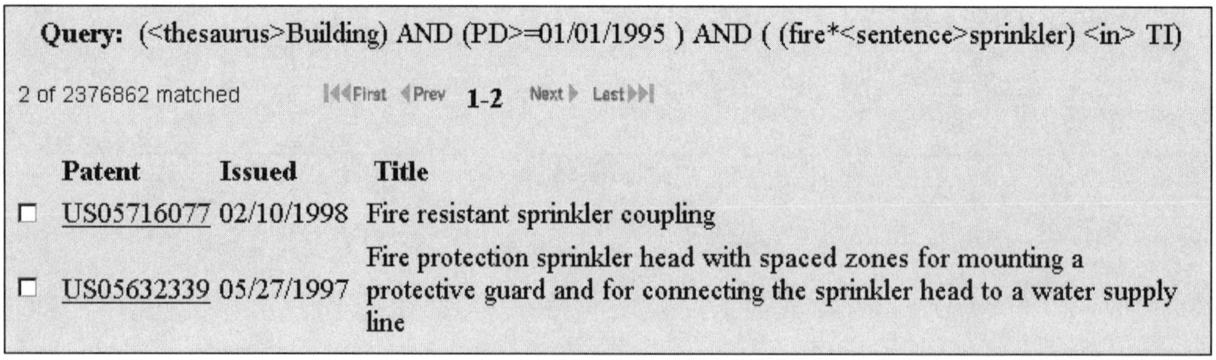

Query: (<thesaurus>Building) AND (PD>=01/01/1995) AND ((fire*<sentence>sprinkler) <in> TI)

2 of 2376862 matched |◀◀First ◀Prev **1-2** Next▶ Last▶▶|

Patent	Issued	Title
☐ US05716077	02/10/1998	Fire resistant sprinkler coupling
☐ US05632339	05/27/1997	Fire protection sprinkler head with spaced zones for mounting a protective guard and for connecting the sprinkler head to a water supply line

Figure 37

A major difference is the use of proximity operators at the IBM site. This has to be measured as a big plus for IBM. Proximity operators allow tremendous flexibility when composing search queries. Another very useful feature of the IBM site is the thesaurus operator. This operator frees the user from the tedious task of finding synonyms for his or her selected keywords.

Summary

Advanced Patent Searching at the PTO Website

- Multiple Boolean operators can be combined with parentheses to produce highly focused searches.

- Wildcards and phrase searches are allowed.
- Search results are summarized in lists. An example is all patents issued to a particular inventor. Arrow buttons can be used to quickly navigate through the list.

Advanced Patent Searching at the IBM Website

- Multiple Boolean operators can be combined with parentheses to produce highly focused searches.
- Wildcards and phrase searches are allowed.
- Proximity searches for multiple keywords are allowed.
- A keyword thesaurus is available.

C H A P T E R

7

Advanced Patent Searching at the PTDL

In this chapter we return to the Patent and Trademark Depository Library (PDTL). Here, we will further develop our expertise with the Automated Patent System (APS). We will compose complex Boolean search expressions and analyze the results. The use of search indexes, first introduced in Chapter 5, will be further explored and APS proximity operators will be explained. Finally, the APS and CASSIS systems will be used to search foreign patent abstract databases. Since this chapter builds upon material covered in Chapters 1 and 5, if you have not read those chapters you should do so now, then return here.

A. APS Advanced Boolean Searches

You will need a library assistant to log you into the APS. As discussed in Chapter 5, the assistant will enter a login ID and password. You will then see the main APS text search window. Make sure you select the data file ALLUS as the patent data to search. This is accomplished with the FILE command as shown in Figure 1, below.

```
=> FILE ALLUS
```

Figure 1

In Chapter 5, we proposed a turn signal canceling invention. We composed a simple Boolean search for the terms Turn and Signal, by using the AND operator. To create advanced Boolean queries with the APS, we make use of parentheses and more than one logical operator. For example, the query:

S turn AND signal AND (motorcycle OR bicycle)

Here we have used the short form of the SEARCH command; just the letter S. This APS search command would return only patents that contained the words Turn, Signal and the word Motorcycle or the word Bicycle. Let's try some advanced search commands at the PTDL and examine the results.

In Chapter 5, we performed an APS search using the command SEARCH TURN AND SIGNAL. This search is repeated in Figure 2, below. Here we have 253,556 matching patents (the number of matching patents will increase with time as additional patents are added to the APS system). Now, by using a more complex Boolean expression, we are able to add the requirement for the keywords Motorcycle or Bicycle. The results of our new search are shown in Figure 3, below. From this figure, you can see that the total number of matching patents (shown at the bottom of the figure) has been reduced from 253,556 to 1,086.

```
=> S TURN AND SIGNAL

FILE  'USPAT'

        663217 TURN
        549459 SIGNAL

   L1  245442 TURN AND SIGNAL

FILE  'USOCR'

        32410 TURN
        16724 SIGNAL
   L2  8114 TURN AND SIGNAL

TOTAL FOR ALL FILES

   L3  253556 TURN AND SIGNAL
```

Figure 2

```
=> S TURN AND SIGNAL AND
(MOTORCYCLE OR BICYCLE)

FILE  'USPAT'

        663217 TURN
        549459 SIGNAL
        5757 MOTORCYCLE
        10509 BICYCLE
    L4  1077 TURN AND SIGNAL AND
        (MOTORCYCLE OR BICYCLE)

FILE  'USOCR'

        32410 TURN
        16724 SIGNAL
        113 MOTORCYCLE
        306 BICYCLE
    L5  9 TURN AND SIGNAL AND
        (MOTORCYCLE OR BICYCLE)

TOTAL FOR ALL FILES

    L6  1086 TURN AND SIGNAL AND
        (MOTORCYCLE OR BICYCLE)
```

Figure 3

```
=> S TURN AND SIGNAL AND
MOTORCYCLE NOT BICYCLE

FILE  'USPAT'

        663217 TURN
        549459 SIGNAL
        5757 MOTORCYCLE
        10509 BICYCLE
    L7  459 TURN AND SIGNAL AND
        MOTORCYCLE NOT BICYCLE

FILE  'USOCR'

        32410 TURN
        16724 SIGNAL
        113 MOTORCYCLE
        306 BICYCLE
    L8  2 TURN AND SIGNAL AND
        MOTORCYCLE NOT BICYCLE

TOTAL FOR ALL FILES

    L9  461 TURN AND SIGNAL AND
        MOTORCYCLE NOT BICYCLE
```

Figure 4

Another Boolean operator that is available with the APS is the NOT operator. You use the NOT operator to exclude certain keywords from the search results. To see how this works, let's change the above query to exclude bicycles from the search results:

S turn AND signal AND motorcycle NOT bicycle

The results from this APS search are shown in Figure 4, below. As you can see, by removing the bicycle-related patents, the search results have been further reduced to 461.

Another nice feature of the APS program is that the results of a previous query can be combined with additional search terms. This allows you to quickly refine your search. Let's say we want to perform the search of Figure 2 (Turn AND Signal) again, but we wish to add the requirement for the keyword Motorcycle. We could then compose the following query:

S L3 AND motorcycle

Here we have substituted the search result label L3 for the Boolean expression "Turn AND Signal." This search would find patents that contained all three keywords: Turn, Signal and Motorcycle. The results are shown in Figure 5. As you can see, adding the additional requirement for the keyword Motorcycle has reduced the number of matching patents from 253,556 in Figure 2 to 538 in Figure 5.

```
=> S L3 AND MOTORCYCLE

FILE  'USPAT'

        663217 TURN
        549459 SIGNAL
        5757 MOTORCYCLE
    L10 535 L3 AND MOTORCYCLE

FILE  'USOCR'

        113 MOTORCYCLE
    L11 3 L3 AND MOTORCYCLE

TOTAL FOR ALL FILES

    L12 538 L3 AND MOTORCYCLE
```

Figure 5

```
=> S ELECTRICAL AND "TURN SIGNAL"

FILE  'USPAT'

        525460 ELECTRICAL
        663217 "TURN"
        549459 "SIGNAL"
        1346 "TURN SIGNAL"
            ("TURN"(W)"SIGNAL")
    L13   856 ELECTRICAL AND "TURN SIGNAL"

FILE 'USOCR'
        28080 ELECTRICAL
        32410 "TURN"
        16724 "SIGNAL"
        58 "TURN SIGNAL"
            ("TURN"(W)"SIGNAL")
    L14 40 ELECTRICAL AND "TURN SIGNAL"

TOTAL FOR ALL FILES

    L15 896 ELECTRICAL AND "TURN SIGNAL"
```

Figure 6

Phrases can also be used with the APS program. For example, to search for the phrase "turn signal," you would enclose the words in double quotes. The quotes are actually optional. The APS program assumes that two keywords appearing in a search command, with a space between them, are actually a phrase. In Figure 6, we search for the keyword Electrical and the phrase "turn signal." Here, we see that there are 896 matching patents. If you have read Chapter 6, you'll recall that great care should be exercised with the use of phrases. If the sequence of words does not exactly match their use in the patent text to be searched, you won't get a match and you could miss a relevant prior art patent.

Wildcards can also be used on the APS system. The wildcard symbols and their meanings are different from the Internet-based search systems previously covered. There are three wildcard symbols used on the APS:

?   An unlimited number of characters, including none. It can be used at the beginning or end of a keyword.

Zero or one character for each # symbol used. It can be used at the beginning or end of a keyword.

!   Exactly one character for each ! symbol used. It can be used anywhere within a keyword.

The ? wildcard symbol has the same functionality as the * wildcard symbol we used at the PTO and IBM websites. For example, suppose we wished to search for electrical turn signals. We could compose the APS query:

S electrical AND "turn signal"

But what if the patent text uses the words "electric turn signal" or "electricity used to operate a turn signal"? Clearly it would be advantageous to capture all occurrences of the word stem Electric. This can be accomplished with the query shown in Figure 7, below.

```
=> S ELECTRIC? AND "TURN SIGNAL"

FILE 'USPAT'

    784608 ELECTRIC?
    663217 "TURN"
    549459 "SIGNAL"
    1346 "TURN SIGNAL"
        ("TURN"(W)"SIGNAL")
L16 983 ELECTRIC? AND "TURN SIGNAL"

FILE 'USOCR'

    41134 ELECTRIC?
    32410 "TURN"
    16724 "SIGNAL"
    58 "TURN SIGNAL"
        ("TURN"(W)"SIGNAL")
L17 46 ELECTRIC? AND "TURN SIGNAL"

TOTAL FOR ALL FILES

L18 1029 ELECTRIC? AND "TURN SIGNAL"
```

Figure 7

Here we have used the search command:

S electric? AND "turn signal"

The question mark (?) has been substituted for any characters, including none, that might follow the word Electric. It's important to provide as much of the keyword stem as possible. Suppose, instead, that we had used the query:

S elec? AND "turn signal"

The APS system will return an error message that states:

TERM 'ELEC?' EXCEEDED TRUNCATION LIMITS - SEARCH ENDED

This means that there are so many words that start with "elec" (electrode, electrodynamics, electrolyte, etc.) that the APS could not handle the command and the search was canceled.

The pound sign wildcard (#) is used to replace one or zero characters. It is most often used to catch the singular and plural forms of a keyword. For example, to search for Turn Signal or Turn Signals, we could compose the following query.

S turn AND signal#

The exclamation mark wildcard (!) is used to replace exactly one character. Unlike the # wildcard, the character must be present. The ! wildcard can be used anywhere within the keyword.

It is used to catch variations in spelling for a particular keyword. For example, the following query would return patents that had the word Automatic as well as the word Automate.

S automat!# AND "turn signal" AND time#

Here we have combined more than one type of wildcard within the same query. The ! wildcard will catch the letter "i" or "e" in Automate or Automatic, and the # wildcard will catch the letter "c" in Automatic. Also notice how we have used the # wildcard to capture the words Timer or Timed. The results of this search are shown in Figure 8.

```
=> S AUTOMAT!# AND "TURN SIGNAL" AND
TIME#

FILE 'USPAT'

    295381 AUTOMAT!#
    663217 "TURN"
    549459 "SIGNAL"
    1346 "TURN SIGNAL"
        ("TURN"(W)"SIGNAL")
    1600262 TIME#
L19 323 AUTOMAT!# AND "TURN SIGNAL"
    AND TIME#

FILE 'USOCR'

    14070 AUTOMAT!#
    32410 "TURN"
    16724 "SIGNAL"
    58 "TURN SIGNAL"
        ("TURN"(2)"SIGNAL")
    94378 TIME#
L20 15 AUTOMAT!# AND "TURN SIGNAL"
    AND TIME

TOTAL FOR ALL FILES

L21 338 AUTOMAT!# AND "TURN SIGNAL"
    AND TIME#
```

Figure 8

USPAT Search Index Characters	
Patent Abstract	/AB
Patent Claims	/CLM
Current Patent Class and Subclass	/CCLS
Inventor Name	/IN
Patent Number	/PN

Table 1

For example, to restrict our APS search to the abstract of the issued patents, we make use of the /AB search index. The following query will search for the phrase "turn signal," the keyword Timer and the keyword Vehicle, all within the abstract of the issued patent.

S "turn signal"/AB AND timer/AB AND vehicle/AB

Figure 9, below, shows the result of an APS search using this query.

B. APS—Using Search Indexes

In Chapter 5, we mentioned the use of search indexes. With the use of a search index we can limit our keyword search to selected sections of the patent. We used the /CCLS search index to search for all the patents issued within a particular class and subclass. Additional search indexes were listed in Table 3 of Chapter 5. This table is repeated below as Table 1 for convenience.

```
=> S "TURN SIGNAL"/AB AND TIMER/AB AND
VEHICLE/AB

FILE  'USPAT'

      34710 "TURN/AB
     171267 "SIGNAL"/AB
        271 "TURN SIGNAL"/AB
             (("TURN"(W)"SIGNAL")/AB)
       6507 TIMER/AB
      73194 VEHICLE/AB
 L22   10 "TURN SIGNAL"/AB AND TIMER/AB
          AND VEHICLE/AB

FILE 'USOCR'

       1534 "TURN"/AB
       4224 "SIGNAL"/AB
         11 "TURN SIGNAL"/AB
             (("TURN"(W)"SIGNAL")/AB)
        207 TIMER/AB
 2538 VEHICLE/AB
 L23    0 "TURN SIGNAL"/AB AND TIMER/AB
          AND VEHICLE/AB

TOTAL FOR ALL FILES

 L24   10 "TURN SIGNAL"/AB AND TIMER/AB
          AND VEHICLE/AB
```

Figure 9

Why search only in the patent abstract? Why not always search through the maximum amount of patent text available? The answer is that you are more likely to get thousands of matching patents that don't really have any bearing on your invention the more patent text you search. Selected keywords like Signal and Timer can occur in many contexts. They are used in literally thousands of different types of inventions. Constructing queries that blindly look for any use of these keywords will often return so many matching patents that the newcomer to patent searching is turned off by having to look at many irrelevant hits.

Searcher's Secret Number 10

One of the keys to getting meaningful search results from the APS system is to construct queries that don't just look blindly for the use of certain keywords, but look specifically for how those keywords are used.

One simple way of controlling the context in which the keywords are used is by selecting which section of the patent they are used in. As discussed in Chapter 1, the abstract is usually one or two paragraphs that summarize the invention in plain English. If your selected keywords and phrases embody significant aspects of your invention, they are highly likely to be found in the abstract.

In Figure 9, we see the advantages of restricting our search to the patent abstract. From the label L24, we see there is a very reasonable number (ten) of patents to review. As you may recall from Chapter 5, to display the patent information referenced by a given L number, we use the DISPLAY command. The short form of the display command is just the letter D. The display command requires three inputs: the search display L#, the answer number range and the display format. But we can use the system display default settings and enter only the search result we want to see.

```
=> D 1

 1. 5,642,094, Jun. 24, 1997, Type-of-stop expectation warning;
Frank Marcella, 340/479, 463, 464, 468 [IMAGE AVAILABLE]

=> D 2

 2. 5,565,841, Oct. 15, 1996, Brake light perception
enhancement system; Sobas R. Pandohie, 340/479, 464, 467, 468
[IMAGE AVAILABLE]

=> D 3

 3. 5,414,407, May 9, 1995, Turn signal monitor circuit; A.
Wilbur Gerrans, et al., 340/475, 457, 477 [IMAGE AVAILABLE]
```

Figure 10

To see the first patent, we need only type in D 1. Similarly, to see the second or third matching patents, we could type in D 2 or D 3. This action is shown in Figure 10, above.

We didn't have to type in an L number because the system default is to use the last L number result, namely L24 from the bottom of Figure 9. Since we didn't type in a display format, the default CIT format was used. As you recall from Chapter 5, this includes the patent number, issue date, title, first inventor and class/subclass information.

From Figure 10, the title of the third listed patent (5,414,407) looks like what we might be looking for. To see the abstract of this patent we need to change the display format from CIT to AB, where AB is one of the display formats shown in Table 4 of Chapter 5. To do that, we just add AB to our display command as shown in Figure 11.

A reading of the abstract of Patent Number 5,414,407 would indicate that the use of a timer circuit to inform a vehicle driver of an activated turn signal has been anticipated by the prior art. Similarly, the abstracts of the 4th and 5th patents (patent numbers 5,264,827 and 5,260,685) of our search results (Figures 12 and 13) show other variations of our invention concept. These results would indicate that the field of this invention (a timing device used to cancel a turn signal) is well established and contains many patents.

Should the inventor abandon this idea and move on to another innovation? Well, the answer is maybe, and maybe not. Though it is unlikely the inventor will be able to obtain broad claims covering many possible versions of the basic invention, it may still be possible to come up with a small improvement that will be patentable. In Chapter 10, we provide a basic discussion of the concepts of novelty, obviousness and anticipation as they relate to patentable material.

```
=> D 3 AB

US PAT NO:    5,414,407 [IMAGE AVAILABLE]        L24: 3 of 10

ABSTRACT:
An indicating circuit provides an indication that a turn signal in
a vehicle is activated. A timer receives an activation signal
representative of the turn signal. The timer provides a reminder
output signal based on the activation signal. The timer provides
the reminder output signal during reminder periods which are
spaced by delay time periods.
The delay time periods are variable in length depending on
operation of the vehicle. An indicator is coupled to the timer for
providing an operator indication, based on the activation signal,
indicating that the turn signal in the vehicle is activated.
```

Figure 11

```
=> D 4 AB

US PAT NO:    5,264,827 [IMAGE AVAILABLE]        L24: 4 of 10

ABSTRACT:
A turn signal reminder circuit for warning a vehicle driver that
the vehicle turn signals may have been inadvertently left
actuated. Turn signal flasher pulses are low pass filtered to
provide a continuous enabling signal which initiates the
operation of an astable, multivibrator timer circuit. The timer
circuit switches asymmetrically between a first occurring
longer-time, partial cycle and a shorter-timer, partial cycle. A
sound alarm is enabled by the timer during each shorter-time,
partial cycle. The alarm is actuated by flasher pulses when the
alarm is enabled, but is disabled and the timer circuit is reset in
response to operation of the vehicle brake. A pulse detecting
circuit for using flasher pulses to turn on the timing circuit has
no large capacitor and this permits miniaturization.
```

Figure 12

```
=> D 5 AB

US PAT NO:    5,260,685 [IMAGE AVAILABLE]        L24: 5 of 10

ABSTRACT:
A vehicle turn signal mechanism includes a lockout device in the
form of an electric timer. The flashing signal is normally
cancelled by a steering wheel sensor that is arranged to
generate a triggering signal for an electromagnetic detent
associated with a signal selector lever. The lockout
device prevents the triggering signal from being generated
except after the steering wheel has been retained in its straight-
ahead position for a predetermined time period.
```

Figure 13

The APS program supports many additional search indexes besides the /AB (patent abstract) index. In fact, there are 60 different search indexes available with the APS program. For detailed information about search indexes and other aspects of the APS, the PTO publishes two useful references. The first manual is called *Text Search Training Workbook for Public Users of the Automated Patent System (APS)*. This manual was developed as a classroom training document for the APS. It contains detailed instructions in the use of search indexes, as well as other aspects of the APS.

The second reference is called *Text Search and Retrieval Reference Manual for the Automated Patent System (APS)*. This manual was designed as an aid for an APS user who has already been trained on the APS system. Its contains an alphabetical guide to all of the APS commands and other useful information.

These manuals are currently priced at $25 each. Of the two, the first is probably the most useful for someone new to the APS. For ordering information regarding either of these manuals, call the PTO at 703-308-3040, or see the latest PTO *Products and Services Catalog*.

C. APS—Using Proximity Operators

Another way to control how the APS system searches for not only the occurrence of your keywords, but their use in context, is with proximity operators. The APS system supports the use of several proximity operators. If you have reviewed Chapter 6, you may recall the use of proximity operators at the IBM Internet website. There, proximity operators came in handy when we wanted to find words that were near to each other, but we didn't know their exact order. The APS system uses the four basic proximity operators shown in Table 2, below.

From the top of Table 2, the proximity operators are listed from the most general conditions to the

Operator	Description	Example
L	Search for keywords in the same patent section, in any order.	s vehicle (L) signal
P	Search for keywords in the same paragraph, in any order.	s vehicle (P) signal
A	Search for adjacent keywords in the same paragraph, in any order.	s timer (A) signal
W	Search for adjacent keywords in the same paragraph, in the order specified.	s turn (W) signal

Table 2

most specific. For example, if you want to search for two words occurring in any order within any given section of a patent, you should use the (L) operator. The search command given at the top of the table returns the results shown in Figure 14.

```
=> S VEHICLE (L) SIGNAL

FILE  'USPAT'

        231014 VEHICLE
        549459 SIGNAL

L25 54760 VEHICLE (L) SIGNAL

FILE 'USOCR'

        10887 VEHICLE
        16724 SIGNAL
L26 1443 VEHICLE (L) SIGNAL

TOTAL FOR ALL FILES

    L27 56203 VEHICLE (L) SIGNAL
```

Figure 14

Here we see that there are 56,203 occurrences of the words Vehicle and Signal within any given section of the patent. This includes the claims, abstract, detailed description and more. To search for words that appear in closer proximity, say within the same paragraph, we should use the (P) operator. Using the same query as above, but replacing the (L) operator with the (P) operator, we get the results shown in Figure 15. As you can see, the number of hits has been reduced from 56,203 to 33,886.

```
=> S VEHICLE (P) SIGNAL

FILE  'USPAT'

        231014 VEHICLE
        549459 SIGNAL

L28 33046 VEHICLE (P) SIGNAL

FILE 'USOCR'

        10887 VEHICLE
        16724 SIGNAL
L29 840 VEHICLE (P) SIGNAL

TOTAL FOR ALL FILES

    L30 33886 VEHICLE (P) SIGNAL
```

Figure 15

These results illustrate the fact that great care should be exercised with the use of the (L) and (P) operators. The fact that (L) and (P) operate over such a large amount of patent text means that many irrelevant hits may often be returned. Using (L) and (P) in conjunction with other operators, or searches for infrequently used keywords, will help reduce the number of hits.

The (A) and (W) operators are for adjacent words. The only difference between them is that with the (A) operator the keywords can occur in any order. With the (W) operator, only the order specified in the search command will return a matching hit. For example, if you want to find occurrences of the phrase "turn signal," use the (W) operator, as shown in Table 2. If you want to find occurrences of the phrase "signal timer" or "timer signal," then use the (A) operator. The APS search results for these two queries are shown in Figures 16 and 17, respectively.

```
    => S TIMER (A) SIGNAL

FILE  'USPAT'

      74039 TIMER
      549459 SIGNAL
   L31 1183 TIMER (A) SIGNAL

FILE 'USOCR'

      2508 TIMER
      16724 SIGNAL
   L32 17 TIMER (A) SIGNAL

TOTAL FOR ALL FILES

   L33 1200 TIMER (A) SIGNAL
```

Figure 16

```
    => S TURN (W) SIGNAL

FILE  'USPAT'

      000217 TURN
      549459 SIGNAL
   L34 1346 TURN (W) SIGNAL

FILE 'USOCR'

      32410 TURN
      16724 SIGNAL
   L35 58 TURN (W) SIGNAL

TOTAL FOR ALL FILES

   L36 1404 TURN (W) SIGNAL
```

Figure 17

The degree of nearness can also be specified for each of the four proximity operators. This is accomplished by placing a number in front of the operator. For example, to look for the words Signal and Timer within four words of each other in any given paragraph, use the following query:

S signal (4A) timer

Operator	Description	Example
nL	Search for keywords within n or fewer intervening patent sections, in any order.	s vehicle (2L) signal
nP	Search for keywords within n or fewer paragraphs, in any order.	s vehicle (4P) signal
nA	Search for keywords in the same paragraph, in any order, with n or fewer intervening keywords.	s timer (8A) signal
nW	Search for keywords in the same paragraph, in the order specified, with n or fewer intervening keywords	s turn (5W) signal

Table 3

Table 3 summarizes the use of numbers with each of the proximity operators.

D. APS and CASSIS— Searching Foreign Databases

Prior art that may determine whether an invention is patentable is not limited to inventions patented in the U.S. International patents must also be considered in any thorough patent search. Patents issued in other countries are considered valid prior art, and will be compared against your invention. This is illustrated by the fact that relevant foreign patent documents are referenced on the front page of U.S. issued patents.

In general, it's not necessary to spend a great deal of time, effort and expense searching for foreign patent references. This is because the patent examiner who processes your application will primarily focus on U.S. patent references. But it's a good idea to take a quick look.

With the APS system you can search through a database of Japanese and European patent abstracts. Searching foreign patents on the Internet is covered in Chapter 8, Section D. The JPOABS file contains the English-language translation of abstracts from unexamined Japanese patent applications. In Japan, patent applications are published 18 months from the application filing date. To use the Japanese abstracts file, issue the following APS command:

FILE JPOABS

A search for the phrase "turn signal" and the keyword Motorcycle would produce the results shown in Figure 18, below.

```
=> S TURN SIGNAL AND MOTORCYCLE

      58697 TURN
     660446 SIGNAL
        259 TURN SIGNAL
            (TURN(W)SIGNAL)
       3869 MOTORCYCLE
L37       13 TURN SIGNAL AND MOTORCYCLE
```

Figure 18

To display the title of the first Japanese patent abstract in the search results, simply enter D 1 as shown in Figure 19, below. To see the abstract of this patent, supply the AB display format command as shown in Figure 20.

Japanese abstracts are broken down into two sections. These are the *PURPOSE* and *CONSTITUTION* of the invention. From Figure 20 we can read that the constitution contains direct references to the patent drawings via numbered components.

```
=> D 1

1. 08-268359, Oct. 15, 1996, STOPLIGHT ARRANGING
STRUCTURE FOR MOTORCYCLE; JUNJI KIKUTA, B62J 6/00;
B62J 6/04
```

Figure 19

```
=> D 1 AB

08-268359                           L37: 1 of 13

ABSTRACT:

 PURPOSE: To improve the visibility of a stoplight from the rear
side thereof by arranging turn signal light at the right and left
sides of a taillight as well as stoplights above the taillight, and
forming the stoplight separately from the taillight.

 CONSTITUTION: A support member 10 extended above is fixed
to the rear end of a body frame 2a, and a bracket 12 is secured
to the upper end of the member 10. In this case, the upper
surface of the bracket 12 has the same height as the top of a
seat 8. Also, a support plate 15 is laid at the back of the member
10, and an opening 15b formed on the upper section of the plate
15 is covered internally with a reflector 14. Furthermore, a bulb
16b as a light source for a stoplight 16 is provided in space
formed out of a reflector 14 and the opening 15b. On the other
hand, a support plate 22 is held on a support member 20 fixed to
the rear section of the frame 2a in a slantingly downward
direction, and a bulb 26b as a light source for a taillight 26 is
provided between the wall sections 22a and 22b of the plate 22.
Also, turn signal light are arranged at the right and left sides of
a taillight lens 27.

 COPYRIGHT: (C)1996,JPO
```

Figure 20

Help is also available with the Japanese abstracts file, and Table 4 lists the available help commands. There are several search indexes available as well, and Table 5 lists some of the most useful.

Command	Description
HELP JPOABS	Information on the contents of the file.
HELP FIELDS	List of search indexes.
HELP FORMATS	List of fixed display formats.
HELP CUSTOM	List of custom display formats.

Table 4
Japanese Patent Abstracts Help Commands

Command	Description
/TI	Title of the invention.
/IN	Inventor's name.
/AB	Text of abstract.

Table 5
Japanese Patent Abstracts Search Indexes

European patents are also frequently referenced as prior art for U.S. patents. With the APS system, you can search through a database of European patent abstracts. The EPOABS file contains published patent abstracts from France, Germany, Great Britain, Switzerland, the European Patent Office, the World Intellectual Property Organization and the United States. To access the EPOABS abstracts file, issue the following APS command:

FILE EPOABS

The range of patent abstract coverage in years varies from country to country. The usage of display and index commands is the same as in the JPOABS file, namely, AB for abstract, TI for title, and so on.

Figure 21

Foreign patent abstracts can also be accessed from the CASSIS computer system. The main menu of the CASSIS program is shown in Figure 21, above. Each boxed and arrowed topic refers to a different CD-ROM. By clicking on a topic with the mouse, you load that particular CD-ROM into the CASSIS system. To access the Patent Abstracts of Japan CD-ROM, click on that topic (bottom left) with the mouse. The CASSIS program will then allow you to perform keyword searches of Japanese patent abstracts. (See Chapter 5 for a refresher on the use of CASSIS menus, and special function keys.)

Summary

APS Advanced Boolean Searches
- Multiple Boolean operators can be combined with parentheses to produce highly focused searches.
- Wildcards and phrase searches are allowed.

APS—Using Search Indexes

- Searches can be limited to a large number of different patent fields.

APS—Using Proximity Operators

- Proximity searches for multiple keywords are allowed.

APS and CASSIS—Searching Foreign Databases

- Abstracts of Japanese and European patents are searchable from the APS system.
- Japanese abstracts can be searched with Cassis.

■

8

Additional Patent Search Resources on the Internet

So far, we have limited our Internet patent searches to the resources provided by the PTO and IBM. In this chapter, we will explore some additional patent search websites. Some of these resources can be accessed without cost, while others charge a fee. The available features will often vary from site to site. Several specialized patent databases have been set up around certain topics. Within these topic areas the entire text of patents can often be searched and viewed. It is also important to look beyond the United States in any thorough prior art search, and a number of overseas intellectual property offices have established Internet websites.

First, we will visit the Source Translation and Optimization (STO) website. This site allows users to search the indented list of subclasses from the *Manual of Classification*. Next, we will visit the Biotechnology patent database. This database allows the user to search through the entire text of issued patents. We will then visit the MicroPatent website. This is one of several Internet patent search services that charge a fee for their use. Finally, we will take a trip overseas and foreign patent offices will be discussed.

A. Exploring the STO

In Chapters 3, 4 and 6, we visited the PTO and IBM websites. In additional to these two resources, there are other Internet patent search facilities that can be accessed for free. One of these sites is the Source Translation and Optimization (STO) Internet patent search system. The STO website was created by Gregory Aharonian as an attempt to demonstrate to the PTO the need for more patent information on the Internet. To get to the STO patent search site, you need to type the following address into your Web browser:

http://metalab.unc.edu/patents/intropat.html

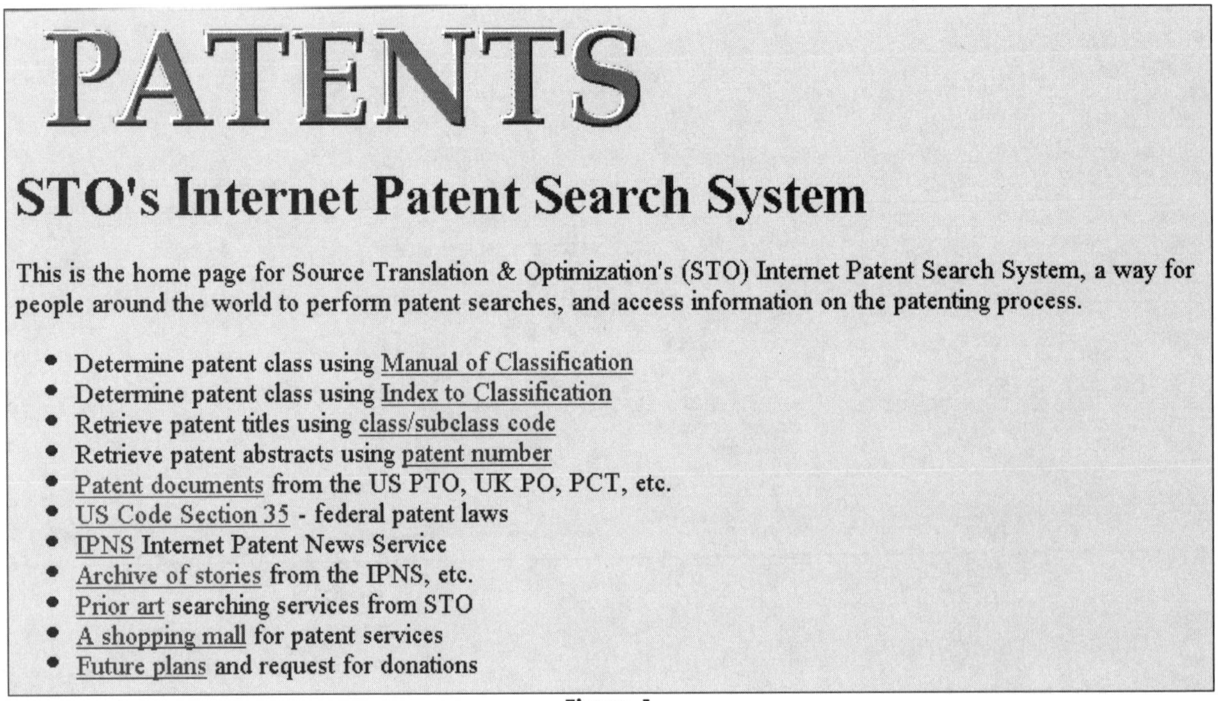

PATENTS

STO's Internet Patent Search System

This is the home page for Source Translation & Optimization's (STO) Internet Patent Search System, a way for people around the world to perform patent searches, and access information on the patenting process.

- Determine patent class using Manual of Classification
- Determine patent class using Index to Classification
- Retrieve patent titles using class/subclass code
- Retrieve patent abstracts using patent number
- Patent documents from the US PTO, UK PO, PCT, etc.
- US Code Section 35 - federal patent laws
- IPNS Internet Patent News Service
- Archive of stories from the IPNS, etc.
- Prior art searching services from STO
- A shopping mall for patent services
- Future plans and request for donations

Figure 1

Figure 1, above, shows a section from the main STO Web page. Here, hypertext links to the available resources are listed as bulleted items. If you reviewed the material in Chapter 5, you may recall that there are three manuals designed to help you determine which class/subclasses your invention falls under. These are:

Index to the U.S. Patent Classification

The Manual of Classification

The Classification Definitions

At the PTO website (Chapter 3), we explained how you can browse the U.S. patent class titles and access the classification definitions. However, you cannot use that site to read the indented list of subclasses from the *Manual of Classification*. This is an important resource because it shows how the various subclasses are related.

The STO site allows you to access a hypertext version of this important document. To access this indented list, just click on the *Manual of Classification* link shown near the top of Figure 1. You will

then be presented with the Web page shown in Figure 2, below. Here, the main patent classes are divided into four supergroups: electronic, chemical, engineering and mechanical.

Each of these are further divided into five to seven subgroups. At the very top of the list is a link to a master list of all patent classes. To select it, just click on it with the mouse. You will then be presented with a numerical list of all U.S. patent classes. The top of this list is shown in Figure 3.

In Chapter 5, we identified Class 116, subclasses 28 and 35, as being relevant to our invention idea for a turn signal canceling device. To see the page from the *Manual of Classification* for Class 116, just scroll down and select Class 116.

In Figure 4, we see a section of the indented list of subclasses for Class 116. This particular section shows subclasses 28 and 35. Here you can clearly see that under subclass 35—Motion and direction—are further related subclasses (pneumatically operated, governor actuated, etc.). As you may

Patent searching using the PTO classification system

The US Patent and Trademark Office uses a classification scheme with 400+ main classes, and tens of thousands of subclasses, to classify all of the 5,300,000+ patents issued since the 1800's. With a few clicks of your mouse, you can obtain a list of titles to patents in any class/subclass. The first is to locate the class that pertains to your technology area.

The 400+ main classes are divided into four supergroups: electronic, chemical, engineering and mechanical, each of which are divided into 5 to 7 groups. A master list of all the classes is also provided. The Manual pages at this Mosaic site are current as of December 1993.

- Master list of all patent classes
- Design patent classes
- ELECTRONIC group
    - Computing and data processing
    - Electricity and electric power
    - Electronics and electronic components
    - Optics - Radiant energy - Photography
    - Communications
    - Other science and engineering, measurement, nuclear
    - Music, education, amusement
- CHEMICAL group
    - Biochemistry
    - Chemical enginering

Figure 2

Index to all US Patent Classes

Click on the patent class number to jump to that class' list of subclasses.

- Class: 2 APPAREL
- Class: 4 BATHS, CLOSETS, SINKS, AND SPITTOONS
- Class: 5 BEDS
- Class: 7 COMPOUND TOOLS
- Class: 8 BLEACHING AND DYEING; FLUID TREATMENT AND CHEMICAL MODIFICATION OF TEXTILES AND FIBERS
- Class: 12 BOOT AND SHOE MAKING
- Class: 14 BRIDGES
- Class: 15 BRUSHING, SCRUBBING, AND GENERAL CLEANING
- Class: 16 MISCELLANEOUS HARDWARE

Figure 3

recall from Chapter 5, the dots or periods to the left of the subclass title indicate how specific that subclass is. The more dots there are, the more specific the subclass. For example, under subclass 35 (Motion and Direction) there is one dot to the left. This refers to a general class of vehicle motion and direction indicators. Subclass 39 (pneumatically operated) has two dots to the left of it, and refers to pneumatically operated motion and direction indicators only.

```
28 R     VEHICLE
28.1     .Transmission indicator
29       .Station indicators
30       .Car and train markers
31       .Steering-wheel-position indicators
32       .Collision-released identification tags
33       .Theft preventing
34 R     .Tire inflation or deflation
34 A     ..Sidewall operated
34 B     ..Internal protuberance operated
35 R     .Motion and direction
36       ..Combined with vehicle control
37       ..Speed controlled
38       ...Governor actuated
39       ..Pneumatically operated
40       ..Lazy-tong operated
41       ..Fan type
42       ..Window-exhibited sign or shutter
43       ...Rotatable
44       ...Sliding
45       ..Movable cover or screen
46       ..Rotatable
47       ...Pointer
48       ....Illuminatedd
49       ...Illuminated casing
50       ..Sliding
```

Figure 4

At the top of each Web page version of the *Manual of Classification* is a quick search feature that allows you to display the titles of all the patents issued within a selected class/subclass combination. This is shown in Figure 5. To use this feature, just enter the class number, followed by a dash, and then the corresponding subclass. Then click Submit Query.

Searcher's Secret Number 11

The STO can be a good resource if you are having trouble finding all of the classes/sub-classes for your invention idea.

After searching the classification definitions and titles using the procedures of Chapter 3, you can jump to the STO website and search the *Manual of Classification*. This indented listing of all of the subclasses within each major class gives you a visual aid towards understanding how the various subclasses are related. By reviewing this indented

PTO Manual of Classification for US patents

What follows are the subclasses from one class of the Manual of Classification for US patents. As you scroll through the list and encounter a class/subclass of interest, you can jump back to the top and retrieve patent titles by entering the class/subclass in the box below.

Enter a class/subclass code here to get a list of patent titles. Use any of the following forms:
363-131 121-55A 14-.5
that is, no embedded spaces, class and subclass seperated by a dash, and any subclass letters capitalized. Currently Design Patent titles (those in the classes of the form Dxx.yy) are not retreivable.

Enter class/subclass code:

Submit Query | Clear

Figure 5

list of subclasses, you may find further classifications of interest.

The STO Internet patent search system provides a wealth of patent-related information and is well worth taking the time to explore.

B. Free Specialized Patent Databases

Several specialized patent databases have been set up on the Internet. These databases are organized around certain topics. One of these topics is biotechnology. The full text of recent biotechnology related patents can be searched at the following web address:

http://www.nal.usda.gov/bic/Biotech_patents

Figure 6 shows the homepage for the Biotechnology Patents and New Technology search system. Presently, the full text of biotechnology patents for the years 1994 and 1995 can be searched for free. Additional patents may be added in the

near future. Other links related to the field of biotechnology can also be found at this location.

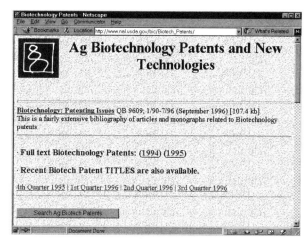

Figure 6

To begin searching biotechnology related patents, click on the button labeled "Search Ag Biotech Patents" at the lower left of Figure 6. You will then see the Web page shown in Figure 7, below.

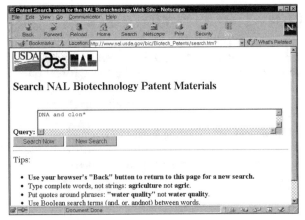

Figure 7

were retrieved. To see the matching patents, simply scroll down the results window. A portion of this window is shown in Figure 9, below.

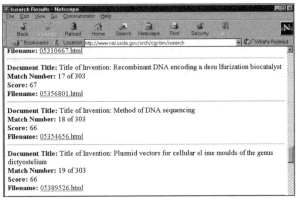

Figure 9

The search screen shown in Figure 7 is very similar to the advanced Boolean search screen used by the PTO in Chapter 6, Section A. Here, we can enter Boolean search expressions and search phrases. Wildcards can also be used for searching.

For example, let's suppose you are working on a project that involves cloning DNA. In Figure 7, we have entered the Boolean search expression "DNA AND clon*". When we click on the button labeled Search Now, shown at the center left of Figure 7, the full text of biotechnology related patents will be searched for the keyword DNA, and the word stem "clon*". This query will find the words clone, cloned, cloning, etc. The search results are shown in Figure 8, below.

In Figure 9, we see a list of the titles of the matching patents that resulted from our search. These patents are scored by the search engine to give you an indication of relevance. This scoring method takes into account the frequency of occurrence of your keywords within the patent text.

Let's suppose that your invention involves an automated method of DNA sequencing. You would then want to review the text of patent number 5,354,656. This patent is listed as item 18 located in the center of Figure 9, above. To review the text of this patent, just click on the patent number shown in the figure.

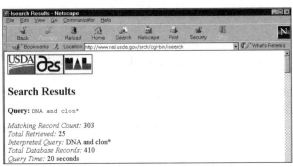

Figure 8

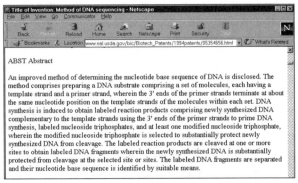

Figure 10

Figure 8 shows the top of the search results screen. Here we see that there were 303 matches for our search query, of which the 25 most relevant

Figure 10 shows the abstract portion of the full text of patent 5,354,656. The entire patent can be reviewed by using the scroll bar. To obtain a print-out of this patent, use the Netscape File...Print function, shown in Figure 11, below.

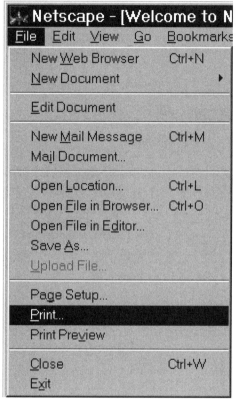

Figure 11

If your invention is related to biotechnology research, you will certainly want to take advantage of this valuable patent search resource. In addition to the biotechnology topic, there are several other free, specialized patent databases on the Internet. Some of these are listed in Table 1.

Name	WWW Address
DNA Patent Database	http://208.201.146.119
*Fullerene Patent Database	http://mgm.mit.edu:8080/ pevzner/Bucky/Patents.html

*Note: A Buckminsterfullerene molecule is a closed cage structure molecule with a carbon network. A Buckyball is a C60 molecule.

Table 1

C. Fee-Based Patent Databases

There are a number of Internet-based patent search systems that charge a fee for their use. Why pay for what you can get for free? Well, that depends on the extent of the service that these companies provide. In some cases, for a nominal fee, you can get access to a patent database that is much more comprehensive than what the PTO or IBM offers. For a larger fee, other firms will perform much of the work for you, including foreign patent searches.

One company that charges a fee for patent and trademark searches is called MicroPatent. To get to the main MicroPatent website, you need to type in the following address:

http://www.micropat.com

The MicroPatent search system has patents issued from January 1964 to the present. As such, it is more extensive than both the PTO and IBM sites, which only go back to the early 1970s. In addition to patents, trademarks issued from April 1884 to the present can also be searched. The homepage of the MicroPatent corporation is shown in Figure 12, below.

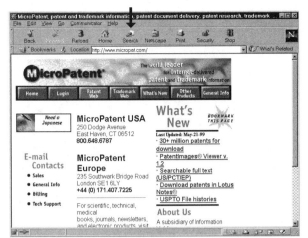

Figure 12

By clicking on the PatentWeb button shown in the upper center of Figure 12, you can access the patent search features of the site. These services require registration. The registration process itself is free. You are only charged for the services that you use. By clicking on the Login area of Figure 13 (lower left), you will be guided through the registration process.

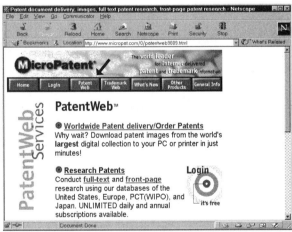

Figure 13

When you register, you will be asked to select a log-in name and a password. You will use this information when you log-in to MicroPatent as a registered user. Simply enter your log-in name and password in the appropriate boxes shown in Figure 14. Then, click on PatSearch Fulltext. The very first time you log-in to MicroPatent, you will have to enter a four-digit code which is emailed to you after registration. This entry screen is shown in Figure 15.

Figure 14

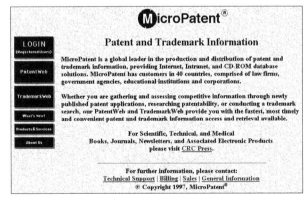

Figure 15

After logging into PatentWeb as a registered user, you will see the Web page shown in Figure 16 above. This Web page has links for ordering patent copies. Although prices change constantly, typical charges are around $5 per patent for a full patent document download. Delivery options include email, fax and postal mail. Figure 16 also shows a link to a handy program called Patent-Image Viewer, which you can download for free. This program allows you to view patent images (drawings) as well as text.

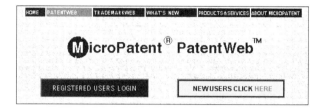

Figure 16

Several other fee-based patent search companies are listed in Table 2, below.

Company	WWW Address
Derwent Scientific and Patent Information	http://www.derwent.co.uk
LEXIS/NEXIS	http://www.lexis.com
Questel - Orbit Patent and Trademark Databases	http://www.questel.orbit.com
QPAT-US	http://www.qpat.com
Patent Services	http://www.patentec.com
Chemical Patents Plus	http://casweb.cas.org/chempatplus

Table 2

D. Overseas Intellectual Property Offices

Should you eventually file a patent application, your patent examiner will first search through U.S. issued patents and then check for any referenced foreign patents. When a patent is issued, any foreign patent references can be found on the front page of the issued patent.

In general, it's not necessary to spend a great deal of time, effort and expense searching for foreign patent references. This is because the patent examiner who processes your application will primarily focus on U.S. patent references. But it's a good idea to take a quick look, especially since a number of these overseas intellectual property offices have established Internet sites. (Searching foreign patents at a Patent and Trademark Depository Library via the APS computer system is covered in Chapter 7, Section D.)

For example, to visit the United Kingdom Patent Office we need to type in the following address:

http://www.ukpats.org.uk/

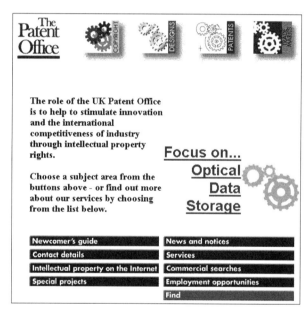

Figure 17

Figure 17 shows the main homepage of the UK Patent Office. You can access the patent search information by clicking on the Services button at the lower right. You will then see the list of available services shown in Figure 18. By selecting the first listed link, Search and Advisory services, you can access patent information services, documentation, databases and costs.

Overseas Intellectual Property Offices on the Internet	
Argentina	http://www.mecoh.gov/ar/inpi
Australia	http://ipaustaralia.gov.au
Austria	http://www.patent.bmwa.gv.at
Belgium	http://www.european-patent-office.org/patlib/country/belgium
Brazil	http://www.inpi.gov.br
Canada	http://cipo.gc.ca
Czech Republic	http://upv.cz/english
China, People's Republic of	http://www.cpo.cn.net
Croatia	http://jagor.srce.hr/patent/eng
Denmark	http://www.dkpto.dk/english
Euraasian Patent Office	http://www.eapo.org
European Patent Office	http://www.european-patent-office.org
Finland	http://www.prh.fi
France	http://www.evariste.anvar.fr/inpi
Georgian Industrial Property Organization	http://www.global-erty.net/saqpatenti
Germany	http://www.patent-und-markenamt.de
Greece	http://www.obi.gr
Hong Kong	http://info.gov.hk/ipd
Hungary	http://www.hpo.hu
Italy	http://www.minindustria.it
Japan	http://www.jpo-miti.go.jp
Korea	http://www.kipo.go.kr
Lithuania	http://www.is.Lt/upB/engl
Luxembourg	http://www.etat.lu/EC
Malaysia	http://www.kpdnhq.gov.my/homepage/english/mainlp.html
Mexico	http://www.impi.gob.mx
Moldova	http://www.agepi.md/index_pages/index_eng.html
Monaco	http://www.european-patent-office.org/patlib/country/monaco
Netherlands	http://www.bie.nl
New Zealand	http://www.med.govt.nz/buslt/int_prop.html
Norway	http://www.patentstyret.no
Peru	http://www.indecopi.gob.pe
Poland	http://www.ibspan.waw.pl
Portugal	http://www.inpi.pt
Romania	http://www.osim.ro/web/eng/indexen.html
Russian Patent Office	http://www.rupto.ru
Singapore	http://www.gov.sg/minlaw/ipos
Slovak Republic	http://www.indprop.gov.sk/ie.htm
Slovenia	http://www.sipo.mzt.si
Spain	http://www.oepm.es
Sweden	http://www.prv.se
Switzerland	http://www.ige.ch
United Kingdom	http://www.patent.gov.uk
World Intellectual Property Organization (WIPO)	http://www.wipo.org

Table 3

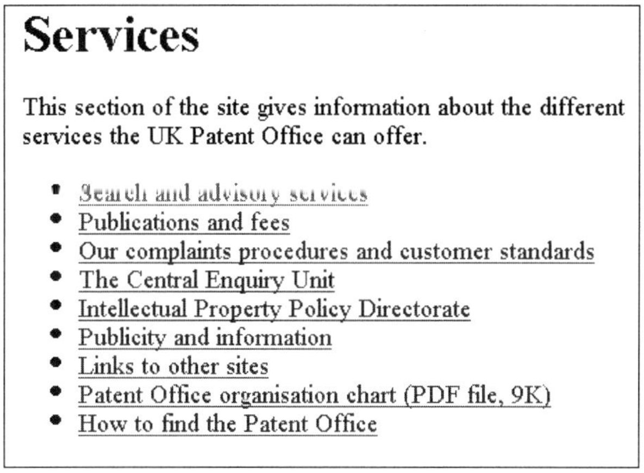

Services

This section of the site gives information about the different services the UK Patent Office can offer.

* Search and advisory services
* Publications and fees
* Our complaints procedures and customer standards
* The Central Enquiry Unit
* Intellectual Property Policy Directorate
* Publicity and information
* Links to other sites
* Patent Office organisation chart (PDF file, 9K)
* How to find the Patent Office

Figure 18

These search and advisory services are not free. The UK site quotes typical full patentability search costs at £500 to £800, depending on subject matter. However, the cost of simpler searches that are limited to computerized databases are a minimum of £270. Several countries that maintain intellectual property offices on the WWW are listed in Table 3, above.

Summary

Exploring the STO

The Source Translation and Optimization (STO) website allows users to search the indexed list of subclasses from the *Manual of Classification*.

Free Specialized Patent Databases

Several free patent databases for special topics have been set up on the Internet. Examples are patent databases for biotechnology-related patents and Buckminsterfullerene patents.

Fee-Based Patent Databases

A number of companies have established Internet patent search systems that charge a fee for their use. Services vary. Users can often access more comprehensive patent data than would be available from free patent search websites.

Overseas Intellectual Property Offices

A number of overseas intellectual property offices have established Internet sites. Patent search services and database collections vary from site to site. ∎

Additional Sources of Prior Art

So far in this book, we have restricted ourselves to patent searching resources. However, prior art is not limited to patented inventions. Any published information, from any corner of the globe, can prevent a patent from being granted. Even unpublished works, such as a Master's thesis, can be considered valid prior art. In this chapter, we will consider other prior art search resources. These resources include Internet search engines, government websites and industrial product and manufacturer listings. As you may recall from Chapter 1, the prior art for a given invention are those prior inventions (whether patented or not) that embody some of the same or similar elements as the current invention.

A. Internet Search Engines

To date, millions of commercial, educational and government websites have been established. These sites provide a wealth of information about current retail products and research into new product concepts. The following Internet Domain Survey statistics were compiled by Network Wizards (www.nw.com) as of July 2000.

Number of commercial website host computers
(addresses with a .COM at the end)   32,696,253
Number of educational website host computers
(addresses with a .EDU at the end)   6,678,055
Number of government website host computers
(addresses with a .GOV at the end)   827,575

So how do you search through all of this information to see if your invention idea has already been produced as a commercial product? Or, perhaps your idea is already the subject of ongoing government research. To efficiently search through millions of Web pages, you make use of a program called a *search engine*. A search engine is a program that keeps track of the content of the various Web pages on the Internet. The search engine then allows the user to seek specific Web pages through keyword searching.

Typically, when a company creates a website, they register it with one or more of the Internet's major search engines. At a minimum, this involves providing a homepage address, contact information and some key search words. For example, if the company manufactures carbon dioxide lasers, then the search terms "laser" and "carbon dioxide" should be linked from the search engine to their Web page.

There are currently around 300 large search engines on the Internet. In addition to using information supplied by registered companies, some search engines run programs called *Web crawlers*. These programs automatically run around on the Internet, read Web site information and add it to the search engine's database.

One of the most powerful Internet search engines is called *Alta Vista* and is run by Digital Equipment Corporation. To get to the Alta Vista search engine, you need to type the following address into your Web browser:

http://altavista.com/

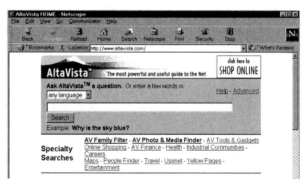

Figure 1

Figure 1, above, shows the keyword entry section of the Alta Vista main search page. Searching by category can be performed by scrolling down the image shown in Figure 1.

Down the left-hand side of Figure 2, we see a series of categories: Computers & Internet, Business & Finance, etc. Let's suppose we have an idea for an invention that will be used in the aerospace industry. To search for relevant topics we select the Business & Finance link. We are then presented with a new column of categories within the topic Business & Finance. These subcategories are then further subdivided as shown in Figures 3 and 4, below.

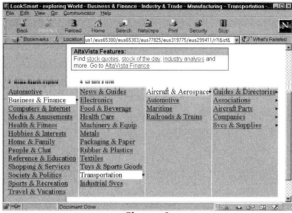

Figure 4

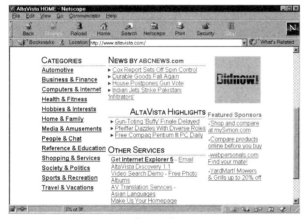

Figure 2

Figure 3

The Alta Vista website allows us to quickly progress through a succession of categories to find the topic we are looking for. In Figure 3, we selected Business & Finance, Industry and Trade, and Manufacturing. This brings us to the series of categories shown at the far right of Figure 3. Since our invention will be used in the aerospace industry, we select the Transportation link. The succession of categories then continues as shown in Figure 4. Here we have selected the Aircraft & Aerospace link, and finally the Companies link. We are then presented with the series of website links shown in Figure 5. All of the listed sites have content pertaining to the aerospace industry.

You can perform a highly focused keyword search of aerospace related sites by using the search entry box shown in Figure 5. Also, if you are not sure where you are in the Alta Vista category structure, a breakdown is written directly below the search entry box. In this case the progression was:

Business & Finance–Industry & Trade–Manufacturing–Transportation–Aircraft & Aerospace–Companies

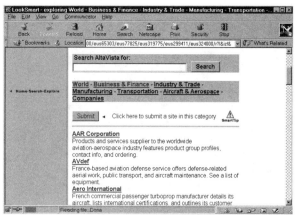

Figure 5

1. Low Temperature Physics
[URL: www.imr.tohoku.ac.jp/soshiki/kenkyu-bu/kobayashilab-e.html]
Low Temperature Physics. Prof. Norio KOBAYASHI Assoc.Prof.
Masafumi SERA Res. Assoc. Takako SASAKI Masahiko HIROI
Terukazu NISHIZAKI. Prof. N. KOBAYASHI...
Last modified 18-Sep-96 - page size 1K - in English [Translate]

2. LOW TEMPERATURE PHYSICS
[URL: www.phys.tue.nl/lt/publicat/pub95lt.htm]
LOW TEMPERATURE PHYSICS. Scientific Publications. 1995.
P.J.M. Peters, P.K.H. Sommerfeld, S. van den Berg, P.P. Steijaert,
R.W. van der Heijden, and...
Last modified 17-Jun-97 - page size 3K - in English [Translate]

3. PHY4403 Low-Temperature Physics (1997/98)
[URL: newton.ex.ac.uk/admissions/ug/modules/PHY4403.html]
PHY4403 (1997/98)LOW-TEMPERATURE PHYSICS. Lecturer: Dr.
Charles Williams. Duration: 20 lectures (10 credits), in Semester II.
Prerequisites: Statistical...
Last modified 17-Jul-97 - page size 4K - in English [Translate]

Figure 7

Keyword searching at the Alta Vista website can also be performed without the use of categories. Let's use the Netscape back arrow to return to the main Alta Vista search page and perform a typical search. Suppose that we have an idea for an invention that involves low-temperature physics. To search the WWW for that topic, we can type in the word Physics, the Boolean operator AND, and the phrase "low temperature," as shown in Figure 6. We then click on the search button at the lower right of the figure. After a few seconds, the search results are returned, with the first few shown in Figure 7, below. Here we see several references to Web pages that contain both the word Physics and the phrase "low temperature." To review any of these references in detail, just click on the title of the reference.

By clicking on the Advanced Search link at the extreme lower right of Figure 6, we see the Alta Vista advanced search Web page shown in Figure 8. This screen allows us to enter Boolean expressions and rank our search results. For example, suppose that we wanted to modify our search to include the phrase "low temperature" or the keyword Cryogenics.

By specifying the keyword Cryogenics in the Rank Results entry box (directly above the Boolean expression entry box), matching Web pages that have this keyword will be listed first in the search results.

Figure 9 shows the results of our advanced search. Also note how we have used the From and To entry boxes to limit our WWW search to Web pages that were written on or after January 1, 1997.

Figure 6

AltaVista A Compaq Internet Service   Search Zones Services
Search the Web for documents in English
cryogenics   Search   Refine
Boolean expression: Range of dates:
Physics AND ("low temperature" OR   **From:** 1/Jan/97
cryogenics)
                                             To:
                                             e.g.: 21/Mar/96
☐ **Count documents matching the boolean expression.**

Figure 8

1. CTI-Cryogenics: Calendar Of Events [text]
[URL: www.ctivacuum.com/lite/tcalendar.htm]
Who We Are | Vacuum Solutions | Sales | Technical Support |
Calendar Of Events | Contact Us | Home. Calendar Of Events. We'll
be at the following events...
Last modified 5-Feb-98 - page size 23K - in English [Translate]

2. CTI-Cryogenics: Calendar Of Events: main frame
[URL: www.ctivacuum.com/enhanced/calmain.htm]
nbsp;   We'll be at the following events in 1997. Make a point of
coming to see us! For your convenience we have provided links to
various...
Last modified 2-Oct-97 - page size 9K - in English [Translate]

3. CTI-Cryogenics: Calendar Of Events: main frame
[URL: www.ctivacuum.com/enhanced/calendar_rt.htm]
We'll be at the following events in 1998. Make a point of coming to
see us! For your convenience we have provided links to various
associations so you can.
Last modified 5-Feb-98 - page size 18K - in English [Translate]

Figure 9

Another important Internet information resource is called Yahoo!. Yahoo has a vast array of searchable categories. To get to the Yahoo website, you need to type the following address into your Web browser:

http://www.yahoo.com/

Figure 10, below, shows the homepage of the Yahoo website.

Here, you'll find a directory of top-level categories, including:

Arts and Humanities	News and Media
Business and Economy	Recreation and Sports
Computers and Internet	Reference
Education	Regional
Entertainment	Science
Government	Social Science
Health	Society and Culture

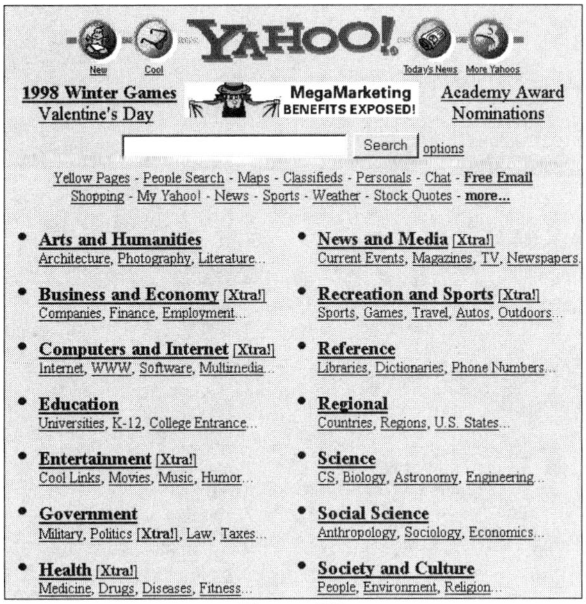

Figure 10

Each of these categories contains thousands of subcategories arranged into additional directories. These directories of categories are arranged in a hierarchical structure. They run from the general to the specific. Yahoo contains over 25,000 categories of topics. Once you have navigated through the Yahoo category structure, you will eventually come to a list of relevant websites.

For example, let's suppose you are developing a new type of laser and you would like to check up on similar research on the WWW. Of the general topics, the one most applicable to laser research would be Science. After clicking on the Science link shown in Figure 10, you will see the science directory of categories shown in Figure 11.

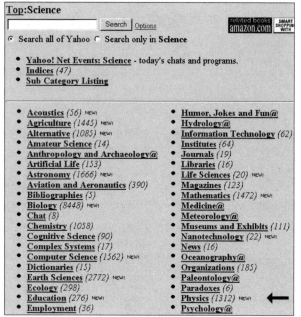

Figure 11

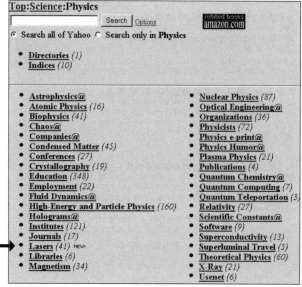

Figure 12

After scanning through the list of available categories, Physics (lower right—Figure 11) would seem to be the most appropriate, so we click on that link. We are then presented with the directory shown in Figure 12. After scanning these categories, we see that Lasers is listed towards the bottom of the left-hand column.

When we click on the Lasers link, Yahoo will give us one of two results: either a further breakdown of categories, such as different types of lasers arranged into a directory, or a listing of websites that have content related to lasers. This is how all of the website links are organized under Yahoo. You proceed from very general to more specific categories, until you can't get any more specific. Then you get a list of websites for that specific topic.

In this case clicking the lasers link of Figure 12, above, brings us to the end of the category chain and we get the results shown in Figure 13. Notice that at the upper left of Figure 13 is our directory chain: Top:Science:Physics:Lasers. This lets us know our current location in the Yahoo hierarchy. Yahoo has over half a million websites divided into its 25,000 categories.

What if you are not sure which category to look under? In addition to browsing, Yahoo will let you search the various categories with keywords. The results are very similar to the search engine process, but with an important difference. The first set of search results returned are Yahoo categories. This is because some Yahoo categories can contain hundreds or even thousands of relevant websites. Returning to the categories first gives you a chance to filter the results by looking under one category at a time. Following the categories are the website listings. If no categories match the keyword search terms, then only the matching websites are listed.

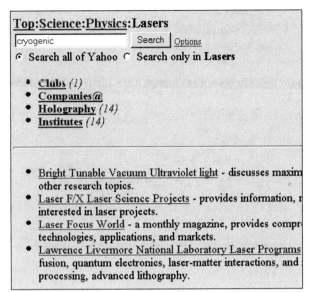

Figure 13

Table 1, below, lists some other popular search engines.

Figure 14

A search can be performed at any point in the Yahoo hierarchy. At the upper left of Figures 11, 12 and 13, you will see a search entry box. This is where you enter your search keywords. For example, suppose we want to review information about cryogenics, but don't know which category to look under. We can enter the word Cryogenic as shown at the upper left of Figure 13. Then, under the keyword entry box, we can select either "Search all of Yahoo" or "Search only in Lasers." We select "Search all of Yahoo" because we want to look for the word Cryogenic anywhere in the Yahoo hierarchy. Selecting "Search only in Lasers" would limit our search to the current topic only. To start the process, we then click on the Search button.

The results of our search are shown in Figure 14, below. At the top of the Figure we see that there are four categories and 120 website matches reported for the keyword Cryogenic. The categories are listed first, followed by the websites.

Search Engine	WWW Address
Deja News	http://www.dejanews.com/
Excite	http://www.excite.com/
Lycos	http://www.lycos.com/
Search.com	http://www.search.com/
WebCrawler	http://www.webcrawler.com/

Table 1

B. The Thomas Register

In the previous section, we looked for companies, products and research facilities that have published information on the WWW. But what about all those companies that don't have Web pages? The Thomas Register industrial database has contact information for over 155,000 American and Canadian companies. Some of these companies have websites, but many do not. When a listed company has an established website, the Register provides a link to that Internet address. When a website doesn't exist, the Register provides contact information such as an address, telephone and fax number.

The register has 63,000 product and service classifications, and provides access to 7,700 online supplier catalogs. You can receive product literature by fax from over 1,000 companies at no charge. To get to the Thomas Register website, you need to type the following address into your Web browser:

http://thomasregister.com

The homepage for the Thomas Register is shown in Figure 15. To use the Register for the first time, click on the "Free Membership" link. Registration is free and the requested information is limited to contact information (for example, your name, company, address, etc.).

Once you have registered, you will be able to search the Register by clicking on the "Search A through Z" area shown in Figure 15. The next screen is shown in Figure 16, below. Searching is a simple, three-step process. First, we decide if we want to search for a company name, product or brand name. Second, we enter a search keyword. Finally, we click on the Search button.

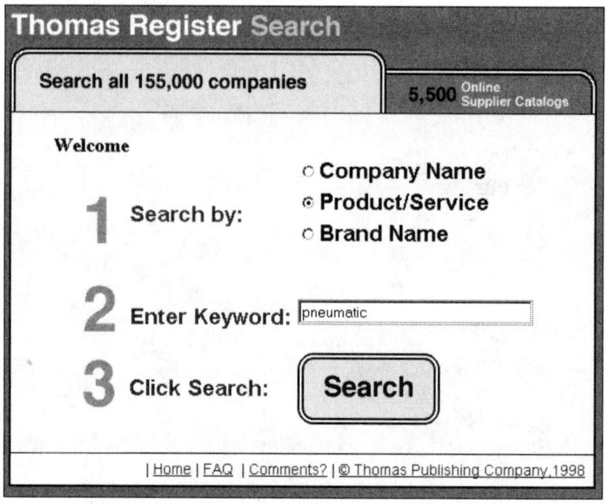

Figure 16

Now let's suppose that we have an invention idea for a pneumatic (air-powered) motor. To search for similar products, we select the Product/Service radio button, type in the keyword Pneumatic and click the Search button.

The results of our search are shown in Figure 17. At the top of the figure, 149 product headings were found. Next to each heading are columns which provide information about available online catalogs, information by fax and WWW links. Looking down the list, we see that item number 5 is Pneumatic Motors. The adjacent column tells us that four companies that make pneumatic motors were found. To get a list of links to those companies, we click on item number 5.

The resulting list of companies is shown in Figure 18. To read the contact information for any of these firms, just click on the title of the company. For example, to extract the contact information for the first listed company, Ingersoll-Rand, just click on it. The resulting Web page is shown in Figure 19.

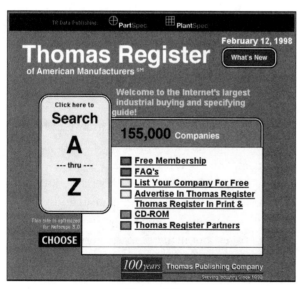

Figure 15

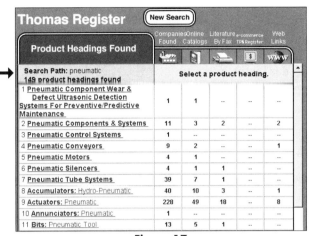

Figure 17

Figure 18

Figure 19

C. Government Websites

The U.S. government spends billions of dollars on research annually. It is quite possible that some of this research could be directly related to your invention ideas. Most government agencies support at least one website, and much of their research information is unclassified and accessible.

One of the most useful of these government websites is run by the Defense Technology Information Center (DTIC). DTIC contributes to the management and conduct of defense-related research, development and acquisition efforts by providing access to, and exchange of, scientific and technical information. To get to the DTIC website, you need to type the following address into your Web browser:

http://www.dtic.mil/

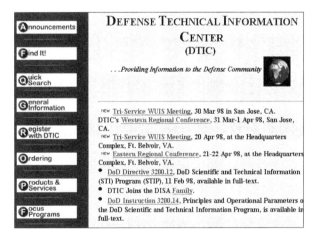

Figure 20

Figure 20 shows a section of the DTIC homepage. The navigation controls for the DTIC site are a series of buttons shown on the left-hand side of the figure. For example, by clicking on the

"Find It!" control (second from the top), you will be presented with the screen shown in Figure 21. This is an alphabetical listing of DTIC developed sites.

Let's suppose that your invention is related to recent Aerospace developments. To see if related research is being performed, you could click on the link titled, "Aerospace in the 21st Century." This would bring up the Web page shown in Figure 22. This series of links was compiled for the Advisory Group for Aerospace Research and Development and it lists new and advanced developments, research and technologies that are expected for the next 20–50 years.

The DTIC website also supports keyword searches. Directly below the Find It! button, on the DTIC homepage, is the Quick Search button. Clicking on this button brings up the Web page shown in Figure 23, below. By selecting the Search button, you get a simple text entry box for keyword searches.

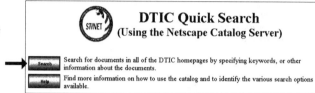

Figure 23

In addition to DTIC, there are a large number of other government websites that offer valuable information for prior art searches. Selected government websites are listed in Table 2, below.

Figure 21

AEROSPACE in the 21st Century Electronic Bibliography

Welcome to Aerospace in the 21st Century! Explore the field of Aerospace and learn what new and advanced developments, research and technologies are expected 20-50 years in the future. Compiled for the Advisory Group for Aerospace Research and Development.

The Future of Aerospace over the next 25-50 years-Publications

- NEW WORLD VISTAS STUDY - USAF Scientific Advisory Board. A look at how science and technology will affect the military. Full text of summary volume available.
- Air Force 2025 Final Report Home Page New! from Air University- Collectively, this diverse group served as a "think tank" to identify the innovative, high-leverage technologies and systems that will enable the United States to continue to set the standard for excellence in air and space power well into the 21st century.
- GLOBAL ENGAGEMENT: A Vision for the 21st Century Air Force Global Engagement A guiding vision for the 21st Century Air Force
- JOINT VISION 2010 -An official document that describes the US defense strategy for the future
- SPACECAST 2020 Technical Report - Volume I - Air University Study

Figure 22

Websites of Selected Government Agencies	
U.S. Dept. of the Interior	http://www.doi.gov
USDA Forest Service	http://www.fs.fed.us
Department of Commerce	http://www.doc.gov
Department of Energy	http://www.energy.gov
NASA Commercial Technology Network (CTN)	http://nctn.hq.nasa.gov
Dept. of Health and Human Services	http://www.os.dhhs.gov
Department of Education	http://www.ed.gov
National Technology Transfer Center (NTTC)	http://www.nttc.edu
Environmental Protection Agency	http://www.epa.gov
Dept. of Transportation	http://www.dot.gov
National Science Foundation	http://www.nsf.gov
U.S. Army Corps of Engineers	http://www.usace.army.mil

Table 2

D. Discussion Groups

Unlike the WWW, where websites all over the world are connected through hypertext links, the Usenet is a collection of thousands of individual newsgroups. Several million people from all over the world subscribe to these newsgroups. Each newsgroup is devoted to a certain topic or subject. With so many topics covered, the odds are that one or more newsgroups will be relevant to your field of invention.

Messages of interest to each group are *posted* (or written) to that group. Newsgroup messages are then read via a newsreader program. To access the Usenet via Netscape, locate the Window item at the upper left of the menu bar as shown in Figure 24. Click on the Window item to get the pulldown menu shown in the figure. Next, scroll down to Netscape News and click once. You will then see the window shown in Figure 25.

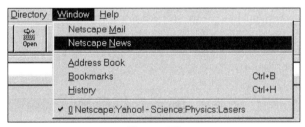

Figure 24

You should have one or more news hosts available. In Figure 25, I have opened the folder for the Netcruiser news host, "nntp.netcruiser." The default setting of the view option is to display only active newsgroups. These are newsgroups that you have subscribed to. As you can see from the Figure, two newsgroups are active: alt.inventors and alt.inventorworld. Messages of general interest to inventors are often posted here.

To see all the available newsgroups, change the Options settings from Show Active Newsgroups to Show All Newsgroups as shown in the figure. Netscape will then load the latest collection of

newsgroups. At last count there were more than 15,000, so this takes a few minutes. The result is shown in Figure 26, below.

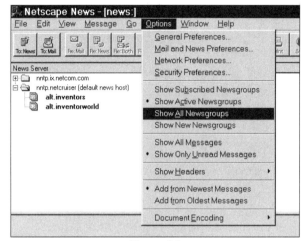

Figure 25

There are topics ranging from aviation (newsgroup name: aus.aviation) to Zenith computer systems (newsgroup name: comp.sys.zenith). There are so many newsgroups that they are often arranged into folders. In Figure 26, we have opened the Alt folder. This folder contains 5,317 different newsgroups. Folders can be opened by clicking on them or clicking on the small plus sign to their immediate left. To the right of the newsgroup name is an empty box. To subscribe to that newsgroup simply click on the box. Netscape responds by placing a check mark within the box. For efficient reading, you can later limit the display to only subscribed newsgroups. This is done by clicking on the Show Subscribed Newsgroups option (see Figure 25).

Past the subscription box are two columns of numbers. The first column gives you the number of unread messages within that group. The second column gives you the total number of messages within the group. To read the messages currently posted within a newsgroup, simply click on the name of the group.

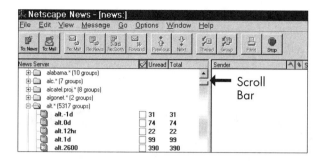

Figure 26

For example, suppose you have an idea for a new circuit board design. You can use the scroll bar of Figure 26 to move down the list of Alt newsgroup headings to the alt.electronics.manufacture.circuitboard newsgroup. Then click on the newsgroup title and the topics of messages currently posted to the group will be displayed to the right. This action is shown in Figure 27 below.

Let's suppose that while designing your circuit board, you've come up with the following questions:

1. How long is a presensitized copper board good for, provided it is kept sealed in a black bag?
2. What does each chemical do in the process?
3. Is tin coating really necessary?
4. After immersing in the developing solution, only the surface layer of the exposed part was wiped away. Is this supposed to happen? Doesn't the entire board still remain as one conductor?
5. Is there a better method?

In order to ask these questions, you need to write or post a message to the newsgroup. To post a message to a newsgroup select File from the Netscape menu and then New News Message. This action is shown in Figure 28. A message window will then pop up, as shown in Figure 29. Notice that the newsgroup name, alt.electronics.manufacture.circuitboard has already been added to the newsgroup destination line. Then, type in a subject line and the body of your message. To post the message to the selected newsgroup, click on the Send button.

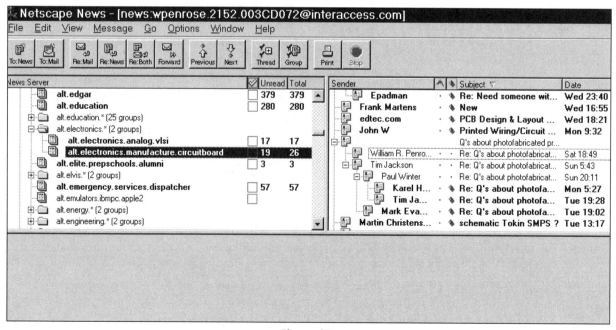

Figure 27

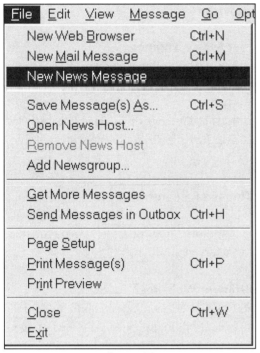

Figure 28

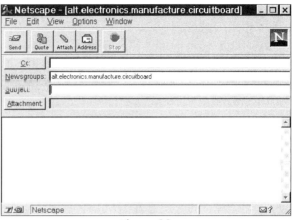

Figure 29

In Figure 30 below, we show a typical response to our message. Notice how the essential parts of the original message are included in the response.

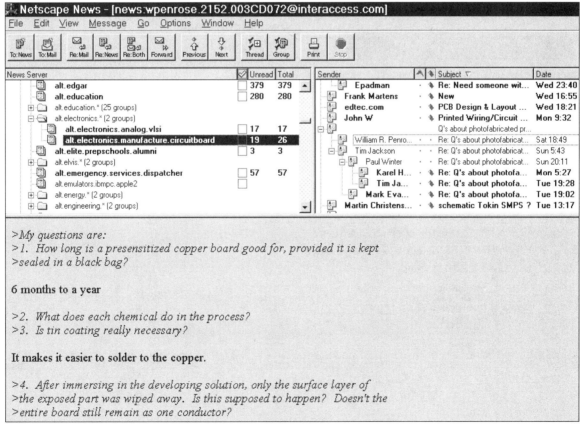

>My questions are:
>1. How long is a presensitized copper board good for, provided it is kept
>sealed in a black bag?

6 months to a year

>2. What does each chemical do in the process?
>3. Is tin coating really necessary?

It makes it easier to solder to the copper.

>4. After immersing in the developing solution, only the surface layer of
>the exposed part was wiped away. Is this supposed to happen? Doesn't the
>entire board still remain as one conductor?

Figure 30

The answers to each question are inserted directly below the question. For example:

Question: How long is a presensitized copper board good for, provided it is kept sealed in a black bag?

Answer: 6 months to a year

The Usenet has millions of readers who like to participate in interesting discussions and answer questions. But they don't like to answer the same questions over and over again. For this reason a "frequently asked questions" (FAQ) list of questions and answers is often posted to each group. Before you post a message to a newsgroup, please read any FAQ postings. Often you will find that your question has been anticipated and the answer already provided.

There are certain rules and conventions for posting messages to Usenet newsgroups. These are generically referred to as *Netiquette*. Some of the most important rules of Netiquette are summarized in Table 3, below:

Rules of Netiquette

1. Post your question or message only to the newsgroup that is the most appropriate. Sending messages to multiple newsgroups is called "spamming" and is very frowned upon.
2. Put a short, descriptive header into the Subject line of your posting. People use these headers to select which messages to respond to.
3. Keep your message short and concise.
4. If you reply to a previous posted message, include the essential parts of the original message in your response, but not the entire original message.
5. Don't use the Net for sending nasty messages (called "flames"), advertising or chain letters.

Table 3

Summary

Internet Search Engines
- Internet search engines, such as Alta Vista, can be used to efficiently search through millions of Web pages.
- Yahoo is a directory of searchable categories. It has over half a million websites divided into 25,000 categories.

The Thomas Register
- The Thomas Register industrial database has contact information for over 155,000 American and Canadian companies.

Government Websites
- The U.S. Government spends billions of dollars on research annually. Most government agencies support at least one website, and much of their research information is unclassified and accessible.

Discussion Groups
- The Usenet is a collection of thousands of individual discussion newsgroups. Each newsgroup is devoted to a certain topic or subject. One or more newsgroups may be relevant to your field of invention.

■

Where Do I Go From Here?

If you used the techniques in this book to search for patents similar to yours at the PTDL and/or on the Internet, you probably have come up with at least a half dozen prior art patents.

Searcher's Secret Number 12

If you haven't found any prior art for your invention idea, you haven't looked hard enough.

So where do you go from here? The next step is to decide if you should go through the effort and expense of filing a patent application in light of your search results.

A. Has Your Invention Been Anticipated by the Prior Art?

In order to get a utility patent (as opposed to a design patent), your patent application has to satisfy four legal criteria. (For a detailed description of what is patentable, as well as the entire patent application process, we highly recommend *Patent It Yourself,* by David Pressman (Nolo).)

1. Your invention has to fit into an established Statutory Class.
2. Your invention must have some Utility. In other words, it has to be useful.
3. Your invention must have some Novelty. It must have some physical difference from any similar inventions in the past.
4. Your invention must be Unobvious to someone who is skilled in the appropriate field.

Let's look at each of these requirements. The first is fairly simple. In order to get a patent, your invention must be either a Process, a Machine, an Article of Manufacture, a Composition of Matter or a New Use invention. Let's look at a few examples:

- *Process.* A process is just the performance of a series of operations on something. Electroplating is an example of a process.
- *Machine.* A machine is a device consisting of a series of fixed or moving parts that direct mechanical energy towards a specific task. An example of a machine with no moving parts would be a screwdriver. A more complex machine would be an automobile engine.
- *Article of Manufacture.* An article of manufacture can be made by hand or machine. As opposed to machines, articles of manufacture are inventions that are relatively simple, with few or no moving parts. Blue jeans and other clothes are good examples.
- *Composition of Matter.* A composition of matter is a unique arrangement of items. Chemical compositions such as glue and plastics are good examples of compositions of matter.
- *New Use Process.* A new use process is simply a new way of using an invention that fits in one of the first four statutory classes.

Virtually all inventions that have some use also fit into one or more of these classes. It's not necessary to decide which class applies to your invention as long as it is arguably covered by at least one of them.

The second criterion your patent application has to satisfy is that it must be useful. Fortunately, any new use will satisfy this requirement. In general, if your invention is operable (if it functions), it will satisfy this requirement. Perpetual motion machines or other devices that violate an established law of physics are examples of inventions that fail this requirement.

The third criterion is novelty. In order to meet this requirement, your invention must be somehow different from all previous inventions. This includes both nonpatented, as well as patented, inventions.

Generally, there are three types of difference categories:

- physical differences
- combinatorial differences
- new uses.

An example of a physical difference between your invention and a previously patented product would be the elimination, replacement or functional modification of a component of the previous device.

As an example of elimination of a component, consider the invention shown in Figure 1 below. The figure shows a side and front view of a fire safety glass window. It consists of four elements.

Element #1. Left-hand side glass segment.

Element #2. A thermal conduction film.

Element #3. Right-hand side glass segment.

Element #4. Heat-conducting metal frame.

For this invention to work, a heat-conducting film is sandwiched between two glass plates. When a sharp temperature rise occurs on either side of the glass, the film conducts the heat away from the window to the metal frame.

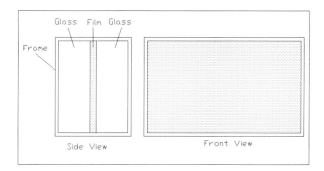

Figure 1

Now consider the invention shown in Figure 2 below. This figure is also a side and front view of a safety glass window. In this case there are three elements.

Element #1. Thermal-conducting wire mesh.

Element #2. Glass segment enclosing the wire mesh.

Element #3. Heat-conducting metal frame.

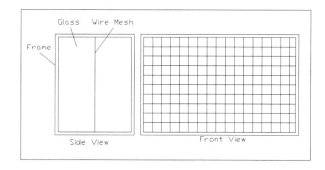

Figure 2

The wire mesh conducts heat away from the glass and into the frame, just as the first invention does. But now, instead of two separate glass elements, there is only one continuous glass element (in which the wire grid is embedded).

As an example of a replacement physical difference, consider the centrifugal water pump shown in Figure 3 below. Centrifugal pumps use impellers to impart energy to the water. For the sake of simplicity, we will identify four essential elements.

Element #1. Pump intake.

Element #2. Impeller.

Element #3. Pump casting.

Element #4. Pump discharge.

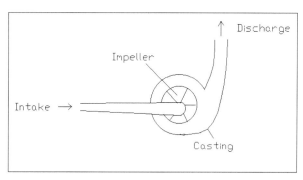

Figure 3

Let us suppose that the impeller is made out of metal. You design a new impeller for this pump that performs as well, but is made out of plastic. This replacement physical difference would satisfy the novelty requirement.

As an example of a functional modification, suppose our water pump vibrates at high pressure (high impeller speed) due to water turbulence. You redesign the blades of the impeller by increasing their pitch. This solves the turbulence problem and allows the pump to operate at high pressure. You have therefore made a functional modification.

A new combination of two different inventions can also be used to satisfy the novelty requirement. An example would be the combination of a hot air balloon (an old invention) and a new high strength lightweight fabric. The lightweight fabric replaces the older balloon material, making the balloon lighter. This provides more lift and lets the balloon carry more cargo.

A new use of an old invention can also satisfy the novelty requirement. As an example, suppose during World War II a sonar engineer developed a sonar receiver that detects the sound of a ship's propeller. Several years later an independent inventor designs a pool alarm that uses the same technology to sound an alarm if a child accidentally falls into a pool. Even though the pool alarm uses the same electronics, it would pass the new use test.

A systematic approach can be made for assessing novelty (except if you publish or publicly use your invention more than one year prior to applying for a patent, then it's no longer novel).

1. Analyze your invention for elements.
2. Analyze each prior art reference for its elements.
3. Compare the elements of each prior art reference to the elements of your invention.
4. If no one prior art reference contains all of the same elements used in the same way and for the same purpose as your invention, then it's novel.

The Prior Art Aspect of a Previously Issued Patent Is Larger Than the Patent's Claims

Novice inventors often confuse the claims of a patent with the concept of prior art anticipation. Don't make the mistake of thinking that if an aspect of your invention hasn't been "claimed" in a prior patent, you can claim it. The claims of the patent only define the legal scope of the inventor's intellectual property. If a claim is violated (infringed upon), an inventor has offensive legal rights. He can sue the infringer. See Chapter 1 for a description of the purpose of each section of a patent.

The fourth criterion is unobviousness. This is the toughest of the patent requirements. Essentially, it means your new concept must be a significant step forward in the field of the invention. In other words, if a skilled worker who is thoroughly familiar with developments in the area of your invention would consider the idea obvious, you would fail this test. As an example, consider the balloon made with new lightweight fabric from the previous paragraph. While this invention qualifies as novel, it would be obvious to a person skilled in the art of balloon making to try using new lightweight materials.

In general, incremental changes are considered obvious since the results could be easily predicted by someone skilled in the related field, whereas changes that produce *new and unexpected results* are considered unobvious.

Oftentimes, new inventions combine elements from two or more previous inventions. Here, the end result must also produce a new and unexpected outcome. For example, electrical circuits can carry alternating currents. A square piece of iron has certain magnetic field properties due to its composition. By combining the two via electrical windings on opposite legs of the iron square, you can create a transformer. By varying the number of turns in the primary and secondary windings (the primary winding is on the voltage supply side of the iron core) you obtain either a voltage increase or decrease (a step-up or a step-down transformer). This is a new and unexpected result.

B. First to File vs. First to Invent and Pending Patent Applications

One of the pitfalls of any patent search is that there is no way to search pending patent applications. Another inventor may have already filed a patent application on essentially the same invention as you. Because pending patent applications are kept confidential, if the patent hasn't been issued yet, you have no way of knowing about it. This is one of the occupational hazards involved in applying for a patent.

If you have a patent application pending, and a patent is issued that covers the essential aspects of your idea, you may still be able to get a patent. How? By proving that you conceived of the invention prior to the inventor listed in the opposing patent.

While most of the world uses what is known as a first to file system (the first person to file a patent application is legally recognized as the inventor), we in the U.S. use a first to invent system. This means that the inventor who can prove to have conceived of the idea first, gets the patent.

To prove when you first conceived of your invention idea, you have to keep legally acceptable records. Nolo publishes an excellent workbook called *The Inventor's Notebook*, where you can record the conception, building and testing of your invention. The notebook walks you through the due diligence process and helps you prove the earliest possible date of invention. It can also help you if your first to invent status is ever challenged by another inventor.

C. Conclusion

In closing, we hope that you have found the information and techniques illustrated in this book both useful and enlightening. By using this resource, the Internet and the nationwide network of PTDLs, the independent inventor can indeed perform a reasonably accurate, preliminary patent search. ■

Patent and Trademark Depository Libraries

(Source: Patent and Trademark Depository Library Program website: current as of February 2001.)

Alabama

Auburn University: Ralph Brown Draughon Library *
334-844-1737

Birmingham Public Library
205-226-3620

Alaska

Anchorage: Z. J. Loussac Public Library
907-562-7323

Arizona

Tempe: Daniel E. Noble Science and Engineering *
Library, Arizona State University
408-965-7010

Arkansas

Little Rock: Arkansas State Library *
501-682-2053

California

Los Angeles Public Library *
213-228-7220

Sacramento: California State Library
916-654-0069

San Diego Public Library
619-236-5813

San Francisco Public Library *
415-557-4500

Sunnyvale Center for Innovation, Invention and Ideas * *
408-730-7290

Colorado

Denver Public Library
303-640-6220

Connecticut

Hartford Public Library
860-543-8628

New Haven: New Haven Free Public Library
203-946-8130

Delaware

Newark: University of Delaware Library
302-831-2965

District of Columbia

Washington: Founders Library, Howard University
202-806-7252

Florida

Fort Lauderdale: Broward County Main Library *
954-357-7444

Miami-Dade Public Library *
305-375-2665

Orlando: University of Central Florida Libraries
407-823-2562

* Denotes APS-Text Access   * * Denotes Partnership PTDL

Tampa Campus Library, University of South Florida
813-974-2726

Georgia

Atlanta: Library and Information Center,
Georgia Institute of Technology
404-894-4508

Hawaii

Honolulu: Hawaii State Public Library System *
808-586-3477

Idaho

Moscow: University of Idaho Library
208-885-6235

Illinois

Chicago Public Library
312-747-4450

Springfield: Illinois State Library
217-782-5659

Indiana

Indianapolis-Marion County Public Library
317-269-1741

West Lafayette: Siegesmund Engineering Library,
Purdue University
765-494-2872

Iowa

Des Moines: State Library of Iowa
515-242-6541

Kansas

Wichita: Ablah Library, Wichita State University *
316-978-3155

Kentucky

Louisville Free Public Library *
502-574-1611

Louisiana

Baton Rouge: Troy H. Middleton Library,
Louisiana State University
225-388-8875

Maine

Orono: Raymond H. Fogler Library, University of Maine
207-581-1678

Maryland

College Park: Engineering and Physical Sciences Library,
University of Maryland
301-405-9157

Massachusetts

Amherst: Physical Sciences Library, University of
Massachusetts/Amherst
413-545-1370

Boston Public Library *
617-536-5400, Ext. 265

Michigan

Ann Arbor: Engineering Library, University of Michigan
734-647-5735

Big Rapids: Abigail S. Timme Library,
Ferris State University
231-591-3602

Detroit: Great Lakes Patent and Trademark Center,**
Detroit Public Library
313-833-3379

Minnesota

Minneapolis Public Library and Information Center *
612-630-6120

Mississippi

Jackson: Mississippi Library Commission
601-961-4111

Missouri

Kansas City: Linda Hall Library *
816-363-4600

St. Louis Public Library *
314-241-2288, Ext. 390

Montana

Butte: Montana Tech of the University of
Montana Library
406-496-4281

* Denotes APS-Text Access   ** Denotes Partnership PTDL

Nebraska

Lincoln: Engineering Library,
University of Nebraska-Lincoln *
402-472-3411

Nevada

Reno: University of Nevada-Reno Library
775-784-6500, Ext. 257

New Hampshire

Concord: New Hampshire State Library
603-271-2239

New Jersey

Newark Public Library
973-733-7779

Piscataway: Library of Science and Medicine,
Rutgers University
732-445-2895

New Mexico

Albuquerque: Centennial Science and
Engineering Library,
University of New Mexico
505-277-4412

New York

Albany: New York State Library
518-474-5355

Buffalo and Erie County Public Library *
716-858-7101

New York Public Library, Science,
Industry and Business Library
212-592-7000

Rochester: Central Library of Rochester
716-428-8110

Stony Brook: Engineering Library,
State University of New York
516-632-7148

North Carolina

Raleigh: D. H. Hill Library, North Carolina
State University *
919-515-2935

North Dakota

Grand Forks: Chester Fritz Library,
University of North Dakota
701-777-1888

Ohio

Akron-Summit County Public Library
330-643-9075

Cincinnati and Hamilton County, The Public Library of
513-369-6971

Cleveland Public Library *
216-623-2870

Columbus: Ohio State University Libraries
614-292-3022

Toledo/Lucas County Public Library *
419-259-5212

Oklahoma

Stillwater: Center for International Trade Development, *
Oklahoma State University
405-744-7086

Oregon

Portland: Paul L. Boley Law Library,
Lewis & Clark College
503-768-6786

Pennsylvania

Philadelphia, The Free Library of *
215-686-5331

Pittsburgh, The Carnegie Library of
412-622-3138

University Park: Pattee Library,
Pennsylvania State University
814-865-6369

Puerto Rico

Mayaguez: General Library,
University of Puerto Rico-Mayaguez
787-832-4040, Ext. 2022

* Denotes APS-Text Access

Rhode Island

Providence Public Library
401-455-8027

South Carolina

Clemson: R. M. Cooper Library, Clemson University
864-656-3024

South Dakota

Rapid City: Devereaux Library, South Dakota
School of Mines and Technology
605-394-1275

Tennessee

Memphis & Shelby County Public Library
and Information Center
901-725-8877

Nashville: Stevenson Science and Engineering Library,
Vanderbilt University
615-322-2717

Texas

Austin: McKinney Engineering Library,
University of Texas at Austin
512-495-4500

College Station: Sterling C. Evans Library,
Texas A&M University *
979-845-5745

Dallas Public Library *
214-670-1468

Houston: The Fondren Library, Rice University *
713-348-5483

Lubbock: Texas Tech University Library
806-742-2282

South Central Intellectual Property Partnership
at Rice University (SCIPPR) * *
713-285-5196

Utah

Salt Lake City: Marriott Library, University of Utah *
801-581-8394

Vermont

Burlington: Bailey/Howe Library,
University of Vermont
802-656-2542

Virginia

Richmond: James Branch Cabell Library,
Virginia Commonwealth University *
804-828-1104

Washington

Seattle: Engineering Library, University of Washington *
206-543-0740

West Virginia

Morgantown: Evansdale Library,
West Virginia University *
304-293-4695, Ext. 5113

Wisconsin

Madison: Kurt F. Wendt Library,
University of Wisconsin-Madison
608-262-6845

Milwaukee Public Library
414-286-3051

Wyoming

Casper: Natrona County Public Library
307-237-4935

* Denotes APS-Text Access   * * Denotes Partnership PTDL

B

Forms

Classification Search Sheet

Class Finder Tool

Classification Search Sheet

	A. Descriptive Words	B. Class Index-Alpha	C. Subclass Index-Xref	D. Subclass Man. of Class.	E. Get List	F. Search Class	G. Got List
1.							
2.							
3.							
4.							
5.							
6.							
7.							
8.							
9.							
10.							

Class Finder Tool

Summary of Searcher's Secrets

1. The more keywords used with the AND operator, the smaller the number of matches obtained and the more meaningful each match is to the searcher.

2. The OR operator is used to widen the scope of the search results.

3. One, and only one, of the keywords combined with the XOR operator will appear in each of the patents in the search results.

4. The ANDNOT operator is used to exclude specific keywords from the search results.

5. Don't limit your patent searches to Internet-based resources. Make the effort to use the tools available at the nearest PTDL.

6. The PTO may use a term you don't expect for a class/subclass title. Use a thesaurus as necessary to find alternative descriptive words for your class titles.

7. First find the most relevant classes and subclasses for your invention. Then review all of the issued patents within those classes.

8. Always start your Internet patent searches at the PTO website. Then proceed to the IBM website to take advantage of the extended range of years covered.

9. When in doubt about the order of evaluation in complex patent search commands, use parentheses to explicitly set the order. Then check the output command at the top of the results report.

10. One of the keys to getting meaningful search results from the APS system is to construct queries that don't just look blindly for the use of certain keywords, but look specifically for how those keywords are used.

11. The STO can be a good resource if you are having trouble finding all of the classes/ subclasses for your invention idea.

12. If you haven't found any prior art for your invention idea, you haven't looked hard enough.

Glossary

Abstract. One or two paragraphs appearing on the front page of an issued patent, summarizing the invention.

AIDS. Acquired Immune Deficiency Syndrome. A severe immunological disorder caused by a retrovirus that results in an increased susceptibility to opportunistic infections.

ANDed Search Commands. The process of combining multiple keywords in a Boolean argument together with AND operators. An example would be: Fire AND Protection AND (Building OR Structure), where Fire, Protection, and the keywords within the parentheses are ANDed.

Answer Set. A collection of search result patents that contain the search terms.

Answer Set L Number. A numbered label that is applied to each collection of search results that has been assembled. The L numbers increase sequentially for each new search.

Antigen. A substance, such as a bacterium, that when introduced into the body stimulates the production of an antibody.

APS. The Automated Patent System text search program.

APS CIT Format. Stands for the Citation display format for patent search results. It includes the patent number, issue date, title, first inventor and class/subclass.

APS Continuous Print Special Function Key. Used to start and stop continuous printing of the contents of the output area of the APS.

APS FILE Command. Used to select the patent text file that will be searched by the APS program.

Examples files are USPAT and USOCR. The FILE command ALLUS selects both of these patent text files.

APS Hold/Resume Special Function Key. Used to stop and start the output area of the APS from scrolling.

APS Input Area. The input area of the APS text search window. This is where you enter your keyboard commands.

APS Message Area. The message area of the APS text search window. This area is used to display system status messages, and provides a list of available special functions.

APS Output Area. The output area of the APS text search window. The system response to your keyboard input is displayed here, along with a copy of your input commands.

APS Save to Disk Special Function Key. Used to save the entire contents of an APS session to a floppy disk.

APS Search Index. Used to limit APS searches to certain sections of the patent. It is added to the end of the search command. An example is /AB to search the patent abstract only.

Baud Rate. The baud rate specifies the number of signal elements transmitted per second. Used to specify the speed performance of a modem.

Boolean Logic. Logic used to combine keywords into more powerful searches. There are four Boolean logical operators that we need to understand; AND, OR, XOR and ANDNOT.

Browser. A computer program that provides a way to look at information on the World Wide Web.

CASSIS. The Classification And Search Support Information System.

CD-ROM. A CD-ROM drive reads computer data that is stored on an optical CD.

Class and Subclass. These are the categories that the PTO uses to classify or sort the various types of inventions.

Class Finder Tool. A visual aid used for finding the relevant classes of an invention.

Click. Pressing the left mouse button down once, and then releasing it.

Copyright. Copyrights are used to protect the *expressive* works of authors, computer programmers, movie producers and other artistic creators.

CPU. Central Processing Unit. The brains of the computer.

CSIR. The Classified Search and Image Retrieval system.

Double Click. Pressing the left mouse button down and releasing it twice, in rapid succession.

Escape Key. The key labeled ESC. Located at the extreme upper left of the keyboard.

FAQs. A list of frequently asked questions, along with the corresponding answers.

Field Codes. At the PTO website, these are characters that precede a keyword. The characters are used to limit the search for that keyword to certain sections of the patent. At the IBM website, the need for field codes has been eliminated through the use of predefined fields.

Governor. A device on an engine that regulates speed, pressure or temperature.

Hard Disk. Used for long-term storage of programs and information. This data remains with your computer after the power has been turned off.

Hit. A match reported by a computer search program, between a keyword and a database. The document that the word occurred in, and sometimes the location of the word, are returned to the user.

Homepage. Electronic documents that are published on the WWW. For multiple documents at the same location, the homepage is the top-level document.

HTML Document. A document that has special codes in it that allow the browser programs (Netscape Navigator, Microsoft Internet Explorer, etc.) to display and link the document with other documents on the Internet.

Hypertext Link. Electronic documents that are published on the WWW are linked together through hypertext links. Usually a word or words on a homepage are highlighted and/or underlined. By clicking on the highlighted word, you move from one document to another.

Intellectual Property. A product of the human mind. Patents, trademarks, trade secrets and copyrights fall under the category of Intellectual Property.

Internet. A worldwide network of interconnected government, business, university and scientific computer networks.

ISDN. An acronym for the Integrated Services Digital Network. It is a numerical phone network.

ISP. Internet Service Provider. A company that provides dialup telephone number access to the Internet.

Keyword Search. The search process carried out by a computer program, where entered keywords are matched with words stored in a database. When the program finds a match, the program will report back the document in which the word was found, and in some cases, the location of the word within the document.

MB. A contraction of the words mega and byte. It stands for one million bytes. A byte is just a word of computer data.

Microfilm Reader. A device that displays images stored on microfilm reels or index cards. A printout of the displayed page can be obtained.

Modem. A device that converts digital computer data into analog data for transmission and reception over standard telephone lines.

Netiquette. Generally accepted rules and conventions used for posting messages to Usenet newsgroups.

Optical Character Recognition Program. A computer program that can extract words from a digital image.

Page Up and Page Down Keys. Used to display an additional page of information of the computer monitor.

Pneumatic. Air operated.

Posting Messages to a Newsgroup. Writing messages of interest to a particular newsgroup.

Preferred Embodiment. Inventor's "best guess" version of the invention configuration, at the time the patent application was written.

Prior Art. Previous inventions that are in the same field, or a closely related field, as the current invention.

Proximity Operators. These operators allow you to search for two or more keywords within a specified number of words of each other. An example would be searching for the words Fire and Protection in any order within a sentence or a paragraph.

Radio Buttons. Radio buttons are circles that can be selected with a mouse click. They are a Windows feature used for selecting one, and only one option, from a group of options. When selected, the circle has a dot in the center.

RAM. Random Access Memory. The temporary memory that the computer uses to run programs.

Scroll Bar. A scroll bar is a Windows feature that lets you use the mouse to see objects that are outside the normal viewing area.

Search Class Cross-Reference. A listing of additional classes that are related to the current subject matter. Located below the current sub-class definition in the Classification Definitions.

Search Engine. A program that keeps track of the content of the various Web pages on the Internet. The search engine then allows users to seek specific Web pages through keyword searching.

Special Function Keys. Row of twelve keys across the top of the keyboard. These keys are labeled F1, F2, etc.

Subscribing to Newsgroups. Allows you to separate retrieved newsgroup messages with the Netscape option "Show Subscribed Newsgroups."

Taskbar. The horizontal gray area across the bottom of the Windows main display area.

Text Search. A document (patent) is searched for matches with one or more keywords, separated by commas. Any occurrence of a keyword causes a hit to be reported. No Boolean operators allowed.

Trade Secret. Generally described as any information that, if kept secret, gives its owner a competitive business advantage. The formula for Kentucky Fried Chicken is one example.

Trademark. A symbol or word associated with a particular product, or a family of products. Examples are Diet Coke and Mr. Coffee.

TXT Document. A document in text format, a common format that any word processor can read.

Usenet. A collection of over 15,000 Internet newsgroups,

Venn Diagram. Graphical representation of Boolean logic.

Web Crawler. A program that automatically accesses website information. Usually called from an Internet search engine.

Web Page. Generic term for any document published on the WWW.

Website. Used to refer to a particular Web page on the WWW. This term is usually accompanied by a WWW location address, such as http://www.upsto.gov.

Wildcard. An asterisk (*), an exclamation point (!) or a question mark (?) that can be used to replace one or more characters (letters) in a keyword.

World Wide Web (WWW). A part of the Internet. Computers on the WWW host websites, where information can be read by browser programs and displayed on the home user's computer monitor. ■

Index

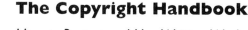

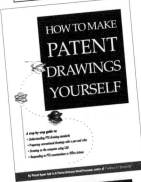

Take 2 Minutes
& Give Us Your 2 cents

Your comments make a big difference in the development and revision of Nolo books and software. Please take a few minutes and register your Nolo product—and your comments—with us. Not only will your input make a difference, you'll receive special offers available only to registered owners of Nolo products on our newest books and software. Register now by:

PHONE
1-800-992-6656

FAX
1-800-645-0895

EMAIL
cs@nolo.com

or **MAIL** us
this registration card

REMEMBER:
Little publishers have big ears. We really listen to you.

fold here

- -

REGISTRATION CARD

NAME _____ DATE _____

ADDRESS _____

_____

CITY _____ STATE _____ ZIP _____

PHONE _____ E-MAIL _____

WHERE DID YOU HEAR ABOUT THIS PRODUCT? _____

WHERE DID YOU PURCHASE THIS PRODUCT? _____

DID YOU CONSULT A LAWYER? (PLEASE CIRCLE ONE)   YES   NO   NOT APPLICABLE

DID YOU FIND THIS BOOK HELPFUL?   (VERY)   5   4   3   2   1   (NOT AT ALL)

COMMENTS _____

_____

_____

WAS IT EASY TO USE?   (VERY EASY)   5   4   3   2   1   (VERY DIFFICULT)

DO YOU OWN A COMPUTER? IF SO, WHICH FORMAT? (PLEASE CIRCLE ONE)   WINDOWS   DOS   MAC

We occasionally make our mailing list available to carefully selected companies whose products may be of interest to you.

❑ If you do not wish to receive mailings from these companies, please check this box.

❑ You can quote me in future Nolo promotional materials. Daytime phone number _____.

PATSE 2.2

NOLO IN THE NEWS

"Nolo helps lay people perform legal tasks without the aid—or fees—of lawyers."

—USA TODAY

Nolo books are ..."written in plain language, free of legal mumbo jumbo, and spiced with witty personal observations."

—ASSOCIATED PRESS

"...Nolo publications...guide people simply through the how, when, where and why of law."

—WASHINGTON POST

"Increasingly, people who are not lawyers are performing tasks usually regarded as legal work... And consumers, using books like Nolo's, do routine legal work themselves."

—NEW YORK TIMES

"...All of [Nolo's] books are easy-to-understand, are updated regularly, provide pull-out forms...and are often quite moving in their sense of compassion for the struggles of the lay reader."

—SAN FRANCISCO CHRONICLE

fold here

nolo

950 Parker Street
Berkeley, CA 94710-9867

Attn: PATSE 2.2